Collins

SO-AJH-439

SAS
Survival
Guide

John 'Lofty' Wiseman

John 'Lofty' Wiseman, a former SAS instructor,
teaches and writes on survival techniques.

First published as
The SAS Survival Guide in 1986

Collins Gem edition first published 1993
This edition published 2010

10   15

Text © John Wiseman 1986, 1993, 2004, 2010
Illustrations © HarperCollins Publishers 1986, 1993

ISBN 978-0-06-199286-5

For information address HarperCollins Publishers,
195 Broadway, New York, NY 10007

HarperCollins books may be purchased for educational,
business, or sales promotional use. For information, please
email the Special Markets Department at SPsales@harpercollins.co

Produced for Collins by Essential Works Ltd.
www.essentialworks.co.uk

Printed and bound in China by South China Printing Co. Ltd

INTRODUCTION

The aim of this book is to prepare you for any survival situation. For 26 years, I had the privilege of serving as survival instructor with the Special Air Service (SAS). Tested in training and operations, these skills form the basis of this book.

I look to identify every danger imaginable and show you how to deal with it, while focusing on what nature can provide: any kit must be considered a bonus.

You also need to have a sense of how your body works in different climates and in different situations – and thereby have an idea of your limits. The best way to learn is to see what the locals do and learn from them.

When training soldiers or civilians, part of my job is to ensure their safety. I cannot do that for the reader, but what I have written has saved lives in the past and can save more in the future. In learning the skills described, readers must be restrained by the need to conserve our environment and to avoid cruelty to animals, and by laws which some techniques may contravene. This is a handbook for situations when self-preservation is paramount, so risks that would otherwise be out of the question may be involved.

Although this is not an official publication, by sharing survival knowledge gained through my SAS experience I aim to help you to be a survivor, too.

Survival is, above all, a mental exercise. Being physically prepared will help increase your confidence and the mental resolve to survive all odds.

John 'Lofty' Wiseman

WARNING

The survival techniques described in this publication are for use in dire circumstances where the safety of individuals is at risk. Accordingly the publishers cannot accept any responsibility for any prosecutions or proceedings brought or instituted against any person or body as a result of the use or misuse of any techniques described or any loss, injury or damage caused thereby. In practising and perfecting these survival techniques the rights of landowners and all relevant laws protecting certain species of animals and plants and controlling the use of firearms and other weapons must be regarded as paramount.

CONTENTS

ESSENTIALS

Survival is the art of staying alive. Mental attitude is as important as physical endurance and knowledge. You must know how to take everything possible from nature and use it to the full, how to attract attention to yourself so that rescuers may find you, how to make your way across unknown territory back to civilisation if there is no hope of rescue, navigating without map or compass. You must know how to maintain a healthy physical condition, or if sick or wounded heal yourself and others. You must be able to maintain your morale and that of others who share your situation.

Any equipment you have must be considered a bonus. Lack of equipment should not mean that you are unequipped, for you will carry skills and experience with you, but those skills and experience must not be allowed to get rusty and you must extend your knowledge all the time.

Think of survival skills as a pyramid, built on the foundation of the will to survive. The next layer of the pyramid is knowledge. It breeds confidence and dispels fears. The third layer is training: mastering skills and maintaining them. To cap the pyramid, add your kit. Combine the instinct for survival with knowledge, training and kit and you will be ready for anything.

ESSENTIALS

BE PREPARED

The Boy Scouts' motto is the right one. Make sure you are physically and mentally prepared before you set out and pack the appropriate gear for what you plan to do.

ASK YOURSELF

- How long will I be away? How much food and water do I need to carry?
- Have I the right clothing/footwear for the climate? Should I take standbys?
- What special equipment do I need for the terrain?
- What medical kit is appropriate?

HEALTH CHECKS

Have thorough health check-ups and ensure you have all the necessary injections for the territories you will cover. Pack a medical kit for all of the group's likely needs.

GROUP EXPEDITIONS

Consider the ability of each member to deal with likely challenges: it may be necessary to drop the unfit. Hold meetings to discuss responsibilities and plans. Nominate a medic, cook, mechanic, driver, navigator, etc. Ensure everyone is familiar with equipment, and carry spares.

RESEARCH

The more detailed your knowledge of the place and people, the better your chances. Study your maps carefully, gain as much knowledge of the terrain as possible: climate; weather conditions; river directions and speed of flow; how high are the mountains/hills; what kind of vegetation/ animal life can you expect?

PLANNING

Divide the project into phases: entry phase, objective and recovery. Clearly set the aim and time scale of each phase. Plan for emergency procedures such as vehicle breakdown, illness and casualty evacuation.

Allow plenty of time when estimating the rate of progress. Pressure to keep to an over-ambitious schedule leads to exhaustion and errors of judgement.

The need to replenish water supplies from local sources will be a major factor in determining the route.

Make sure someone knows where you are planning to go and your times of departure and expected arrival. Keep them informed at prearranged stages so that failure to contact will set alarm bells ringing. Boats and aircraft are strictly controlled in this respect. If you are hiking in the hills inform the police and local mountain-rescue centre of your proposed plan.

Contingency plans

Be prepared. What will you do if a vehicle breaks down, or if weather conditions prove more severe than anticipated? If in a party, how will you regroup if separated? What happens if someone falls ill?

P.L.A.N.

The main elements of survival in order of priority are:
Protection – ensure you are protected from any harm.
Location – draw attention to your position, for rescuers.
Acquisition – look for food and water. Ration supplies.
Navigation – good navigation will keep you on route. If you are stranded, stay where you are.

ESSENTIALS

ESSENTIALS

EQUIPMENT

Clothes should be well-fitting but not restrictive, giving protection from cold and rain while keeping the body ventilated. Carry waterproofs, a change of clothes and extra warm garments. Layer in cold climates. Synthetics such as Gore-tex™ and fleece are versatile and useful. Wool is excellent in cold and wet climates, while cotton works well in the tropics.

Sleeping bag

Down bags are light and give better insulation than man-made fibres. When wet, however, down loses its insulating properties and is difficult to dry out. If you don't have a tent, a bivouac bag of breathable material will keep you dry.

Backpack

Must be strong, waterproof, with tough, adjustable webbing secured to the frame, and a comfortable belt to take the weight on the hips – the body's strongest pivot. External frames are best: although heavier and prone to snag on branches, they can take awkward, heavy loads, and even an injured person. The frame should allow an airspace between the pack and your back to reduce perspiration. Zip-fastened side pockets are best.

STOWING KIT

Pack so you know where everything is and the first things you need are on top. If it's wet, stow items in polythene bags. Tent and heavy kit go on top, but don't make the pack too high as it will be hard to balance in strong wind. Keep damageable food in containers.

ESSENTIALS

RADIO

A necessity for long, remote expeditions. Prearrange a
signals plan with twice-daily scheduled calls to base
giving your location and plans. Base can supply weather
updates and other info, and monitor the frequency for
emergency calls if necessary. Select frequencies that will
work in the areas you are going to. At least two group
members should be able to operate the radio. An
emergency plan will go into operation if you miss two
consecutive calls from base. In this case, go to or stay at
the last reported location and await contact.

G.P.S.

A G.P.S. (Global Positioning System) receives signals
from satellites and can locate your current position anywhere in the world. They are relatively easy to use, with a
95 per cent accuracy rate. The satellite transmission must
not have any obstructions in its way, so make sure you're
out in the open when using one. G.P.S. is not effective
unless you can identify where you are, so do not use it as a
substitute for basic map-reading and navigating, but for
confirming or correcting your navigation. As with any
battery-operated piece of equipment, use sparingly.

MOBILES

Mobile phones offer a helpful supplement to radio
contact, and can be a life-saver in emergency situations.
Check your network coverage before an expedition.
Charging can be a problem, but small, hand-held
manual chargers can now be bought. Remember, it
takes less power to listen than to transmit.

ESSENTIALS

SURVIVAL KIT

The items shown on p. 19 can be crucial in the fight for survival. They should be stored in a small container, such as a tin about 100 x 75 x 30mm. Polish the inside of the lid to make a reflecting surface. Seal with a strip of adhesive tape (a), which can be removed and replaced, to make it waterproof. Pack it with cotton wool (for fire lighting) to keep contents from rattling. Make a habit of always having it with you - do not get separated from it.

Check regularly, changing contents that deteriorate. Never leave the tin open or lying on the ground.

1 **MATCHES** Preferably waterproof, but non-safety matches can be 'showerproofed' by dipping heads in melted candle fat. Snap off half to save space.

2 **CANDLE** Shave square for packing. Tallow ones can be eaten in emergency or used for frying, but difficult to store in hot climates. Other kinds inedible.

3 **FLINT** Processed flint with saw striker.

4 **MAGNIFYING GLASS** To start fire in sunlight.

5 **NEEDLES AND THREAD** Several needles, including at least one with a very large eye to take sinew and coarse threads. Wrap length of strong thread round the needles. They can be used for repairing or making clothes in an emergency.

6 **FISH HOOKS AND LINE** Selection of hooks and split lead weights, plus as much line as possible.

7 **COMPASS** Liquid-filled type with luminous button is best. Make sure it is in working order and that you know how to use it. Pointer is prone to rust: check it is on its pivot and swings freely.

ESSENTIALS

8 **BETA LIGHT** Small, self-illuminating, and reliable for about 15 years. Ideal for map-reading.

9 **SNARE WIRE** Preferably brass. 60–90cm (24–36in).

10 **FLEXIBLE SAW** Remove handles and grease before storing. To use, fit wooden toggle handles.

11 **MEDICAL KIT** Pack medicines in airtight containers with cotton wool. Label carefully with full dosage instructions and expiry date. Do not exceed recommended dosages or take with alcohol. The following items are only a guide:

Analgesic Pain reliever for mild/moderate pain.

Intestinal sedative For acute/chronic diarrhoea.

Antibiotic For general infections. Carry enough for a full course.

Antihistamine For allergies, insect bites/stings.

Water sterilising tablets Use when you cannot boil suspect water.

Anti-malaria tablets Essential in areas where malaria is present.

Potassium permanganate Add to water and mix until pink to sterilise, deeper pink to make antiseptic, full red to treat fungal diseases, e.g. athlete's foot.

12 **SURGICAL BLADES** At least two scalpel blades of different sizes.

13 **BUTTERFLY SUTURES** To hold edges of wounds together.

14 **PLASTERS** Waterproof, assorted sizes.

15 **CONDOM** Makes good water-bag: holds 1 litre (1¾ pints). Fill from a source with pressure, like a waterfall.

SURVIVAL POUCH

In addition to your survival tin, pack a pouch and keep it handy for emergencies. Carry it on your belt.

POUCH Must be waterproof, large enough to take a mess tin, with a positive fastening that will not come undone and a strong loop to hold it on your belt.

FUEL Preferably solid hexamine fuel tablets in their own stove container (1). Use sparingly when a wood fire is inconvenient. They make excellent fire-lighters. Stove unfolds to form an adjustable pot stand (2).

SIGNAL FLARES (3) to attract attention. Carry red and green miniflares (4) and a discharger (5). Beware: these are explosives! Remove discharger and screw on to flare (6). Withdraw flare and point skywards at arm's length. Pull trigger to fire. Use with care; do not waste (see p. 281).

ESSENTIALS

ESSENTIALS

MESS TIN Aluminium cooking utensil. Pack kit inside.

TORCH (7). Keep batteries reversed to avoid switching it on accidentally. LED torches use less battery power.

MARKER PANEL Fluorescent strip for signalling, *c.* 30 x 200cm (12 x 79in). A silver thermal blanket is ideal.

MATCHES (8) Pack in waterproof container.

BREW KIT (9) Tea bags, sachets of milk and sugar.

FOOD Tube of butter (10). Dehydrated meat (11). Chocolate (12). Salt tablets (13) or electrolite powder which contains vitamins, salt and other minerals.

SURVIVAL BAG Heat-insulated bag 60 x 200cm (24 x 79in) of reflective material that keeps you warm and free of condensation.

SURVIVAL LOG Written log of all events. It will become a valuable reference and training tool.

KNIVES

A knife is an invaluable asset in a survival situation. It should be packed with checked-in luggage when flying. Current UK knife law states knives with blades shorter than 7.62cm (3in) that fold into the handle are legal.

CHOOSING A KNIFE

A multi-bladed penknife is useful, but if you can carry only one knife take something stronger, a general-purpose blade that will do all likely tasks efficiently and comfortably, from cutting trees to skinning animals and preparing food. Some have built-in compasses or hollow handles for your kit, but any advantages are offset by the fact that such handles may break or the compass lose its accuracy and, if you lose the knife, you lose everything.

FOLDING KNIVES: Should have a good locked position. A wooden handle is more comfortable to use.

Handle (a) is ideal: a single rounded piece of wood, the knife tang passing through it and fastened at the end. Handle (b) is riveted and would cause blisters, (c) could easily break. The sheath (d) must have a positive fastening and tunnel belt loop.

ESSENTIALS

You are only as sharp as your knife. It must be sharp and ready for use. Don't misuse your knife by throwing it. Keep it clean, oiled and in a sheath when not in use.

PARANG: The Malayan name for a knife with a large curved blade like a machete. Too large for everyday use, it is ideal in the wilds for cutting down trees and building shelters and rafts. The ideal parang size is 30cm (12in) overall blade length, with a blade 5cm (2in) at its widest, weighing no more than 750g (1½lb). The end of the blade should be bolted into a wooden handle.

The parang blade has three different edges: (b) does the heavy work of chopping wood and bone; (a) is finer and used for skinning; (c) is for carving and delicate work. The curved blade enables maximum effort to be applied when cutting timber and the blade arrives before the knuckles, offering protection.

The sheath must have positive fastenings to keep the parang secure and a loop for fixing to a belt. Some sheaths have a pocket on the front for a sharpening stone.

ESSENTIALS

☠ There is a danger that the cutting edge may come through the side of the sheath. NEVER hold the sheath on the same side as the cutting edge when drawing the parang. Always grip the side AWAY FROM THE CUTTING EDGE.

SHARPENING A KNIFE

Sandstone, quartz and granite will sharpen tools. Rub two pieces together to make them smooth. A double-faced stone with a rough and smooth surface is ideal. Use the rough surface first to remove burrs, then the smooth one to get a fine edge.

To sharpen the blade, hold the handle in the right hand. Use a clockwise circular motion and apply steady pressure on the blade with the fingertips of the left hand as you push away. Keep the angle constant and push the knife into the stone for a sharp, not round, edge. Keep the stone wet. Don't drag the blade towards you under pressure; this produces burrs. Reduce the pressure for a finer edge. Work counter clockwise on the other side.

Blade profile: A is too steep and will soon wear; B is good; and C is too fine and will chip.

Get in the habit of checking all your equipment regularly, especially after negotiating difficult terrain. A check of all pockets and possessions should be second nature.

ESSENTIALS

FACING DISASTER

It is no use giving up. Only positive action can save you.
People can survive seemingly impossible situations if
they have the determination.

SURVIVAL STRESSES

The survival situation will put you under physical and
mental pressure. You will have to overcome some
or all of the following stresses:

Fear and anxiety

Pain, illness and injury

Cold and/or heat

Thirst, hunger and fatigue

Sleep deprivation

Boredom

Loneliness and isolation

Can you cope? You have to.

Self-confidence is a product of good training and
sound knowledge. These must be acquired before you face
a survival situation. Confidence will help you overcome
the mental stresses. Physical fitness will give you the
resources to cope with fatigue and loss of sleep. The fitter
you are the better you will survive. Start training now.

Pain and fever call attention to an injured part and
prevent you using it. It is important to treat any injury as
soon as possible, but pain may have to be overcome and
controlled in order to seek help and avoid the risk of
further injury or death.

ESSENTIALS

WATER

Ordering your priorities – food, fire, shelter and water –
is one of the first steps to survival.

In general, an adult can survive for 3 minutes without
air; 3 days without water; 3 weeks without food. Water
should therefore be prioritised. Don't wait until you run
out of it; seek a new source of fresh running water. All
water can be sterilised. A 1-litre jug (1¾pt) can be made to
last 4 days in a survival situation. If necessary, the last
¼ litre (½pt) can be made to last 3 days, by dividing it into
three, then drinking half of the day's ration at midday, and
the balance at night, for 3 days.

The human body loses 2–3 litres (3½–5¼ pints) of
water each day. Loss of liquids through respiration and
perspiration increases with work rate and temperature.
Vomiting and diarrhoea increase loss further. This must be
replaced either by actual water or water contained in food.

HOW TO RETAIN FLUIDS

**To keep fluid loss to a minimum, take the
following precautions:**

- Avoid exertion. Just rest. Don't smoke.
- Keep cool. Stay in shade. If there is none, erect a
cover.
- Do not lie on hot ground or heated surfaces.
- Don't eat, or eat as little as possible – digestion uses
up fluids, increasing dehydration. Fat is especially hard
to digest.
- Never drink alcohol. This takes fluid from vital organs
to break it down.
- Don't talk. Breathe through the nose, not the mouth.

ESSENTIALS

FINDING WATER

- Look in valley bottoms where water naturally drains. If there is no stream or pool, look for patches of green vegetation and dig there.
- Dig in gullies and dry stream beds.
- In mountains look for water trapped in crevices.
- On the coast dig above the high-water line, or look for lush vegetation in faults in cliffs: you may find a spring.

Be suspicious of any pool with no green vegetation growing around it, or animal bones present. It is likely to be polluted. Check edge for minerals which might indicate alkaline conditions. Always boil water from pools. In the desert, lakes with no outlets become salt lakes: their water must be distilled before drinking.

DEW AND RAIN COLLECTION: Use as big a catchment area as possible, running the water off into containers. A covered hole in the ground lined with clay will hold water. If you have no impermeable sheeting, use metal sheets or bark to catch water.

Use clothing to soak up water: tie clean cloths around the legs and ankles and walk through wet vegetation. These can be sucked or wrung out.

RATION YOUR SWEAT NOT YOUR WATER!
If you have to ration water, take it in sips. After going without water a long time, don't guzzle when you do find it. Take only sips at first. Large gulps will make a dehydrated person vomit, losing even more of the valuable liquid.

ANIMALS AS SIGNS OF WATER

Mammals

Most animals require water regularly. Grazing animals are usually never far from water as they need to drink at dawn and dusk. Converging game trails often lead to water; follow them downhill. Meat eaters are not good indicators – they get moisture from their prey.

Birds

Grain eaters, such as finches and pigeons, are never far from water and drink at dawn and dusk. When they fly straight and low they are heading for water. When returning from water they fly from tree to tree, resting frequently. Water birds and birds of prey do not drink frequently and are therefore not good indicators.

Insects

Bees are especially good indicators. They fly at most 6.5km (4 miles) from their nests or hives. Ants are dependent on water. A column of ants marching up a tree is going to a small reservoir of trapped water. Such reservoirs are found even in arid areas. Most flies keep within 90m (100 yards) of water.

Reptiles

They collect what little moisture they need from dew and their prey. Not good indicators.

Humans

Tracks usually lead to a well, bore hole or soak. It may be covered with scrub or rocks to reduce evaporation. Replace the cover.

ESSENTIALS

ESSENTIALS

CONDENSATION

Trees can draw moisture from a water table 15m (50ft) or more below ground, too deep for you to dig. Let the tree pump it up for you by tying a plastic bag round a healthy, leafy branch or placing a polythene tent over vegetation. Evaporation from the leaves will produce condensation in the bag.

Keep the mouth of the bag at the top with a corner hanging low to collect water.

Suspend tent from the apex or support with padded stick. Avoid foliage touching the sides or it will divert droplets from collecting in plastic-lined channels at the bottom.

Even cut vegetation will produce

condensation when placed in a large plastic bag. Keep foliage off the bottom with stones so that water collects below it, and don't let it touch the sides. Keep the bag taut with stones. Support the top on a padded stick. Arrange the bag on a slight slope so condensation runs down to the collecting point.

ESSENTIALS

Solar still

Dig a hole approximately 90cm (36in) across and 45cm (18in) deep. Place a collecting can in the centre, then cover the hole with a sheet of plastic formed into a cone. Roughen underside of sheet with a stone to ensure droplets run down it. The sun raises the temperature of the air and soil below, producing vapour. Water condenses on the underside of the plastic, running down into the container. This is especially effective where it is hot by day and cold at night. This kind of still should collect at least 570ml (1 pint) over a 24-hour period.

The still doubles as a trap. Insects and small snakes, attracted by the plastic, slide down into the cone or wriggle beneath it and drop into the hole.

A solar still can be used to distil pure water from poisonous or contaminated liquids.

Use stones or weights to secure edges. Fix can so that trapped creatures can't tip it over. If feasible use a syphon to lower level (a) to draw off water without disturbing the still.

ESSENTIALS

URINE AND SEA WATER
Never drink either – never. But both can produce drinking water if distilled – and sea water will provide you with a residue of salt.

DISTILLATION

Pass a tube into the top of a water-filled covered container, placed over a fire, and the other end into a sealed collecting tin which should be set inside another container providing a jacket of cold water to cool the vapour as it passes out of the tube. You can use any tubing, e.g. pack frames. To avoid wasting water vapour, seal around the joins with mud or wet sand.

An easier method is a variation on the desert still. Take a tube from a covered vessel in which polluted or saltwater is to boil. Set the other end under a solar still. A sheet of metal, bark, or leaf weighted down, will cover the vessel and help direct the steam into the tube.

WATER FROM ICE AND SNOW

Ice produces twice as much water as snow for half the heat. To heat snow, melt a little in a pot and gradually add more. If you fill the pot, a hollow will form at the bottom as the snow melts, making the pot burn. Surface snow yields less water than lower layers.

Sea ice is salt (no good for drinking) until it has aged. Old sea ice is bluish and has weathered, rounded edges; the bluer it is the better for drinking. New sea ice is white and rough. But beware of even old ice that has been exposed to seaspray.

WATER FROM PLANTS

ESSENTIALS

WATER COLLECTORS: Plants often trap water in cavities. Old, hollow joints of bamboo fill up with water: shake them – if you hear water, cut a notch at the base of each joint and tip the water out.

Traveller's Tree Ravenala madagascariensis, *one of the banana family, can hold 1–2 litres (2–4 pints) of water between the bases of the chevron of leaf stalks.*

VINES: Those with rough bark and shoots about 5cm (2in) thick can be a useful source of water. But beware: not all have drinkable water and some yield a sticky, milky sap which is poisonous. Some vines cause skin irritation on contact, so collect the liquid in a container or let it drip into your mouth rather than put your mouth to the stem. To obtain water from a vine select a stem and trace it upwards. Reach as high as possible and cut a deep notch in the stem. Cut off the same stem close to the ground and let the water drip from it. When it ceases to drip cut a section from the bottom and go on repeating this until the vine is drained. Do not cut the bottom of the vine first as this will cause the liquid to run up the vine through capillary action.

ESSENTIALS

ROOTS: In Australia the water tree, desert oak and bloodwood have their roots near the surface. Pry the roots out and cut them up into 30cm (12in) lengths. Remove the bark. Suck out the moisture, or shave to a pulp and squeeze over the mouth.

PALMS: The buri, coconut and nipa palms all contain a sugary fluid which is drinkable. To start it flowing, bend a flowering stalk downwards and cut off its tip. If a thin slice is cut off the stalk every 12 hours the flow will be renewed, making it possible to collect up to a quart each day. Nipa palms shoot from the base so that you can work from ground level, but on grown trees of other species you may have to climb up to reach a flowering stalk.

Coconut milk from ripe nuts is a powerful laxative; drinking too much would make you lose more fluid.

CACTI: Water is stored in the fruit and bodies, but some cacti are very poisonous. Avoid contact with the spines, which can be difficult to remove and can cause festering sores.

The barrel cactus (see p. 97) can reach a height of 120cm (48in) and is found in the southwestern United States through to South America. The spine-covered outer skin is very tough: the best method is to cut off the top and chop out pieces from the inside to suck, or smash the pulp within the plant and scoop out the watery sap. A 100cm (40in) barrel cactus will yield about 1 litre (1¾ pints) of milky juice and this is an exception to the rule to avoid milky-sapped plants.

ESSENTIALS

Saquarro cactus of Mexico and USA grows to 5m (2in) and holds lots of fluid – but it is poisonous. Collect and place in a solar still to evaporate and recondense overnight.

Prickly pears have big 'ears' and produce oval fruits which ripen to red or gold. Their large spines are easy to avoid. Both fruit and 'ears' are moisture-laden.

WATER FROM ANIMALS

Animal eyes contain water which can be extracted by sucking them.

All fish contain a drinkable fluid. Large fish, in particular, have a reservoir of freshwater along the spine. Tap it by gutting the fish and, keeping the fish flat, remove the backbone, being careful not to spill the liquid, and then drink it.

If water is very scarce be careful not to suck up the other fish juices in the flesh, because they are rich in protein, and fluid will be taken from your vital organs to digest them.

Desert animals can also be a source of moisture. In northwestern Australia, aborigines dig for desert frogs that burrow in the ground. They store water in their bodies and it can be squeezed out of them.

ESSENTIALS

SALT

Salt is essential for water retention. A normal diet includes a daily intake of 10g (⅓oz). The body loses salt in sweat and urine and you need to replace that loss. The need for replenishment, however, will depend on your situation. If you are on reduced food or water rations, salt is the first thing to cut from your diet as it increases dehydration.

> The first symptoms of salt deficiency are muscle cramps, dizziness, nausea and tiredness. The remedy is to take a pinch of salt in half a litre (¾ pint) of water. Break up salt tablets and dissolve an appropriate amount in water or isotonic drinks, if available. Do not swallow them whole.

If your supplies run out and you are near the sea, saltwater contains about 15g (½oz) of salt, but do not drink it as it is. Dilute it with plenty of freshwater to make it drinkable, or evaporate it to get salt crystals.

Inland, salt can be obtained from some plants such as the roots of hickory trees in North America or of the nipa palm in Southeast Asia. Boil the roots until all the water evaporates and black salt crystals are left.

If no direct salt sources are available then rely on getting it second hand through animal blood, which is a valuable source of minerals.

SURVIVAL LOG

Keep a record of all events, particularly discoveries of edible plants and other resources. It becomes a valuable reference and making it helps keep up morale.

CLIMATE AND TERRAIN

It is vital to research conditions in the areas you plan to visit, but a knowledge of climate zones will help if accident throws you into unfamiliar territory.

Temperate climates cover much of the globe, and offer the best chances for survival without special skills. Heavy winter conditions may call for polar skills.

CLIMATE ZONES

POLAR REGIONS: Latitudes higher than 60°33′ north and south, but polar skills may be needed at very high altitudes everywhere. Arctic conditions occur in Alaska, Canada, Greenland, Iceland, Scandinavia, former USSR.

TUNDRA: Treeless zone south of the polar cap. The subsoil is permanently frozen and vegetation stunted.

NORTHERN CONIFEROUS FOREST: Found between Arctic tundra and temperate lands. Winters long and severe. Trees and plants flourish along the great rivers that flow to the Arctic Ocean. Elk, bear, squirrels and birds are plentiful. Dense growth makes the going difficult.

SURVIVAL SCENARIO
If the weather or conditions in your camp change, should you revise your survival strategy?
You should have a strategy for every scenario. As situations change, so should your strategy. Be flexible and be prepared to adapt.

CLIMATE AND TERRAIN

DECIDUOUS FOREST: Oak, beech, maple and hickory are the main species in America; oak, beech, chestnut and lime, in Eurasia. The rich soil supports many plants. Survival is easy, except in very high altitudes where tundra or snowfield conditions apply.

TEMPERATE GRASSLAND: Found in central continental areas of North America and Eurasia. Hot summers, cold winters and moderate rainfall have made these the great food-producing areas.

MEDITERRANEAN REGIONS: Lands bordering the Mediterranean are semi-arid, with long hot summers and short dry winters. Trees are few, water is scarce.

TROPICAL FORESTS: Equatorial rainforest, subtropical rainforest and montane forest all feature high rainfall and rugged mountains, which drain into large, swift-flowing rivers, with coastal and low-lying regions as swamp land.

SAVANNAH: Tropical grassland found in Australia, Venezuela, Colombia, Brazil and Africa. Grass grows up to 3m (10ft). Temperatures are high all year round. Water is scarce, but where it is found there will be lush vegetation and plenty of wildlife.

DESERT: One-fifth of the earth's land surface is desert, of which only small parts are sand; most is flat gravel cut by dried-up water courses (wadis). Very high temperatures occur by day, falling to below freezing at night. Survival is difficult.

POLAR REGIONS

Winter temperatures are well below freezing and
hurricane-force winds can whip snow 30m (100ft) into
the air. A 32kmph (20mph) wind brings a -14°C (7°F)
thermometer reading down to an actual temperature of
-34°C (-30°F). Days vary from total darkness mid-winter
to 24-hour daylight midsummer.

TRAVEL

Establish shelter as near to the aircraft or vehicle as
possible. Move only if rescue improbable. Cold dulls the
mind – plan while you can still think clearly.

Navigation is difficult in featureless terrain, and the
going treacherous. Don't move in a blizzard. Sea ice turns
to slush in summer and the tundra is boggy.

Don't make shelter near water, the habitat of black fly,
mosquito and deerfly. Cover skin, wear a net over the head
and burn green wood to keep them at bay.

Navigation

Compasses are unreliable near the Poles, so be guided by
the constellations and travel by night. By day use the
shadow stick method (see p. 230).

Do not use icebergs or distant landmarks to fix
direction: floes move constantly, and relative positions
change. If breaking ice forces you to another floe, leap
from and to a spot at least 60cm (24in) from the edge.

• Avoid icebergs – they can turn over without
warning, particularly with your added weight.
• Avoid sailing close to ice-cliffs – huge masses of
ice can break off without warning.

CLIMATE AND TERRAIN

CLIMATE AND TERRAIN

Observe birds: in the thaw wildfowl fly to land; seabirds fly out to sea by day, returning at night.

Clouds over open water, timber or snow-free ground appear black below; over sea ice and snow-fields, white. New ice produces greyish reflections, mottled ones indicate pack ice or drifted snow.

Follow rivers: travel downstream – by raft or on ice – except in northern Siberia where rivers flow north. On frozen rivers keep to edges and outer curve on bends. Where rivers join, follow the outside edge or take to outer bank. If river has many bends, take to land.

 ICE-COLD WATER IS A KILLER
Falling into icy water knocks the breath out of you. The body loses muscular control, consciousness fades, death follows in 15–20 minutes. RESIST! Take action. Move fast for land. Roll in snow to absorb water. Get to shelter and dry kit at once.

CLOTHING

Severe cold freezes exposed flesh in minutes. Cover every part of the body. Wear a drawstring hood; a fur trim prevents breath freezing on the face and injuring the skin. If clothing has no drawstrings, tie sleeves above cuffs, tuck trousers in to prevent heat escaping. If you sweat, loosen collar or cuffs, or remove a layer.

Outer garments should be windproof, but not waterproof, which could trap vapour inside – animal skins are ideal. Underlayers should trap air for insulation. Wool is best for inner garments. It does not absorb water and is warm even when damp. Cotton absorbs moisture and rapidly loses heat when wet.

CLIMATE AND TERRAIN

Footwear

Mukluks, waterproof canvas boots with rubber soles, are ideal. They should have an insulated liner.

Wear 3 pairs of socks, graded in size to fit over each other and not wrinkle. To improvise footwear use layers of fabric. Canvas seat covers make good boots.

(See Trench foot, p. 328.)

Snow shoes: Skiing is fine for firm snow but snow shoes are best in soft snow. Lift each foot without angling it, keeping shoe as flat to the ground as possible.

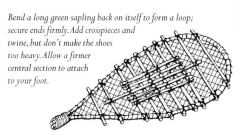

Bend a long green sapling back on itself to form a loop; secure ends firmly. Add crosspieces and twine, but don't make the shoes too heavy. Allow a firmer central section to attach to your foot.

SHELTER

Get out of the wind! Look for natural shelter to improve on, but avoid sites where a snowdrift, avalanche or rock fall might bury you. Avoid snow-laden trees (branches may fall) unless lower boughs are supported (see p. 168).

Don't block every hole against draughts. You must have ventilation, especially if your shelter has a fire.

CLIMATE AND TERRAIN

C.O.L.D.

The key to keeping WARM

Keep it **C**lean – Dirt and grease block air spaces!

Avoid   **O**verheating – Ventilate!

Wear it **L**oose – Allow air to circulate!

Keep it **D**ry – Outside and inside!

FIRE

Fuel sources are limited: driftwood, seal and bird fat, fuel from wreckage – in extreme cold drain oil from sump before it congeals. Can be used solid if drained on ground. High octane fuel can be left in the tanks.

On the tundra, willow, birch scrub and juniper may be found (see p. 177).

Cassiope is a low, spreading heather-like plant with tiny leaves and white bell-shaped flowers. It contains so much resin it burns when wet.

WATER

In summer water is plentiful. Pond water may look brown and taste brackish but vegetation growing in it keeps it fresh. If in doubt, boil it.

In winter melt ice and snow. Do not eat crushed ice, it can injure your mouth and cause further dehydration. Thaw snow enough to mould into a ball before sucking it.

Remember – if you are already cold and tired, eating snow will further chill your body.

CLIMATE AND TERRAIN

FOOD

Best chances for survival are along coasts where food supplies – fish, seals, seabirds – are dependable.

ANTARCTIC: Lichens and mosses are the only plants. Most birds migrate in autumn, but penguins stay. They are easiest to catch when nesting.

ARCTIC: Arctic foxes sometimes follow polar bears to scavenge their kills. Northern wildlife is migratory and availability depends on season.

TUNDRA AND FOREST: Plants and animals available year round. Tundra plants are small compared to temperate species (see p. 95).

> **☠ POISONOUS PLANTS**
> The majority of Arctic plants are edible – avoid water hemlock, baneberry and Arctic buttercups. Other poisonous species include lupin, monk's hood, larkspur, vetch, false hellebore and death camas. Best avoid fungi too – make sure you can distinguish them from lichens!

ANIMALS FOR FOOD

Caribou (reindeer), musk-ox and elk (moose) inhabit the Arctic, as do wolves, beaver, mink, wolverines and weasels. Foxes, living in the tundra in summer and open woodland in winter, are an indication of other, smaller prey – like mountain hares, squirrels and small burrowing rodents.

Bears and walruses are very dangerous. Leave them alone unless you are armed.

CLIMATE AND TERRAIN

Hunting and trapping

Tracks in snow are easy to follow, but leave a trail of bright flags to guide you back to base. Make them high enough not to be covered by a fresh snowfall.

Caribou can be lured by waving a cloth and moving on all fours. Ground squirrels and marmots may run to you if you are between them and their holes. Kissing the back of your hand makes a sound like a wounded mouse or bird and attracts prey. Find a concealed, downwind position. Be patient. Keep trying.

If you have a projectile weapon (gun, bow, catapult) which can be fired from ground level, lie in ambush behind a screen of snow, or make a screen of cloth.

Owls, ravens and ptarmigans are relatively tame and easy prey in winter. Many birds have a summer moult which makes them flightless. Eggs are edible at any stage of embryo development.

Seals provide food, clothing and blubber. They are most vulnerable on the ice with their pups (produced March–June). Newborn pups cannot swim. Out of the breeding season, catch seals by their cone-shaped breathing holes (narrower on the upper surface of the ice). In thick ice flipper and toothmarks show where the seal has been keeping the hole open. Club the animal then enlarge the hole to recover the carcass.

Polar bears feed on seals and fish. Most are curious and will come to you. Treat with respect and caution.

> Always cook meat: muscles carry the Trichinosis worm. Never eat seal or polar bear liver, which can have lethal concentrations of Vitamin A.

Preparing meat

Bleed, gut and skin while carcass is warm. Roll hides before they freeze. Cut meat into usable portions and freeze. Do not reheat meat – eat leftovers cold. Leave fat on all animals except seals. Remove seal fat; render it down before it can turn rancid and spoil meat.

> Rodents – squirrels, rabbits – carry Tularemia, which can be caught from ticks or handling infected animals. Wear gloves when skinning. Boil meat.

ARCTIC HEALTH

Frostbite, hypothermia and snow blindness are the main hazards. Efforts to exclude draughts in shelters can lead to lack of oxygen and carbon monoxide poisoning.

Thinking can become sluggish. Keep alert and active, but avoid fatigue and conserve energy for useful tasks. Sleep as much as possible – you won't freeze in your sleep unless you are so exhausted you cannot regenerate the heat you lose to the air. Exercise fingers and toes to improve circulation. Take precautions against frostbite (see p. 327–8).

Avoid spilling petrol on bare flesh. It will freeze at once and damage the skin.

Don't put off defecation – this can cause constipation. Try to time it conveniently before leaving your shelter so you can take waste out with you.

> Snow glare can cause blindness. Protect the eyes with goggles or a strip of cloth or bark with narrow slits cut for eyes. Blacken underneath the eye with charcoal to reduce glare further.

CLIMATE AND TERRAIN

MOUNTAINS

Snow-covered peaks offer no food or shelter. Climbing and negotiating icefields call for skills which must be learned in mountaineering schools.

If disaster strands you on a mountainside and rescue is unlikely, travel by day to the valleys where food and shelter are available. At night and in bad visibility this is too dangerous. Find shelter until visibility improves.

Shelter among rocks or wreckage (see p. 157). Salvage blankets from a crashed plane and cover up to prevent exposure. A plastic bag makes an improvised sleeping bag. On stony ground sleep on your stomach; on a slope sleep with your head uphill.

JUDGING TERRAIN

As you descend it is difficult to see what is below. Try moving along a spur to see what is below. The far side of a valley will give you an idea of what's on your side. The ground can fall steeply between a distant slope and a foreground bluff. Scree slopes are deceptive, appearing continuous until you are very close to a cliff.

DESCENT

Negotiating cliffs without a rope is very dangerous. Never attempt a high cliff. In the event of a plane crash it is less risky to wait for rescue than to climb.

On steep cliffs face the rock. For less steep rock faces with deep ledges, adopt a sideways position using the inside of your hand for support. For easier crags, descend facing outwards with the body bent and where possible carry weight on the palms of the hands.

CLIMATE AND TERRAIN

Descending by rope

With a rope it is possible to abseil down sheer cliffs. Use a doubled rope unless someone is left above to untie it or you are prepared to leave it behind, in which case use an undoubled rope for twice the descent.

ABSEILING: Loop rope around a firm anchor (test with full bodyweight). Avoid sharp edges. Pass both ends of rope between legs from front, bring round to left of body, over right shoulder and down across back. Hold rope in front with left hand and at back with right. Plant feet firmly against slope about 45cm (18in) apart, and lean back. Let rope round body carry your weight. Do not try to support yourself with your upper hand. Step slowly downwards. The lower hand controls rate of descent. Pay the rope out one hand at a time.

Make sure you are in a firm position before hauling the rope down and that you have planned your next move. Once the rope is down you may have no way of retracing your steps.

Abseiling can be dangerous. If possible, pad out shoulders and groin, and use gloves to prevent damage from friction. Never attempt unless accompanied by an expert or in a survival situation.

ASCENT

Climbing up, holds are easier to see, but it is safer to go round than over obstacles to avoid getting stuck. Plot a route from the bottom; keep body away from the rock, feet flat, and look up. Don't overstretch. Always keep three points of contact. Reach for a hold with one hand or foot, test it and seek a hold for the next hand.

To ascend fissures use the chimney technique. Place your back against one surface and wedge your legs across the gap to the other. Slowly move up.

Ascending with ropes

BELAYING: One person makes the ascent with a light line attached around the waist with a bowline, then hauls up the rope. At each stage of the ascent there must be a ledge to accommodate everyone and a tree or rock for an anchor. Secure the rope with a loop tied in a figure-of-eight or an overhand knot.

The belayer ties on with a bight (loop) or two bights to steady himself, and passes climbing rope over head and down to hips, making a twist around the arm closest to the anchor and takes up any slack. The climber ties on with a bowline around the waist and begins to mount. The belayer takes in rope to keep it taut. The anchor, belayer and climber should be in a straight line.

To take up rope pull in with right hand, push away with left so it passes behind back. Slide right hand out for more rope. Bring hands together and hold both parts of rope in right hand, while the left slides in towards the body to take up slack. Be ready to arrest rope, in case climber falls. Bring rope tight around body by bringing hands together.

☠ **FALLING ROCK CAN KILL**
On loose rock always test holds gently and never pull outwards on a loose hold. Be careful that your rope does not dislodge rocks. Even small falling rocks can inflict serious injury. If you knock a piece down, shout a warning to those below.

SNOW AND ICEFIELDS

If not equipped with proper ice axe and crampons and skilled in their use, try to keep clear of mountain ice.

On steep slopes climb in zigzags, kicking steps and driving snow axe or stick in sideways for stability. For gentle slopes dig in heels and use walking stick. On steep slopes descend backwards driving stick into snow for support and as a brake if you slip. Never use this method where there is any risk of avalanche.

SECURITY ROPES: A party crossing a glacier should be tied together at not less than 9m (30ft) intervals. The leader should probe the snow with a stick for crevasses. Ropes fixed to a firm anchor at both ends can prevent falls: tie short rope round waist in a bowline and tie on to main rope with a Prusik knot. This will slide along to allow descent but will arrest any falls.

If one of the group falls into a crevasse he must be hauled out with care: pressure of a rope on the chest can cause asphyxiation. Pass a looped rope down to put a foot in to take the weight. If the faller is unconscious three people in manharness hitches will be needed to pull him out. Speed is vital: temperatures in a crevasse are very low and the victim will rapidly weaken.

CLIMATE AND TERRAIN

AVALANCHES

Avalanches are a serious hazard in all high mountain regions. They usually occur on slopes of 30°–45° within 24 hours of a snow fall. After a major fall of several hours' duration, wait a day for snow to settle. Rain or a rise in temperature after a snow fall increases the risk, as does heavy snow falling in low temperatures, because it does not have time to stabilise.

MAIN AREAS OF DANGER

Snow-covered convex slopes.

Lee slopes where snow has accumulated.

Deep snow-filled gullies.

PRECAUTIONS

• Irregular, or timbered slopes are safest.

• The heat of the sun on snow can cause avalanches, so before noon travel in shaded areas, while after noon, keep to slopes that have already been exposed to sun.

• Avoid small gullies and valleys with steep side walls.

• Stick to ridges and high ground above avalanche paths – you are more likely to trigger a slide but, if you do, have a better chance of being on top of the debris or not being carried down at all.

• When crossing dangerous ground, rope together and use belays, always keeping at least 50 feet apart.

• Always look out for avalanche activity, even if you do not see it happening. Assess where avalanches started, their direction, and how long ago they took place. They will be a guide to where others are likely to occur.

SEASHORES

Most seashores offer abundant sources of food and
excellent prospects for survival.

CLIMATE AND TERRAIN

SANDY BEACHES: Burrowing species – molluscs, crabs,
worms – are left below the sand when the water recedes.
They attract feeding birds.

It may be possible to find freshwater in the dunes and it
is here that plants will grow. Dunes tend to be full of
insects, so don't make camp there.

MUDDY SHORES AND ESTUARIES: Where a river joins the sea
it deposits sediment, forming large mud flats. These
support many species of worms and molluscs and provide
a feeding ground for birds and animals.

ROCKY SHORES: If the cliffs are not too sheer, rock-pools
may form – these teem with life. Rocks form an anchor
for weed and sea urchins and crevices where octopus and
other cephalopods can live.

Soft rocks, such as chalk, marl and limestone, erode
quickly and have smooth surfaces. Hard rocks fracture in
chunks and provide good nesting sites for birds.

PEBBLE BEACHES: Continual movement of pebbles makes a
difficult habitat for most plants and animals.

TIDES: These vary according to location and season.

HIGH-TIDE LEVEL INDICATORS
- A line of debris along the beach.
- Change in sand texture.
- Weed, shells and colour changes on cliff faces.

CLIMATE AND TERRAIN

SHORE SAFETY

• Time the tides and study their pattern to avoid being cut off by an incoming tide or swept out by the ebb.

• Always check access from a beach or rocky shore. Keep an eye on the tide so you do not get cut off.

• Look out for strong currents, especially off headlands. Sandbanks and submerged rocks are also dangerous. Where a beach falls steeply into deep water there will be a strong undertow. If you enter the water, have a safety line round the waist and a firm anchor on shore.

SWIMMING

When fishing or swimming stay within your depth and watch for large waves which can knock you off your feet. If caught in the undertow of a large wave, push off the bottom and swim to the surface. Swim to shore in the trough between waves. When the next wave comes, face it and submerge. Let it pass and swim in the next trough shorewards.

If forced off shore by a strong current do not fight it – swim across it, using side stroke, and make for land further along the coast. Side stroke is not the strongest or fastest stroke, but it is the least tiring.

If being swept on to rocks, face land, adopt sitting position, feet first to absorb the shock. Wear shoes.

A relaxed body floats best, so stay calm. It is difficult to sink in saltwater. The main danger is in swallowing the water. Women are more buoyant than men and float naturally on their backs. Men float naturally face down, but don't forget to lift your head out to breathe!

WATER

• Freshwater is best obtained from small river outlets – large rivers tend to be polluted and full of silt.

• Seek pools among dunes (see p. 28).

• Freshwater rock-pools can be identified by the growth of green algae which is not grazed by molluscs (saltwater molluscs cannot survive in freshwater).

• Look for water trickling through rock, especially where mosses and ferns grow – it will be drinkable.

If stranded on a rocky outcrop offshore the only source of water may be the sea. Never drink sea water without distilling it. It can be used for cooking – but do not eat until you have a supply of freshwater.

FOOD

Hunt for fish and molluscs in rock-pools at low tide, and dig for molluscs and other creatures in sand.

Only eat molluscs collected live. Bivalves (oysters, mussels, etc.) should close tightly if tapped. Gastropods, (winkles, whelks) have a trap-door entrance to the shell, which should close tightly if the shell is shaken. Limpets and abalones are anchored to rocks. Prise off with a knife. If they are hard to dislodge they are good to eat – only sick or dead ones come off easily.

Bivalves can build up dangerous concentrations of toxic chemicals in polluted areas. In tropical zones mussels are poisonous in summer, especially when seas are reddish or phosphorescent. In the Arctic, black mussels are poisonous at any time of year.

CLIMATE AND TERRAIN

Don't expose yourself to parasites and pollutants: cook shell foods by boiling for at least five minutes.

On most coasts the best time to fish from the shore is about two hours after high water. Make use of the tide by building fish traps (see p. 152).

Hunt octopus at night: attract them with a light, then spear them. To kill an octopus, turn it inside out: place hand inside the fleshy hood, grab the innards and pull hard – alternatively, stab it between the eyes, or bang it against a rock. The flesh is tough but nourishing. Boil the body and roast the tentacles.

Seashore plants differ according to the climate. Gather when weather or tide prevent you taking food from the sea (see p. 105).

> Seaweeds are a valuable contribution to diet but the blue-green algae sometimes found on freshwater pools is very poisonous.

Sea cucumbers live on the seabed or in the sand. They look like warty black cucumbers, up to 20cm (8in) long. Boil for five minutes. Sea urchins cling to rocks just below the low-water mark. Boil, split open and eat the egg-like inside, but avoid if their spines don't move when touched or if they smell bad when opened.

You can also fish for seabirds by leaving baited hooks among offal on flat rocks or throwing baited hooks into the air to be taken on the wing. Hunt on the ground for eggs that are easy to collect before risking raiding cliff nests.

See also *Reptiles* and *Crustaceans* (p. 115 and p. 156).

DANGERS

Beware in water too murky to see through
When foraging, wear shoes to protect from spines, which can inflict a painful wound. If you get pricked and the spine breaks off, trying to squeeze it out may push it in deeper. Most will work their way out after a few days.

Well-camouflaged creatures like stingrays can lie hidden: prod the bottom with a stick and stir up sand and rocks in front of you as you go. Stingray wounds can be soothed with very hot water.

Don't put your hands into underwater crevices – you could get bitten.

Always approach a coral reef with caution
Both the reef and its inhabitants – e.g. cone shells, which shoot a poisonous barb – can present dangers.

Lagoon fish are often poisonous – even species which are edible in the open sea. Fish from the reef on the seaward side of the lagoon instead.

If stung by a jellyfish do not pull the tentacles off or wipe away the slime with your hand – you will only get stung more. Use seaweed or a cloth, or wipe the sting with sand.

Octopuses have a hard beak and a few can give a poisonous bite, e.g. the blue-ringed octopus.

Shark attacks occur in very shallow water. Beware!

Keep clear of snakes in the water – they are highly poisonous. If found on shore, pin them with a forked stick – they make a good meal.

See pp. 350–356 for a more detailed guide to coastal perils.

CLIMATE AND TERRAIN

CLIMATE AND TERRAIN

ISLANDS

Islands offer a special challenge, with acute isolation to be overcome. Explore the island and establish a daily routine. If it has been inhabited in the past, remains of buildings will offer shelter. If you find caves make sure they are not tidal and won't be flooded or cut off by spring tides, which are higher than normal.

On a barren outcrop, shelter may simply mean finding a place out of the wind. Food will be whatever clings to the rocks and what you can haul from the sea.

RESOURCES

Take care not to over-exploit limited resources. Lack of water is the reason many islands are uninhabited. Catch and store rainwater and distil seawater. Lush vegetation is a sign of springs and streams.

Distilling seawater takes lots of fuel, e.g. driftwood, dried seaweeds, or seal blubber. Have a fire only when necessary. Search beaches after every tide for flotsam.

Coconut palms

Tropical islands are rarely desert islands – they usually offer plenty to eat. Coconut palms grow throughout the tropics and subtropics, providing fronds for shelter, husks for ropes, and milk and meat.

To remove the husk, force it over a sharpened stake or split it with a hand axe. Extract the milk by piercing one of the dark eyes of the nut before smashing it open to get at the meat. Coconut milk is safe and refreshing – a large nut may hold 1 litre (1¾ pints). Do not drink from young (green) or old (dark brown) nuts as there is a risk of diarrhoea. The meat is indigestible in large amounts: eat a little at a time. Extract the oil by exposing chopped white meat to heat – sun or fire – and collecting oil as it runs off, or by boiling and skimming the oil as it rises to the surface. Rub it on to protect against sunburn and chafing from saltwater, to repel insects, as a salve for sores and blisters or, mixed with wood ash, as soap.

CLIMBING PALMS: If you need to climb to reach nuts, tie a strap of strong cloth and slip it round your ankles. Adjust it to hold your feet close to the trunk and press the soles of your feet inward to grip the tree.

ATTRACTING RESCUE

- Lay out signals by arranging rocks, seaweed or anything that contrasts with surroundings.
- Polish metal with sand to make signalling mirrors.
- If you see a ship, try to make contact on a VHF radio.

MOVING ON

In a group of islands, you may be able to move on when resources are exhausted on the first. If land is in sight, study tides and currents. Float something you can observe and note its progress. It may be possible to swim, but use a flotation aid, e.g. an empty box or coconuts. Time your swim so the ebb takes you out from your island and the high tide takes you to the new island. Build a raft in cold climates – from autumn to spring seal carcasses will float; lash several together to support your weight.

CLIMATE AND TERRAIN

CLIMATE AND TERRAIN

ARID REGIONS

Utilise any available shade, protect from the sun, cut
moisture loss and restrict activity during the hot days.

When great temperature differences between night
and day occur, condensation is a source of water.

When rain does come – years can pass with none at all
– it may be in torrential downpours which create flash
floods, before being quickly absorbed.

Dust or sandstorms reduce visibility. Protection is
needed against sand entering every orifice.

WATER

Water is vital. If you have it, ration it immediately. If you
are stranded during a desert crossing, you should have
planned your route bearing in mind oases, wells and
waterholes. Wells may require a container lowered on a
line. Small waterholes in wadi (watercourse) bottoms are
often seasonal, and covered with a stone or brushwood.

Away from known waterholes, dig at the lowest point
of the outside bend of a dry stream bed or the lowest point
between dunes. Do not dig in the heat of day – you will
sweat liquid you may not be able to replace. Always
balance fluid loss against possible gain (see p. 27).

Life expectancy depends on water available and your
ability to minimise perspiration. Without water you will
last 2½ days at 48°C (118°F) in the shade, doing nothing. If
you must walk to safety the distance you cover will relate
to the water available. With none, at 48°C, walking at night
and resting by day, you could cover 40km (25 miles).
Walking by day you would cover 8km (5 miles) before

collapse. At 48°C with 2 litres (3½ pints) of water you
might cover 56km (35 miles) and last 3 days.

Drink 1½ litres for every 2 lost (3:4 pints). Less fluid
will not result in less sweat. If more fluid is drunk than
needed it will be excreted and used to no purpose.

> **?** **SURVIVAL SCENARIO**
> **If you were in the desert and had to choose
> between carrying hessian or water, which
> would be more useful?**
> In desert conditions, the hessian is vital, of course.
> Water will be of no use at all if you cannot build a
> shelter to shade you from the blazing sun.

CLIMATE AND TERRAIN

SHELTER AND FIRE

Find immediate shade. In the evening cool build a shelter.
Do not stay in a metal vehicle. Use it to support a shelter
or an aircraft's wing as shade. Pile rocks into a windbreak
and make use of wadi walls (except when flash floods seem
likely). Use the double-layer technique for cooling (see
p. 161). If using fabrics, leave edges loose by day to aid air
circulation. Weight them down with rocks at night. Avoid
lying on hot ground: air can circulate under a raised bed.

Light a fire for warmth at night, for boiling water, and
signalling. Desert scrub burns easily. In barren land, fuel
and oil mixed with sand will burn. Dung is flammable.

CLOTHING

Clothing helps reduce fluid loss and gives protection from
sunburn and insect bites, as well as warmth at night.
Clothes should be light and loose-fitting, with air space

CLIMATE AND TERRAIN

between the garments and the body. Copy the flowing, layered garments of the Arab world. Trousers give more protection from insects and guard against serious sunburn on the legs. Cover the head and feet.

> Keep covered! Apart from risking severe sunburn, an uncovered body will lose sweat by evaporation. Keep clothing loose with a layer of insulating air. Sweating will then cool you more efficiently.

HEADGEAR: A hat with a piece of cloth attached to the back will protect but, better still, copy Arab headwear: make a handkerchief into a wad on top of the head, fold diagonally a piece of cloth about 120cm (47in) square, place it over the handkerchief, long edge forward, and secure with a cord tied round head. This traps pockets of air, and protects from sand. Wrap round the face for warmth at night.

EYE PROTECTION: Sunglasses may not be enough. Soot from the fire smeared below the eyes will reduce glare. Shield eyes from glare and windborne sand with a strip of material. Cut narrow slits to see through.

FOOTWEAR: Do not walk barefoot until your feet have hardened or they will burn and blister. Do not leave tops of feet exposed. Puttees keep sand out of boots; wrap them round the feet over open sandals.

FOOD

Heat causes loss of appetite – don't force yourself to eat. Protein foods increase metabolic heat and water loss. If water is scarce, keep eating to a minimum and try to eat only moisture-containing foods, e.g. fruit and vegetables. Food spoils quickly in the desert. Once open, eat stores at once or keep covered and shaded.

Vegetation is scarce (see p. 97), but deserts often support a variety of animal life. Insects, reptiles, rodents and some small mammals burrow or hide during the day. Large mammals are an indication that there is water close at hand.

HEALTH

Most desert illnesses are caused by excessive exposure to sun and heat. They can be avoided by keeping head and body covered and remaining in the shade.

- Constipation and pain in passing urine are common, and salt deficiency can lead to cramps.

- Heavy sweating coupled with garments that rub can block the sweat glands and result in an uncomfortable skin irritation known as prickly heat.

- Heat cramps, leading to heat exhaustion, heat stroke and serious sunburn are all dangers. A gradual increase in activity and daily exposure to the sun will build up a defence, provided that plenty of drinking water is available.

- Keep moist areas of the body – crevices of armpits, groin and toes – clean and dry to prevent infection.

DESERT SORES
Even the most trivial wound will become infected if not dealt with straightaway. Pull out thorns as soon as possible. Where the skin is broken, a large and painful sore may develop which could prevent walking. Bandage all cuts with clean dressings and use what medical aids are available.

CLIMATE AND TERRAIN

TROPICAL REGIONS

Everything in the jungle thrives, including disease and
parasites. Even if saturated by perspiration, clothing
affords protection from stings and bites.

Except at high altitudes, equatorial and subtropical
regions are characterised by high temperatures, heavy
rainfall and oppressive humidity. Violent storms may
occur towards the end of the summer. In choosing camp
sites make sure you are above potential flooding.

EQUATORIAL RAINFORESTS: Temperatures range from
30°C (86°F) to 20°C (68°F) at night. Jungle trees rise
from buttress roots to 60m (197ft). In this primary jungle
the canopy prevents light reaching the jungle floor. It is
relatively cool, with little undergrowth to hamper
movement, but visibility is limited. It is easy to lose a
sense of direction and difficult for rescuers to spot you.

SECONDARY JUNGLE: Along river banks and the fringes of
the jungle sunlight does penetrate to the floor and growth
is prolific. Undergrowth reaches heights of 3m (10ft) in a
year. Moving is slow, hot work, hacking a way with a
parang or machete (see p. 249).

SUB-TROPICAL RAINFORESTS: Found within 10° of the
Equator, these forests have a season of reduced rainfall,
even drought, with monsoons coming in cycles. More
deciduous trees grow here and undergrowth is dense.

Rescue signals must be set in clearings (often found
near river bends), or – better – on rafts on the river.

MONTANE FORESTS: At altitudes above 1000m (3280ft). The Ruwenzori Range of central Africa is typical: a crater-like landscape covered in moss between ice-capped peaks. Plant growth is sparse, trees stunted and distorted. Low branches make the going hard. Nights are cold, days hot and misty. Survival is difficult: make your way down the slopes to tropical rainforest.

SALTWATER SWAMPS: In coastal areas subject to tidal flooding, mangrove trees thrive, reaching heights of 12m (40ft). Their tangled roots are an obstacle above and below the waterline. Visibility is low and passage difficult. Sometimes channels are wide enough to raft, but generally progress is on foot. You won't starve – fish, molluscs, aquatic animals and vegetation are plentiful – but it is a hostile environment with water leeches, cayman and crocodiles. Where river channels intersect the swamp you may be able to make a raft.

　　If forced to stay in a swamp determine the high-tide level by the line of salt and debris on the trees, and fit a raised bed above it. Cover yourself for protection against ants and mosquitoes. Build your fire on a platform using standing deadwood for fuel. Decay is rapid in a swamp – choose wood that is not far decayed.

FRESHWATER SWAMPS: Found in low-lying inland areas, their thorny undergrowth makes the going difficult and reduces visibility – but survival is easy and swamps are often dotted with islands so you won't be chest-deep in water all the time. There are often navigable channels and raw materials available from which to build a raft.

SHELTER

There are ample materials for building shelters in most tropical regions. Where temperatures are high and shelters exposed to the sun, make roofs in two layers with an airspace 20–30cm (8–12in) between to aid cooling. Double layers of cloth will help keep out rain if angled (see p. 161).

FIRE

Everything is likely to be damp. Take standing dead-wood, shave off the outside and use that to start your fire. Dry bamboo and termite nests make good tinder.

FOOD

A wide variety of fruits, roots and leaves are available. Banana, papaya, mango and figs are easily recognised, but you may find the wealth of tropical foods bewildering. See pp. 99–104 for a detailed guide. If you're not sure, use the edibility tests described on p. 69 before you risk eating plants.

A wide range of mammals, reptiles, birds and fish can be hunted, trapped and fished (see pp. 107–156). Fish are easily digested, but in the tropics they spoil quickly. Clean thoroughly, discard entrails and eat as soon as possible. Do not preserve them by smoking or drying.

> Fish in slow-moving water may be infested with tapeworms and other human parasites: boil for 20 minutes. Water itself may be infected with amoebas which cause dysentery: always boil.

DANGERS

Insect attack
Slashing your way through the jungle you may disturb bee, wasp or hornet nests. Any bare skin is vulnerable to attack. Run! Don't drop anything – you won't want to go back for it. Sunglasses will help protect the eyes. Insects, desperate for salt, will make for the sweaty parts of your body. Protect armpits and groin against their painful stings.

Mosquito protection
Wear a net or T-shirt over your head, especially at dawn and dusk. Better, take a strip of cloth 45cm (18in) deep and long enough to tie round your head; cut it to make a fringe of vertical strips hanging from a band that will dangle round your face and over your neck.
Keep covered at night, including your hands. Oil, fat or mud spread on hands and face may help repel insects.
Use bamboo or a sapling to support a tent of clothing and large leaves rigged over your upper half.
A smoky fire will help keep insects at bay.

Cover your feet
Good footwear and protection for the legs is essential. Wrap bark or cloth round legs and tie it to make puttees as a defence against leeches and centipedes.

Beware hairy caterpillars
Always brush off in the direction they are travelling or small irritant hairs may stay in your skin and cause an itchy rash, which may fester in the heat.

CLIMATE AND TERRAIN

CLIMATE AND TERRAIN

Beware invaders

Keep clothing and footwear off the ground so that scorpions, snakes and spiders don't creep in. Shake out clothes and check boots before putting them on; be wary when putting hands in pockets.

Centipedes

These nestle for warmth in the more private body regions - take care on waking. Protect armpits and groin against stinging insects attracted by sweat.

Leeches

Their bite is messy but not painful. Left alone they drop off once they have had their fill. Do NOT pull them off – the head may come off leaving the jaws in the bite, which could turn septic. Remove with a dab of salt, citric acid from fruit, alcohol, a burning cigarette end, an ember or a flame.

Beware the Candiru

This minute, almost transparent Amazonian catfish, about 2.5cm (1in) long, is reported to be able to swim up the urethra of a person urinating in the water – where it gets stuck by its dorsal spine. The chance of this happening is remote, but don't take the risk. Cover your genitals and don't urinate in the water.

River dangers

Rivers can be home to dangerous creatures such as piranhas, stingrays and electric eels. Look out for crocodiles or alligators and take care in handling catfish, which have sharp dorsal fins and spines on their gill covers.

See pp. 340–356 for a guide to dangerous creatures and p. 319 for first aid procedures if bitten or stung.

FOOD

The survivor must understand the body's nutritional needs and how to meet them. This chapter provides details of how to trap, snare, hunt and fish, along with a miniature field guide to edible plants.

FOOD VALUES

A healthy body can survive on reserves stored in its tissues, but food is needed to supply heat and energy, and to recover after hard work, injury or sickness. Seventy calories per hour are required just for breathing and basic bodily functions. Work or major activity can burn up over 5,500 calories daily. Save calories: do not squander energy.

> A balanced diet is as important as having enough to eat. Vary your diet: it must include a range of elements which provide the right proportions of fat, protein, carbohydrates, minerals and vitamins.

CARBOHYDRATES: Easily digested, a primary source of energy, they prevent ketosis (nausea due to breakdown of body fats). They come in two forms: sugars, found in sugar, syrup, honey, treacle and fruits; and starches, roots, tubers (always cook) and cereals. One gram (0.035oz) produces 4 calories.

FATS: A concentrated form of energy. Lengthy digestive process requires plenty of water. Found in animals, fish, eggs, milk, nuts and some vegetables and fungi. One gram (0.035oz) produces 9 calories.

FOOD

PROTEINS: Main sources are meat, fish, eggs, nuts, grains, pulses, dairy produce and fungi. Worms are the richest source. One gram (0.035oz) produces 4 calories.

MINERALS: Phosphorus, calcium, sodium, potassium, chlorine, magnesium and sulphur are among those required in quantity. Only small amounts are needed of fluorine, iron and iodine. All are vital to good health.

TRACE ELEMENTS: These include strontium, aluminium, arsenic, gold and tiny amounts of other chemicals.

VITAMINS: While Vitamins D and K are synthesised by the body, most come from external sources. The average person naturally has a 28-day supply of vitamins within their body. Vitamin C is first that will need to be replenished, Vitamin A the next. Herbs will help with the first; shoots and leaves (that rabbits eat) with the second.

FOOD PLANTS

There are few places without some kind of edible vegetation. Plants contain vitamins, minerals, protein and carbohydrates. Some contain fat. All provide roughage.

> Do not assume that because birds or mammals have eaten a plant it is edible by humans. Monkeys give some indication but no guarantee that plants are safe.

TESTING NEW PLANTS

Always adopt the following procedure when trying new plants as food. Never take short cuts. One person only should complete the whole test. If in any doubt at any stage of the test, do not eat.

FOOD

EDIBILITY TEST

INSPECT: Try to identify. Ensure the plant is not slimy or worm-eaten. Don't risk old, withered plants.

SMELL: Crush a small portion. If it smells of bitter almonds or peaches – discard it.

SKIN IRRITATION: Squeeze some juice or rub slightly on tender skin (e.g. under upper arm). If discomfort, rash or swelling is experienced, discard it.

LIPS, MOUTH, TONGUE: If there is no irritation so far, proceed to the following stages, waiting 15 seconds between each to check that there is no reaction:

Place a small portion on lips
Place a small portion in corner of mouth
Place a small portion on tip of tongue
Place a small portion under tongue
Chew a small portion.

In all cases, if discomfort is felt, e.g. soreness to the throat, irritation, stinging or burning, discard it.

SWALLOW: Ingest a small amount and wait five hours. During this time drink or eat nothing else.

EATING: If no reactions, e.g. soreness to mouth, repeated belching, nausea, stomach or abdominal pains are experienced, plant may be considered safe.

Should stomach trouble occur, drink plenty of hot water; do not eat again until the pain goes. If it is severe, induce vomiting by tickling the back of the throat. Swallowing some charcoal will also induce vomiting and may absorb the poison at the same time. White wood ash mixed to a paste with water will relieve stomach pain.

FOOD

GATHERING PLANTS

Gather plants systematically. Take a container on foraging trips to stop the harvest being crushed, which makes it go off.

LEAVES AND STEMS: Young growth will be tastier and more tender. Old plants are tough and bitter. Nip off leaves near stem – tearing them off may damage them.

ROOTS AND TUBERS: Choose large plants. If difficult to pull up, dig round plant to loosen, then prise out with a sharpened stick.

FRUIT AND NUTS: Pick only ripe, fully coloured fruits from large plants. Hard green berries are indigestible. Peel fruits with tough, bitter skins. When nuts are ripe they begin to fall from the tree. Shake the tree or throw a stick to knock other nuts down.

CAUTION! Some seeds and grains contain deadly poisons. Taste, but do not swallow. Carry out edibility test (p. 69) and reject any seed that is unpalatable, bitter, or has a hot, burning taste, unless a positively identified pepper or spice.

The heads of some grain plants may have enlarged, black, bean-like structures in place of normal seeds. These carry a poisonous, hallucinogenic fungal disease that can be lethal. Reject the whole head.

FOOD

FUNGI: Medium-sized are easy to identify and less likely to suffer insect damage. Pick whole fungus to aid identification. Keep fungi separate until identified – poisonous ones will contaminate other food.

IDENTIFYING PLANTS

Only a small selection of plants can be described and illustrated here. Knowledge of even one or two plants that grow widely and at most times of year could make the difference between survival and starvation. Begin by learning these few thoroughly. Temperate zones: dandelion, nettle, dock, plantain; Sub-tropical and tropical zones: palm, fig, bamboo; Arid and desert zones: mescal, prickly pear, baobab, acacia (not in the Americas); Polar zones: spruce, willow (north), lichens (north and south), many temperate plant species which grow here in summer; Coastal zones: kelp and laver.

IDENTIFICATION AIDS (WITH KEY FOR ILLUSTRATIONS, PP. 73–106)

● *Location:* Plants grow only in suitable habitats. Learn these and you can eliminate impossibilities.

▲ *Shape and size:* Is it tall and woody? Short and soft-stemmed? Bushy and branched?

◆ *Leaves:* Large or small? Spear-shaped or rounded? Toothed or lobed edges? Uniform in colour?

❖ *Flowers:* Seasonal, but if present note colour, size, shape, single or clustered, where on plant.

Fruits and seeds: Fleshy? Hard? Note colour, shape, size, single or clustered, pods or capsules, etc.

Roots: Unless unusual, no help to identification.

FOOD

PLANTS TO AVOID

• Avoid any plant with milky sap, unless positively identified as safe (e.g. dandelion).

• Avoid red plants, unless positively identified.

• Avoid fruit which is divided into five segments, unless positively identified as a safe species.

• Avoid plants with tiny barbs on stems and leaves: these hooks will irritate mouth and digestive tract.

• Avoid old or wilted leaves – some develop deadly toxins when they wilt, e.g. blackberry, raspberry, plum, peach and cherry. All may be eaten safely when young, fresh and dry.

• Avoid mature bracken – it destroys Vitamin B in the body and can be lethal. Eat only tightly coiled 'fiddle-heads'. All northern temperate ferns are edible when young, but some are too bitter to be palatable and others have hairy barbs that must be removed before eating: break off young tips, close hand over stalk and draw frond through to remove the 'wool'.

POISON !

 There are two common poisons in the plant world, both easily detectable:

Hydrocyanic acid *(Prussic acid)*: tastes and smells of bitter almonds or peaches. Most notable example is the Cherry Laurel: crush a leaf and memorise the smell. Discard all plants with this smell.

Oxalic acid: the salts (oxalates) occur in plants such as Wild Rhubarb and Wood Sorrel. Recognisable by the sharp, dry, stinging or burning sensation when applied to the skin or tongue. Discard all plants which fit this description.

FOOD

EDIBLE PLANTS

In spring and summer young shoots are tender. Some may be eaten raw; many are best cooked. Wash in clean water, rub off hairs and boil in a little water so they cook in the steam. Leaves are rich in vitamins and minerals. Do not overcook.

1 **White Mustard** ▲ 60cm (24in). ● grassy wasteland, Eurasia. Stem: hairy. ◆ crinkly, deep-lobed. ❖ pale yellow. To eat: pick young. Cook whole plant. Peppery leaves and flowers can also be eaten raw.

2 **Shepherd's purse** ▲ 60cm (24in). ● wasteland. ◆ rosette; lobed, spear-shaped. ❖ small, white. To eat: boil leaves and mix with other plants.

3 **Primrose** ● grassy and shady spots. ◆ crinkly, tapering; basal rosette. ❖ long stalked, 5-petalled pale to bright yellow (pink, in some forms). All parts edible; young leaves are best. Primula genus, includes **Cowslip** (3a) and **Oxslip** (3b).

FOOD

4 **Dandelion** ● widespread.
◆ deep-lobed rosette. ❖ large,
yellow to orange. Eat young leaves
raw; boil old ones, change water to
remove bitter taste. Boil roots or
roast for coffee.

5 **Chicory** ● grassy wasteland.
▲ 1.3m (4ft). ◆ thick, hairy basal;
leafy spikes. ❖ blue, dandelion-
like. Prepare as Dandelion.

6 **Wild Sorrel** ● grassy
wasteland. ▲ 1m (3ft).
◆ long, arrow-shaped.
❖ Spikes, tiny red and green
flowers. Cook young leaves to
reduce sharp taste.

7 **Buckwheat** ● open grassy
spots, temperate climate.
▲ 60cm (24in). Stem: red.
◆ spear-shaped. ❖ clusters; small,
pink or white. Seeds make grain.

8 **Curled Dock** ● grassy
wasteland. ▲ 1m (3ft).
◆ long, narrow with wavy-
margin. ❖ whorls, small green.
Boil young leaves. Change water
to remove bitterness. Rubbing
with dock leaves soothes nettle
stings. Many varieties exist:
prepare as above, use sparingly.

FOOD

*Some plants have edible stems.
If they are soft, peel off outer
stringy parts, slice, then boil.
Inner pith of some stems, e.g.
elder, can be extracted by
splitting stem, and eaten. Use
fibrous stems to make twine.*

9 **Dead-nettles** Smaller than
stinging nettles. ◆ heart-shaped,
no stinging hairs. ❖ white (9) or
pinkish-purple (9a). Boil leaves.
10 **Stinging Nettles** ● widespread.
▲ young plants 15–20cm
(6–8 in). ◆ toothed, narrow ovals
covered in stinging hairs.
❖ green spikes. Boil for 6 minutes
at least to destroy acid. Dry and
store leaves.
11 **Ribwort** or **English
Plantain** has spear-shaped leaves
and shorter flower-spikes than the
Greater Plantain. ● dry ground.
Prepare as Greater Plantain (below).
12 **Buck's horn Plantain** ● dry
sandy and rocky areas. Small with
narrow, jagged leaves. ❖ short spikes.
Prepare as Greater Plantain.
13 **Greater** or **Rat's tail Plantain**
● grassy wasteland. ◆ broad, oval.
❖ distinctive spikes, tiny yellowish-
green and brown flowers. Prepare
rather bitter young leaves like spinach;
use expressed juice for wounds, or
decoction of whole plant for chest
complaints.

FOOD

14 **Galingale, Nutgrass** or **Chufa**
● common in and by freshwater.
▲ 1.5m (5ft). Stems: 3-angled.
◆ long, strap-like. ❖ forked,
clustered olive-brown flowerhead
turns yellow with fruit. Peel and
boil tubers, or dry and grind for
flour or coffee substitute.

15 **Cat's tail** or **Reedmace**
● in and by freshwater.
▲ 2–5m (6–15ft). ◆ long,
narrow, greyish. ❖ dark brown,
sausage-shaped. Rootstock / stems:
eat raw or boiled; cook leaves like
spinach, shoots like asparagus. Mix
pollen and water to make dough;
bake or cook on end of a stick.

16 **Reeds** ● in and by freshwater.
▲ up to 4m (13ft) ◆ grey-green.
❖ spreading, brown-purple
flowerheads on tall canes. Cook root.
Punctured canes exude edible gum.

17 **Flowering rush** ● Eurasia; in
and by freshwater. ▲ 1.5m (5ft).
◆ rise from roots; very long,
strap-like, 3-angled.
❖ pink, 3-petalled. Peel and
boil rootstock.

18 **Bracken** ● widespread. Old
fronds are harmful: eat only young
shoots or fiddleheads, drawing
off woolly parts and boiling for 30
minutes. Eat sparingly. Roots can be
boiled or roasted.

FOOD

Many herbs grow wild.
Most can be dried, but not in
direct sunlight.

19 **Tansy** ● grassy wasteland.
▲ 90cm (36in). ◆ toothed, dark
green, feathery leaflets.
❖ button-like, bright yellow.
Poisonous in quantity; leaves and
flowers make a wormifuge tea.
Strong smell keeps flies away.

20 **Marjoram** ● Eurasia; warm,
dry grassy areas. ▲ 60cm (24in).
◆ small, oval, stalked. ❖ clusters,
small purple-pink. Use infusion for
coughs and digestive complaints;
chewed leaves relieve toothache.

21 **Ramsons** ● Eurasia; woody
areas. ◆ bright green. ❖ white, star-like
at top of stem. Wild garlic. Use any part.

22 **Borage** ● Eurasia; grassy wasteland.
▲ 30–60cm (12–24in). ◆ pointed, oval.
❖ blue, star-shaped. Smells like
cucumber. All parts edible raw or
cooked. Use infusion for fevers.
Stems produce salt when cooked.

23 **Wild Angelicas** ● damp grassy and
woody areas. ▲ 1.5m (5ft). Stems: hollow,
sometimes purplish. Opposite pairs of broad,
toothed leaves. ❖ heads of tiny greenish
white or pink flowers. Boil aromatic leaves,
stems and roots. Use an infusion for colds
or externally for stiffness. Do not confuse
with water hemlock.

FOOD

ROOTS AND TUBERS

Roots are starchiest between autumn and spring. All roots should be thoroughly cooked. Scrub in clean water, boil until soft, then roast on hot stones in embers. To cook more rapidly, cut into cubes. Use a sharpened stick to test if they are done.

1 **Wild Parsnips** ● grassy wasteland. ▲ 1m (3ft). ◆ hairy, pungent with toothed leaflets. ❖ tiny, yellow, dense heads. Eat roots raw or cooked.

2 **Comfrey** ● ditches, damp areas. ▲ 1m (3ft). ◆ spear-shaped, taper to stem. ❖ clusters of cream or mauve bell-shaped flowers. Eat root raw or cooked. See p. 330ff for other uses. Do not confuse with foxglove.

3 **Salsify** or **Oyster Plant** ● dry wasteland. ▲ 60–90cm (24–36in). ◆ long, grass like. ❖ large, purple, dandelion-like. Cook root and young leaves.

4 **Woolly Lousewort** ● N. American tundra. Hairy, low-spreading. ❖ pink. Root: yellow. Eat raw or cooked. Beware: some other louseworts are poisonous.

FOOD

5 Jerusalem Artichoke
● wasteland. Sunflower-like: very tall, hairy. ◆ large rough oval leaves, ❖ large, yellow. Do not peel before cooking.

6 Wild Calla or **Bog Arum**
● by water. ▲ small. ◆ long-stalked, heart-shaped. ❖ green, finger-like organ enclosed in leaf-like hood, pale on inside, from which red berries arise. Roots must be cooked. Avoid other parts.

7 Arrowheads
● aquatic. ▲ 30–90cm (12–36in). ◆ large; arrow- or spear-shaped, strap-like below water. ❖ three rounded petals. Tubers edible raw, but best cooked.

8 Water Chestnut
● Eurasia, aquatic. ◆ diamond-shaped, floating. ❖ small, white. Grey, hard 2.5cm (1in), two-horned seeds are edible raw or roasted.

Flowers of some plants are edible, e.g. limes, basswoods, roses, hops, elder, primrose, camomile. Best used for teas and in medicinal infusions.

FOOD

FRUITS

Many fruits are familiar from cultivated forms. From summer on they are an important food source.

1 **Barberry** ● scrub, dry moorland. ▲ 3m (9ft). ◆ oval. ❖ yellow. Thorns in groups of three stems. Berries: bright red, very acid, rich in Vitamin C.

2 **Wild Rose** ● Temperate areas. Resemble straggly, unshowy garden roses: thorned stems, ❖ white or pink. Seedcases (hip) rich in Vitamin C: chew to extract juices, or crush and boil to a syrup.

3 **Brambles (Blackberry)** and **Wild Raspberry** ● scrub, woods, open ground. ◆ toothed. ❖ white, sometimes pinkish. Berries: juicy, segmented, ripen from green through red to purplish black in late summer. Raspberry bushes are less straggly, ripen to red earlier in summer. Eat raw.

4 **Dewberries** Like brambles, but berries are smaller with fewer segments than blackberry.

5 **Wild strawberry** ● dry grassy areas, woodland. Small, scrambling plants. Fruits (hidden under leaves) resemble small cultivated strawberries. Eat fruit fresh.

FOOD

6 **Hawthorn** ● scrub, wasteland. Spiny shrubs or small trees. ◆ deep-lobed leaves. ❖ clusters, white or pink. Berries: red. Flesh is creamy. Eat raw. Young spring shoots edible, too.

7 **Crab Apple** ● scrubland, woods. Short, spiny trees. ◆ oval, toothed, downy; reddish brown twigs. ❖ white, pink or red flowers. Fruit looks like cultivated apple. Very bitter. Eating too many causes diarrhoea. Best cooked with other fruit.

8 **Wild Cherry** ● woodland. ▲ 24m (79ft). ◆ small, pale green to red. Shiny red-brown bark. ❖ white or pinkish. Fruits are red or black: some kinds taste sour.

9 **Blackthorn** or **Sloe** ● Eurasian scrub, woodland. ▲ 4m (13ft). Bush with dark brown twigs, long thorns. ◆ oval. ❖ white. Small blue-black fruits are very acid and best cooked down to jelly.

To make jelly: boil fruit, then simmer until mushy. Allow to cool and store in airtight container. Fruits lacking in pectin (the setting agent) may be supplemented by adding pectin-rich fruit, e.g. crab apple.

FOOD

10 **Juniper** ● mountainous and
northern areas. ▲ 5m (15ft).
Tall or small prostrate bush.
◆ grey-green, needle-like.
Avoid young green berries;
cook ripe blue-black ones with
other food.

11 **Rowan** or **Mountain Ash**
● woods, rocky areas. ▲ 15m
(50ft). Smooth, greyish bark.
◆ small toothed leaflets. ❖ white.
Clusters of small orange berries.
Taste sharp, raw. Best cooked
down to jelly.

12 **Wild Mulberry**
● woods. ▲ 6–20m
(18–60ft). ◆ oval, sometimes
deeply lobed. ❖ on catkins. Red or
black fruits look like 5–7cm
(2–3in) long blackberries.
Edible raw.

13 **Wild grapes** ● widespread
in warm climates. Straggly, high-
climbing. ◆ large, heart-shaped,
coarsely toothed. ❖ greenish. Grapes
amber to purple. Eat fruit raw.
Boil young leaves.

*Some fruits can be dried for
storage. Lay them in a single
layer on a sheet, out of direct
sunlight. Protect from any
moisture, e.g. rain and dew.
The process takes 10 days.*

FOOD

NUTS

Nuts supply proteins and fat.

1 **Pine** ● temperate and
northerly areas. Cone-bearing trees.
◆ clusters of slim evergreen
needles. Heat mature cones to
release seeds. Edible raw, but
tasty roasted (and keep better).
Needles and bark also edible.

2 **Walnut** ● temperate areas
▲ to 30m (99ft). ◆ many
toothed, narrow leaflets; furrowed
bark. Blackish-brown nuts are first
enclosed in a thick green husk.

3 **Pistachio** ● warm climates
Mediterranean east to Afghanistan.
Trees. ▲ to 10m (33ft). ◆ small
oval leaflets. Clusters of nuts with
green kernel and reddish skin.
Eat raw or parch on embers.

4 **Oak** Occur in great variety.
◆ many have lobed leaves, all bear
acorns. Shell and boil several times,
changing water to ease bitterness,
or steep in cold water 3–4 days.
Can be buried with ash and charcoal,
watering occasionally. Then roast.
Good flour or coffee substitute.

5 **Hazel** ● thickets, wasteland.
Tall shrubs. ◆ toothed, oval to heart-
shaped. ❖ brown-yellow catkins.
Nuts come in ovoid, leafy, bristly or
hairy husks.

FOOD

EDIBLE PLANTS

The following are a further selection of the food plants
available. If you can find none of the plants illustrated or
described here, use standard edibility tests. Although
one part may be edible, another may be poisonous.
Test leaves, stems, roots, etc. separately.

Currants and Gooseberries
Bushy shrubs in woods, scrub and wasteland. Leaves
toothed, maple-like. Flowers small, 5-petalled, green-
white to purple. Red, purple-black, or yellow berries.
Eat currants raw. Cook gooseberries.

Wild Onions
Long, grass-like leaves; cluster of 6-petalled purplish,
pink or white flowers tops stem. Easily detectable by
smell. Edible bulb may be 25cm (10in) underground.

Thistles
Spiny, ridged stems; spear-shaped, prickly leaves,
purple flowers. Remove prickles, boil young leaves.
Peel tender shoots: eat raw or boiled. Cook roots of
young stemless plants. Eat nut at base of flower head.

Clovers
Abundant in grassy areas. Trefoil leaflets and dense
rounded heads of small flowers of white to greenish-
cream or shades of red. Leaves best boiled.

Wild Rhubarb
In open grassy places, from southern Europe to China.
Resembles cultivated rhubarb, but leaves ragged and
dissected. Eat stalk only, other parts are harmful. Boil.

Violets
Damp woods. Veined, crinkly, heart-shaped leaves;
violet, yellow or white flowers. Cook young leaves.

FOOD

POISONOUS PLANTS

Contact poisons

1 **Poison Sumac** ● swamp-lands in southeastern USA.
▲ 2–6m (6–18ft). ◆ hairless, oval leaflets in opposite pairs; dark-spotted smooth bark; clusters of white berries.

2 **Poison Oak** ● N. American woods. Resembles poison ivy, but is smaller, always upright.
◆ oakleaf-shaped. Berries.

3 **Poison Ivy** ● N. American woods. ▲ 0.6–2.1m (2–7ft), trailing or upright. ◆ 3-part, variable.
❖ greenish. Berries: white.

4 **Jewelweed** ● often found near poison ivy. ❖ pale yellow or orange spotted. Seed pods that pop. Juice eases irritation from contact poisons.

Poisons by ingestion

5 **Death Camas** ● N. America; grassy, rocky, lightly wooded places.
▲ 30–60cm (12–24in). ◆ long, strap-like, rising from base.
❖ 6-part, in clusters, green-white. deadly. Do not confuse with wild onions or lilies.

6 **Thorn-apple** or **Jimson Weed** ● widespread in temperate areas and in tropics.
▲ 90cm (36in). ◆ jagged-toothed, oval. ❖ solitary, large white trumpet. Fruits: spiny. Sickly smelling. All parts deadly.

FOOD

7 **Foxglove** ● wasteland.
▲ 1.5m (5ft). ✤ rosette of basal
leaves. ❖ tall, leafy spike, tube-
shaped purple, pink or yellow.
All parts highly toxic.

8 **Monk's hood** ● damp woods,
shady areas. ◆ palm-shaped,
segmented. ❖ hairy, hood-like,
purple-blue or yellow. Poisonous.

9 **Hemlock** ● grassy wasteland.
▲ 2m (6ft) Hollow purple-
spotted stems. ◆ coarsely toothed,
lighter below. ❖ dense clusters,
tiny, white. White roots.
Bad smelling. Very poisonous.

10 **Water Hemlock/Cow-bane**
● near water. ▲ 0.6–1.3m
(2–4ft). Stems: purple-streaked,
branching. Hollow rootstock.
◆ small 2–3 lobed, leaflet.
❖ clusters, tiny white. Smells bad.
One mouthful can kill.

11 **Baneberry** ● woods.
▲ 30–60cm (12–24in). ◆ toothed
leaflets. ❖ small, usually white,
at end of stem. Berries: white
or black. ALL parts cause
dizziness, vomiting.

12 **Deadly Nightshade**
● Eurasia; woods and scrub.
▲ 1m (3ft). ◆ oval. ❖ solitary,
bell-shaped, purple or greenish.
Berries: shiny black. All parts poisonous,
especially berries.

FOOD

Some poisonous plants are easy to mistake for edible species. Do not take risks: identify carefully. Learn to recognise the following in addition to those illustrated:

Buttercups
Occur in great variety of sizes worldwide. All have glossy yellow flowers. Avoid: all cause severe inflammation of intestinal tract.

Lupins
Habitat: grassland, clearings. 30–90cm (12–36in). Spikes of 'pea-flowers', blue, violet, pink, white or yellow. All parts cause fatal intestinal inflammation.

Vetches or Locoweeds
Grassland, meadows. 15–45cm (6–18in). Small spear-shaped leaflets in opposite pairs; spikes of 5-petalled pea-flowers, yellow-white, pink, lilac, purple.

False Helleborines
Wet, swampy areas, grassland. 0.6–2.6cm (0.2–1in). Lily-of-the-Valley-like leaves, drooping clusters of white or greenish-yellow flowers. Can be lethal.

Henbane
Bare ground by sea. Sticky hairs, toothed oval leaves. Flowers: cream, streaked purple. Bad smell. Deadly.

Virginia Creeper
Vine-like climber. Long-stalked, palm-shaped leaves, toothed leaflets. Clusters of small blue berries, smaller than wild grapes. As a principle, no plant with edible blue berries is vine-like with tendrils.

Buckthorns
Shrubs, sometimes small trees. Woods, scrubland. Leaves oval, fine-toothed. Berries: black and bitter-tasting. Violent purgative. Avoid.

FOOD

TREES

BARK

Outer bark is inedible, but the thin inner bark of certain trees can be eaten in spring, when sap has started to flow. Peel back bark near bottom of tree or from exposed roots to reveal inner layer. Can be eaten raw, but boiling will reduce to gelatinous mass which can be roasted and ground for use as flour.

Trees with best inner bark: Slippery Elm; Tamarack; Basswood; Birch; Aspen; Poplar; Maple; Spruce; Willow (including ground-hugging Arctic ones); Pine.

Other uses for inner bark: Birch bark may be removed in large sheets and used to make shelters, river craft and containers. Tear into strips for lashings.

Gums and resins: Some trees, when cut, bleed sap which hardens into a lump. If soluble in water this is gum; if not, it is resin. Both are nutritious. Some types are highly inflammable and ideal for lighting fires.

Birch and maple syrup: Cut a V-shape in the bark, collect the sugary sap that runs out. Below the V make a hole in the trunk, insert a leaf as a drip spout to run sap into container. Collect sap daily and boil to thicken down into a syrup.

Spruce tea: Steep fresh, green spruce needles in hot water to make a tea. Do not boil – boiling destroys Vitamin C. Alternatively, chew tender young needles, whose starchy green tips are particularly pleasant in spring. Spruces occur in the far north and are an important source of nourishment.

POISONOUS TREES

FOOD

The following trees contain irritants or poisonous substances. Do not eat any part of them.

Yew: Straggling evergreen tree or shrub with flaky bark, dark green needles and red, berry-like fruit.

Cedar: Large, spreading, scented evergreens with erect cones.

Horse Chestnut and **Buckeye:** Tall, with hand-shaped leaves, sticky buds and white, pink or yellow flowers. Do not confuse their poisonous, spiky-cased nuts with those of Sweet Chestnut.

Laburnum: Small, broad-leafed tree with three-part leaves and long sprays of yellow flowers.

Black locust: N. American tree with dark grey bark, oval leaflets in opposite pairs, clusters of white flowers and bean-like seed pods.

California Laurel or **Oregon Myrtle:** Short-trunked N. American evergreen, averaging 16m (50ft) with oval leathery leaves, clusters of yellowish flowers and green to purple berries. The foliage is pungently aromatic.

Moosewood or **Moosebark:** Occurs northeastern US. 12 m (40 ft); light, white-striped bark, oval to spear-shaped leaves, olive to brown above, broad-petalled yellow-green flowers and winged fruits.

Hickory: divided, often palm-shaped leaves, catkins and, usually, rounded nuts. Some varieties have edible nuts, sap and roots, but do not eat until the species is positively identified.

See also p. 104.

FOOD

FUNGI

PREPARING FUNGI: Reject suspicious, discoloured or maggoty parts. Clean, slice and boil. Many bracket fungi are bitter and tough: cook thoroughly. Tender ground fungi can be added to soups and other foods.

> Fungi must be positively identified before eating. No reliable edibility tests exist – deadly kinds do not taste unpleasant and no symptoms may appear for some hours after eating. There is no truth in folk tales that a fungus is not poisonous once peeled or cooked, or that toxic kinds change colour when cooked.

STORING FUNGI: Collect all you can when available and separate caps from stems. Place on rocks in sun, caps gill-side up. With *Boletus* species, remove spongy tissue under cap. When dry, store in airtight containers. To use, soak in water then eat raw, or add to soups.

IDENTIFYING THE POISONOUS AMANITAS
- To avoid mistaking *Amanitas* for edible varieties:
- Avoid fungi with white gills, a volva (cup-like appendage at base of stem) and stem rings.
- Avoid fungi that are wormy or decomposing.
- Unless positively identified – discard.

OTHER USES FOR FUNGI
- Many bracket fungi make excellent tinder.
- Razor-strop fungus can be used to sharpen knives.
- Giant puffball will staunch and soothe bleeding cuts.
- Tree fungi can be used in treating burns.

FOOD

EDIBLE FUNGI

Learn to recognise the small
selection illustrated here — and
stick to them.

cap

gill

ring

stem

volva

1 *Fistulina hepatica*
(Beefsteak fungus).
Tree fungus. Found
in autumn on oaks.
Reddish above, pinkish
below. Rough texture.
Resembles large tongue.
Exudes blood-coloured juice.
Young specimens are best. Soak to
soften, stew thoroughly.

2 *Armillaria mellea* (Honey fungus).
Grows on broad-leaved trees,
conifers and stumps, spring to autumn.
Tawny yellow, brown-flecked caps
3–15cm (1¼–6in) across, white
gills, white flesh and bootlace roots.

3 *Lycoperdon giantea* (Giant
Puffball) Grows on the ground.
Resembles a 30cm (12in) football.
In woods and grassy places late
summer to autumn. Smooth, white,
leathery. Yellows with age. Weighs up to
9kg (20lb). Simmer or fry young ones.

4 *Cantharellus cibarius* (Chanterelle).
Apricot-scented, egg-yellow, funnel-
shaped, 3–10cm (1¼–4in) across.
Pronounced, forking gills. Grows in
groups under trees, especially beech, from
summer on. Stew for 10 minutes.
Do not confuse with *Cortinarius speciosissimus*.

FOOD

Agaricus *fungi. Avoid any that stain yellow when cut or bruised, or that smell of carbolic. Some young buttons are hard to distinguish from the deadly Amanitas.*

1 **Agaricus campestris** (Field mushroom). Grassy places in autumn, rarely by trees. White cap to 10cm (4in) across, browning slightly in older specimens. Pink gills later turn dark brown. Eat raw or cooked.

2 **Agaricus augustus** In clusters in woodland clearings, summer and autumn. Smells of anise. Scaly, light brown cap to 20cm (8in) across. Young gills pink, later turn dark. Ringed stem.

3 **Lepiota procera** (Parasol) By broad-leaved woods and in grassy clearings summer to autumn. Tastes of almonds or Brazil nuts. Brownish cap, later with dark scales, to 30cm (12in) across with creamy white gills and slender stem with double white ring and brown bands.

4 **Coprinus comatus** (Shaggy Ink Cap). In groups, open grassland, summer/ autumn. Cylindrical cap with white or pale brown scales. Gills begin white, turn pink then dissolve into black inky mess. Gather young ones with pale gills. Poisonous if eaten with alcohol.

5 **Boletus edulis** In woodland clearings, autumn. Swollen stem, white flesh. Sponge-like pores instead of gills. Dry well. Avoid any with pink or red spores.

POISONOUS FUNGI

Do not use any fungi you can't positively identify.

1 *Amanita virosa* (Destroying Angel).
White. Large volva, scaly stem,
cap to 12cm (5in) across. Woodland,
summer/autumn. Sweet, sickly
smelling. Deadly.

2 *Amanita phalloides* (Death Cap).
In woodland, especially oak or beech.
Green-olive cap, to 12cm (5in) across.
Pale stem, large volva, white gills and flesh.
Lethal.

Symptoms for Destroying angel/Death cap
appear 8–24 hours after eating: vomiting,
diarrhoea, thirst, sweating, convulsions.
Apparent recovery after one day, then a
relapse followed in 90% of cases by
death from liver failure.
No known antidote.

3 *Amanita pantherina*
(Panther Cap). In woodland,
especially beech. Brownish, white-
flecked cap to 8cm (3in), white gills,
2–3 hoops at base of stem.
Can be fatal.

4 *Amanita muscaria* (Fly Agaric). In pine
and birch woods in autumn. Bright red cap,
flecked with white, to 22cm (9in).
Causes severe gastro-intestinal
disturbance, delirium, hallucinations,
convulsions, then coma-like sleep.
Victim usually recovers.

FOOD

5 *Entoloma sinuatum* (Leaden
Entoloma). In groups in grassy areas
and woods, especially beech and oak,
summer/autumn. Dull grey-white,
deeply convex cap to 15cm (6in)
across. Yellowish gills turn pink. Firm
white flesh smells of meal, bitter almond
and radish. No ring on the stem.
Deadly.

6 *Inocybe patouillardii* In broad-
leaved woods, especially beech,
summer/autumn. Begins whitish,
turns yellow-brown. Cap to 7cm
(2¾in), often split at margin. Whitish
gills turn olive-brown. Stains red when
bruised. Confusable with *Agaricus* when
young, but lacks ring on stem.
Causes vertigo, blindness, sweating,
dilated pupils, delirium. Can kill.

7 *Paxillus involutus* In woods,
especially birch. Solid yellow-brown
cap with rolled rim to 12cm (5in)
across. Yellow-brown gills, straight
stout stem. Deadly. Do not confuse
with chanterelle.

8 *Cortinarius speciosissimus*
In coniferous woods in autumn.
Reddish to tawny brown. Flattish
cap 2–8cm (¾–3¼in). Rusty-
brown gills. The lighter-
coloured *C. orelanus* is also
poisonous, found in broad-leaved
woodland. Both have radish-like
smell. Deadly.

ARCTIC AND NORTHERN PLANTS

In addition to these hardy Arctic plants, many temperate species occur in summer in the far north.

1 **Red Spruce** ● dry areas, N. America. ▲ 23m (75ft). Dark or yellow-green needles round hairy twigs. Rough dark bar. Pendant cones. Eat young shoots raw or cooked. Infuse needles for teas. Boil edible inner bark.

2 **Black Spruce** ● moist areas, N. America. ▲ smaller than red spruce, shorter needles. Other similar species occur in America and northern Eurasia. Use as red spruce.

3 **Labrador Tea** ● N. America. ▲ 30–90cm (12–36in). ◆ narrow, rolled edges, whitish or hairy below. ❖ 5-petalled, white. Infuse leaves for tea.

4 **Arctic Willow** ● tundra. ▲ 30–60cm (12–24in). Mat-forming shrub with rounded leaves, shiny above. Yellow catkins. Eat spring shoots, leaves, inner bark, young peeled roots. High in Vitamin C.

5 **Ferns** ● moist areas in summer, far northern woods, by tundra. Eat only young fiddleheads up to 15cm (6in). Remove hairs. Steam to cook.

FOOD

FOOD

6 **Cloudberry** ▲ 30cm (12in).
Bramble-like. ◆ palm-shaped. ❖ white.
Berries: at top of plant, pink, ripening to
orange/amber. Eat raw.

7 **Salmonberry** ● N. America, Europe.
Like a small Wild Raspberry. Thornless,
with 3-part leaves. ❖ purple-red.
Berries: red or yellow. Eat raw.

8 **Bearberry** ● Arctic regions. Small, mat-
forming, woody evergreen. ◆ club-
shaped. ❖ pink or white. Berries: red,
in clusters. Cook.

9 **Iceland Moss** Lichen. Forms tufted,
grey-green or brownish mats to
10cm (4in), composed of strap-shaped
branches. Soak for several hours, then
boil well.

10 **Reindeer Moss** Lichen.
▲ 5–10cm (2–4in). Often grows in
large clumps. Hollow, roundish, grey stems,
antler-like branches. Soak several
hours, boil well.

11 **Rock Tripe** Lichen. Roundish,
blister-like grey or brown growths
attached to rocks by a central stalk.
Some kinds warty, pebble-like;
others smooth. Can cause irritation if
eaten raw. Soak in water overnight,
then boil well. Then roast to make
them crunchy.

If you kill a caribou, eat the
fermented lichens in its stomach.

FOOD

DESERT PLANTS

Water is vital to desert survival.
Know the water-bearing plants.
Eat only if you have no water.

1 **Barrel Cacti** ● southwest USA.
▲ 1.2m (4ft). Yields up to 1 litre
(1¾ pints) milky sap – an exception to the
rule to avoid milky sap. Slice off the top,
smash inner pulp, then drink.

2 **Prickly Pears** ◆ thick, jointed, pad-
like leaves. ❖ red or yellow. Egg-
shaped, pulpy fruit. Eat peeled fruit
raw. Cut away spines, peel and cook
tender young pads. Roast seeds for
flour. Tap stems for water. Beware:
very prickly. In Africa, do not
confuse with spurges (which have
milky sap).

3 **Carrion Flowers**
● southern / tropical Africa.
Large plants; short succulent stems
branch off into leaves like fat spines.
❖ star-shaped, some hairy, give off stench
of rotting meat when mature.
Tap stems for water.

4 **Mescals** ● Africa, Asia, Europe,
Americas – moist tropical areas and
desert. ◆ rosette of thick, sharp-
tipped leaves from which rises a long
flower stalk. Stalks not yet in flower
are edible when cooked.

5 **Wild Gourds** ● Kalahari, Sahara east to India.
Mat-forming, vine-like. Orange-sized fruit. Roast seeds, cook
young leaves, eat flower raw, chew stems and shoots for water.

FOOD

6 **Date Palm** ● near water,
India to N. Africa. Tall, slender palms
crowned with tuft of leaves up to 4m
(16ft) long. Eat fruit and growing tip
raw. Cook young leaves. Sap from
trunk can be boiled down.

7 **Baobab** ● Africa to Australia.
Large tree with swollen, ridged
trunk, 9m (30ft) diameter.
Tap roots for water. Fruit,
10–20cm (4–8in) long, and
seeds are edible raw. Boil tender
young leaves.

8 **Acacia** ● Africa to northern
Australia. Many kinds, all
thorny, scrubby, medium-sized
trees with small leaflets.
Globular, 1cm (⅓in)
flowerheads, white, pink or
yellow. Tap roots for water.
Roast seeds. Boil young leaves
and shoots.

9 **Carob** ● Mediterranean, Sahara,
Arabia to India. ▲ to 15m
(50ft). ◆ shiny, evergreen,
paired, 2 or 3 to a stem.
❖ small, red. Flat leathery seed
pods contain sweet pulp – eat
raw. Hard brown seeds can be
ground and cooked as porridge.

FOOD

TROPICAL PLANTS

1 **Sago Palm** ● damp lowlands.
▲ 10m (33ft). Spiny trunk.
◆ long, arching. Spongy inner pith
provides sago.

2 **Nipa Palm** ● brackish estuaries
in SE Asia. ▲ 6m (20ft). ◆ long, fern-
like, clustering at base to form
'trunk'. Yields sugary sap, delicious
fruit and edible growing tip.

3 **Banana** or **Plantain**
● all over tropics. ▲ 3–10m
(10–33ft). Large, strap-like, usually
split light green leaves. Eat buds,
growing tips, young stems and inner
parts of roots. Always cook hard fruit.

4 **Fish-tail Palm** ▲ average 10m (33ft).
Smooth ringed trunk, long arching leaves,
oval or wedge-shaped leaflets. Use as sago
palm. Do not eat fruit.

5 **Coconut Palm** ● moist tropics.
▲ to 30m (99ft). Large clusters
of nuts hang at base of leaves.
Coconut is inside large, smooth husk.
Growing tip, milk and flesh of nut
are edible. Boil sap down.

Growing tip, enclosed by
crown of leaves or bases of
leaf stems, is edible in most
palms – eat if not too bitter.
Avoid fruit unless positively
identified.

FOOD

6 **Bignay** ● SE Asian forests.
▲ 10–13m (33–43ft).
Evergreen shrubs. ◆ shiny,
15cm (6in). Fruits: currant-like,
many-seeded, 1 cm (⅖in) across.
Ripen from green to white to
red then black. Edible raw, but
best jellied.

7 **Mango** ● moist places.
Medium to large evergreen
tree. ◆ narrow, dark green
clusters. Fruit: oval, 7.5–13cm
(3–5in); ripens from green to
orange. Eat fruit raw. Leaves
may cause allergic reaction.

8 **Sweet Sop** ● widespread.
▲ 5–6m (15–18ft). Tree.
◆ oval to spear-shaped.
❖ magnolia-like flowers. Fruit:
aromatic, pulpy, green-grey,
segmented.

9 **Sour Sop** ▲ to 12m
(39ft). Fruit: avocado-like,
green, leathery, spiny. Weigh
up to 2kg (4.4lb).

10 **Wild Fig** ● tropical,
subtropical areas, some species in
deserts. Straggly trees, aerial
roots, leathery evergreen
leaves, rounded at base. Fruit:
pear-shaped, grow direct from
branch. Edible raw. Avoid any
that are hard and woody, or hairy.

FOOD

11 **Ceylon Spinach** ● most tropical areas. Vine-like. ◆ thick, circular to oval or heart-shape, green to purple-red. ❖ fleshy, purplish. Cook young leaves and stems.

12 **Tamarind** ● widespread. Densely branched tree. ▲ to 25m (82ft). ◆ Evergreen leaflets. ❖ pale yellow, red-streaked. Eat pulp of brown seed pods raw. Use seeds and young leaves as pot herb. Peel and chew bark.

13 **Peanut** ● widespread. Small bushy plant. ◆ oval, in pairs. ❖ yellow flowers and stalks leading to wrinkled pods. Nuts ripen underground and keep well.

14 **Yam Beans** ● in large patches in most of tropics. Climbing plants with knotty, turnip-like root. ◆ irregular, 3-part. Tubers are crisp, sweet, taste of nuts. Seeds are harmful raw: boil well.

Food deteriorates rapidly in the tropics. Do not pick more than you need.

FOOD

15 **Water Spinach** ● by fresh water, SE Asia. Usually floating plant. ◆ green leaves. ❖ white. Old stems are stringy. Boil young leaves and shoots.

16 **Lotus** ● aquatic, Asia, Africa, N. America. ◆ long-stalked, bell-shaped blue-green leaves stand clear of water. ❖ pink, white or yellow. Boil young leaves, peeled stems and rootstalk. Remove bitter embryo and boil or roast ripe seeds.

17 **Water Lily** ● lakes, rivers, streams in tropical Africa, India, Americas. ◆ heart-shaped, float on water. Large edible tubers; cook stems; seeds are bitter but nourishing.

18 **Wild Yam** ● occurs in variety in light forest and clearing in tropical and subtropical areas. Twining, vine-like stems, some kinds bear edible aerial tubers leading to underground tubers. Store well if kept dry. Some are poisonous raw; so always cook: peel tubers, boil and mash.

19 **Wild rice** ● widespread in tropics. ▲ 90–120cm (36–48in). Coarse grass. Thresh and winnow grains to remove husks; boil or roast and pound to store as flour.

20 **Sugarcane** ● cultivated all over tropics, grows wild. Coarse, tall, aromatic, thick-stemmed grass. Chew canes raw to extract sweet juice.

21 **Millets** Grasses several feet tall, with sausage-like heads of grain. Pound to a meal and use in stews or as porridge.

22 **Bamboo** ● moist areas. Rapid growing, edible young shoots (22a) are at base of plant. Split tough outer sheath and cook like asparagus. Seeds of flowering plant are also edible. Take care: plants under tension may shatter or whiplash.

In addition to plants illustrated here, you will recognise relations of cultivated varieties such as avocado and citrus fruits. Always apply edibility test to unknown plants, using very small amounts.

FOOD

POISONOUS TROPICAL PLANTS

1 **Physic Nut** ● wooded areas in tropics.
Small tree. ◆ large, lobed, ivy-like.
❖ small, green-yellow. Fruit: yellow,
apple-sized with 3 large seeds. Seeds taste
sweet but are violent purgative.

2 **Strychnine** ● mainly in India, but other
species occur throughout tropics. Small
tree. ◆ oval, opposite pairs. Fruit:
orange-like, white to yellow-red. Seeds
are deadly.

3 **Castor Oil Plant** ● scrub and wasteland
all over tropics. shrub-like. ◆ arranged like
fingers of a hand. ❖ yellow, spikes.
Prickly 3-seeded pods. Seeds are violent
purgative, sometimes fatal.

4 **Duchesnia** ● waste ground in warm
parts of Asia, N. America. ◆ 3-part, trailing.
❖ yellow, not white. Fruit: red,
strawberry-like and highly poisonous,
can be lethal.

Other plants to avoid

White Mangrove ● mangrove swamps.
Pale bark, pencil-like roots. ◆ spear-
shaped/oblong. ❖ yellow. Round white
berries. Sap blisters skin; can blind.

Nettle Trees ● widespread, often near
water. ◆ spear-shaped, sharp-toothed.
❖ drooping spikes, like common nettle.
Sting like a nettle's, only worse. Poisonous seeds.

Pangi ● SE Asia (mainly Malaysia). Tree. ◆ heart-shape,
in spirals. ❖ green spikes. Clusters of large brownish,
pear-shaped fruit. All parts poisonous, especially fruit
(contains prussic acid).

SEASHORE PLANTS

The following thrive in salty conditions, but many other edible plants occur near the coast.

1 **Oraches** ● salty ground, some occur inland. Pale-stalked.
◆ pale green, spear-shaped.
❖ small, green-white spikes.
Cook young leaves.

2 **Sea Beet** ● European coasts. Sprawling, red-tinged. ◆ long-stalked, dark green. ❖ small green clusters. Boil leaves or eat raw.

3 **Sea Rockets** ▲ 30cm (12in).
◆ fleshy, blue-green, lobed.
❖ lilac/purple. Egg-shaped seed pods. Peppery leaves and young pods can be eaten raw or as pot herb.

4 **Glassworts** or **Marsh Samphire**
● widespread in saline areas, mud flats. Plump, greenish yellow jointed stems up to 30cm (12in) high. ❖ minute, scarcely visible at junction of stems.
(**Rock Samphire** is no relation – grows on shingle and cliffs; cook and suck fleshy hairless stems and grey-green leaves.)

5 **Scurvy grass** ▲ 25cm (10in). ◆ dark green, heart- or kidney-shaped. ❖ small, white or pink. Very bitter, leach in water. Rich in Vitamin C.

FOOD

FOOD

SEAWEEDS

Occur anchored to bottom in shallow waters, or floating on open sea. Coastal weeds are often stratified: green forms grow in surface waters, red in shallow water, brown a little deeper. Wash seaweeds in freshwater before eating, to remove salt.

1 **Sea Lettuce** ● on rocks and stones in Atlantic and Pacific, especially where water runs into sea. Light green leaves. Wash and boil.

2 **Enteromorpha intestinalis** ● rock pools and salt marshes in cool waters. Pale green; pod-like unbranched fronds up to 50cm (20in). Whole plant is edible in early spring, fresh or dried and pulverised.

3 **Kelps** ● rocky shores of Atlantic and Pacific. Short cylindrical stem; thin, long, wavy olive-green to brown fronds. Edible raw but best boiled.

4 **Lavers** ● Atlantic and Pacific. Thin, satiny red, purple or brown fronds. Boil till tender, then mash. Use as relish or mix with grains to make cakes.

Some seaweeds are purgatives. Use the edibility test on p. 69.

FOOD

ANIMALS FOR FOOD

Your humane instincts must be balanced against the expediencies of survival. Study each species' habits: where it sleeps, what it eats and where it waters. Learn how best to make a kill, what traps to set. The younger the animal, the more lean the meat. Most species put on extra fat to see them through the winter.

FINDING GAME

TRACKS AND SIGNS: If you can read the subtle signs that animals leave, you know what hunting/trapping methods to use.

Only large, powerful mammals venture out by day. Most small mammals eat at night, as do those that feed on them. Trails between watering/feeding places and homes are clearest on wet ground, snow and damp sand. Determine the age of the track by its sharpness and moisture content: the clearer it is, the more recent.

In the early morning, check tracks from ground level. If dew and spider's webs have been disturbed, the tracks are fresh. Tunnels through undergrowth and broken twigs along a track will indicate the size of the animal responsible. If trampled leaves have not wilted and broken twigs are green and supple, trail is fresh.

FEEDINGS SIGNS: Gnawed bark, discarded food, and remains of prey reveal an animal's presence and suggest bait for traps. For details, see pp. 108–119.

DROPPINGS: Size and quantity indicate type of animal; old droppings will be hard and odourless, fresh ones wet and still smelling. Flies draw attention to them.

FOOD

Break open a dropping to check for clues as to what the animal has been eating, then bait your trap accordingly. Copious bird droppings indicate presence of nesting sites. Seed-eating birds' droppings are small and mostly liquid (indicating water within reasonable range); meat-eaters' pellets contain indigestible parts of prey.

ROOTINGS: Some animals turn over ground in search of insects and tubers. Crumbly, fresh earth means it has been recently dug. A muddy wallow is a sign of pigs.

SCENT AND SMELL: Listen to noises and register smells. In cold climates a large animal's breath forms a cloud of condensation which can be seen from afar.

BURROWS AND DENS: Some are easy to find. Hidden ones may be given away by tracks or droppings nearby.

MAMMALS

The following tracks are not to scale. Most are typical of a family of animals, varying according to species. Where two are shown, track 1 is right front, track 2 is right hind.

WEASEL GROUP

Stoats, mink, martens and polecats are all secretive and have sharp, dangerous teeth.

Traps: Spring snares with bait bars and deadfalls. Bait with offal or birds' eggs.

Tracks: Indistinct except in soft ground. Five well-spaced claws and toes, hair on main pad often smudges. Fore and rear prints overlap.

FOOD

WILD DOGS

Foxes and other species are found from deserts to the Arctic. Wolves are confined to northern wilderness. Canines can be very dangerous. Their superb senses make it pointless to stalk them.

Remove anal glands before cooking. Boil thoroughly.

Traps: Snare foxes: try stepped-bait or toggle, bait-release, baited-hole-noose. Minimise human scent.

Tracks and signs: Walk on toes. Print shows four pads and claw tips – outer pad shorter than inner, with large main pad to rear. Elongated, tapering droppings show remains of fur, bones, insects. Fox scent pungent. In soft ground, fox dens can be dug out.

WILD CATS

Occur on all continents except Australia and Antarctica, but not common. Secretive and generally nocturnal. Kills of big cats may be scavenged if unattended, but beware big cats. Small cat meat is like rabbit. Stew thoroughly.

Traps: Bait powerful spring snares with offal, blood or meat. Cats have fast reactions and may leap clear of deadfall traps.

Tracks and signs: Walk on toes, claws retracted when walking (except Cheetah). Droppings elongated, often hidden. Strong-smelling urine.

FOOD

MONKEYS AND APES

Confined to tropics, usually live in extended family groups, often in trees. Even small monkeys can inflict a bad bite. Intelligent and difficult to stalk. Very edible.

Traps: Perch or baited spring-spear trap, spring snare or hole-noose. Bait with fruit or colourful objects.

Signs: Few take trouble to conceal themselves and most are noisy.

SEALS

Track shows belly drag in centre. Arrow indicates direction of travel. See p. 44 for details.

BATS

Found in all except very cold climates. Active at night. Hibernating meat-eaters. Plump fruit bats are especially good eating. Remove wings and legs, gut and skin like a rabbit. Vampire bat can transmit rabies: keep well-covered if sleeping rough within its range.

Traps: Knock from roosts when sleeping by day.

Signs: Roosting colonies easy to spot. Often in caves.

CATTLE

Live in herds near water. Bison and other wild cattle are found in N. America (protected species), Africa and S.Asia. Old bulls are particularly dangerous.

FOOD

Traps: Powerful snares, spring traps and deadfalls.

Tracks and signs: Two heavy, distinct hoofmarks, narrow at top, bulbous at rear. Droppings are like cow pats. They make excellent fuel.

WILD SHEEP AND GOATS

Sheep tend to live in small flocks in inaccessible places. Goats are even more sure-footed than sheep and almost impossible to approach.

Traps: Snares or spring snares on trails. In rocky areas natural obstructions are ideal for deadfalls.

Tracks and signs: Cloven hooves, two slender pointed marks not joined, tip splayed in sheep, sometimes in goats. Illustration: domestic sheep (left), chamois (right). Globular droppings like domestic sheep.

DEER AND ANTELOPES

Deer, found in well-wooded country on every continent except Australia, vary from the moose to tiny forest deer of the tropics. Antelopes and gazelles are equally varied and widespread. All are shy and elusive, with superb hearing and smell. Most active at dawn and dusk, and – except

those in arid areas – are never far from water. Meat smokes well. Use hides and antlers.

FOOD

Their horns are weapons and can gouge and stab.

Traps: Snare or deadfall small types. Leg-spring snares, spear traps and deadfalls for larger. Bait with offal.

Tracks and signs: Cloven hooves form two oblongs. Reindeer marks are rounded. The illustration shows, in relative scale, roe deer front and hind track (top); and reindeer (bottom).
Note dew-claw impression on reindeer track. When walking, front and rear prints overlap; and when running they are spaced. Droppings oblong to round pellets, usually in clumps.
Look for scrapes on saplings, nibbled and frayed bark. Also long scratches where antlers have been rubbed.

WILD PIGS

Some have thick hair, and all are pig-shaped with snouts and tusks. They are hard to stalk – listen for snores and creep up on sleeping ones!

Meat must be well-boiled. Their tusks inflict severe injury, often dangerously close to femoral artery on the upper leg. Beware!

Traps: Strong spring snares, deadfall, pig spear traps.

Tracks and signs: Cloven hooves leave deer-like marks. Droppings are often shapeless, never long, firm or tapering. Look for ground disturbed by mudwallows or rooting.

FOOD

RABBITS AND HARES

Rabbits are widespread and easy to catch. Most live in burrows, often in large numbers and using well-worn runs – the places to set snares. Hares do not live in burrows and tend not to have regular runs.

Traps: Simple snares. A spring snare will lessen the chance of your meal being stolen by other prey.

Tracks and signs: Hairy soles leave little detail on soft ground. Combination of long hind and short front feet is distinctive. Hares have 5 toes on front feet, but inner is short and seldom leaves print. Hind foot narrower, 4-toed. Rabbit similar but smaller. Droppings small, hard round pellets. Bark nibbled at bottom of trees, leaving two incisor marks. Rabbits thump a warning.

RABBIT STARVATION

It is not possible to survive on rabbit alone, no matter how many you eat. The body needs minerals and vitamins which rabbit does not provide: make sure to balance your diet with vegetation.

SMALL RODENTS

Rats, mice, guinea pigs, cavies, capybara, coypu and other members of the rodent family may be tempted into cage traps – most species are too small to snare. Tracks of different kinds are not easy to distinguish. Rats carry disease. When gutting, take care not to rupture the innards. Cook thoroughly.

FOOD

SQUIRRELS AND PRAIRIE DOGS

Occur everywhere except
Australasia and the Poles,
hibernating in cold areas.
Alert and nimble, most are
active by day and night.
Beware of their sharp teeth
– they are savage in
defence. Ground-living varieties make burrows. Most
are excellent eating.

Traps: Small spring snares attached to bait bars.
Use split fruit or an egg to attract. For tree squirrels,
set 5cm (2in) loop snares on a pole leaned against
a trunk.

Tracks and signs: Chewed bark, gnawed nuts,
cones beneath a tree or an untidy nest of twigs.

KANGAROOS

With wallabies and other relatives, limited to Australia.
Large kinds can strike a powerful blow with hind feet.
Most active at night. Edibility fair, but difficult to catch.

Traps: Deadfalls, spring snares.

Tracks and signs: Two prints resembling giant rabbit
tracks (front legs not used for locomotion).

OPOSSUMS

Small nocturnal scavengers
of S. America and USA.
Similar, unrelated animals
found in Australasia.

Traps: Bait with fruit, eggs, etc. Very inquisitive.

FOOD

RACCOONS

Cat-sized nocturnal animals
with bushy banded tail and
black mask. Found widely
in N. America.

Traps: Bait a spring snare.

CAMELS

Range wild in desert country. Can spit and inflict
powerful bites. They require a very powerful spear or
projectile weapon.

REPTILES

CROCODILES AND ALLIGATORS

Found in most subtropical and tropical areas. Avoid
large ones. In areas where they live, always assume
they are about for they can lie unseen underwater.
Their tails can inflict a scything blow almost as
damaging as their teeth. Tail meat is very tasty.

Traps: Set by water for small crocs only, or catch on
line with stick wedged in bait to lodge in gullet. Kill with
a sharp blow between the eyes.

LIZARDS

Some are venomous (see p. 348). Most are timid, but
big iguanas and monitors can inflict a bad bite and
have powerful claws. Small ones move fast, but try to
catch by the tail. Can sometimes be trapped in a pit or
may fall into a solar still.

FOOD

TURTLES AND TORTOISES

Most live in water, emerging to lay eggs. A few are terrestrial. Net or drag them. On land use a stick to turn them on their backs. Avoid jaws and flippers. Kill with a blow to the head. Cut through belly and discard guts, head and neck. Best boiled. Very rich, eat in small amounts. Tortoises retract heads – stab, then roast ungutted in embers. When shell splits they are ready.

AMPHIBIANS

Frogs are all edible, but skins may be poisonous so remove before cooking. Active at night near water. Dazzle with a light and club them.

Toads have warty skins and may be found far from water. Most have highly toxic skin – do not eat it.

SNAKES

Avoid poisonous or large ones. Use forked stick to pin down behind head. Strike head with another stick. Tree snakes can be clubbed. Club again to make sure!

Never pick up or get close to a snake until you are sure it is dead. Some can feign death convincingly.

BIRDS

All birds are edible, but some taste better than others. Game birds are good to eat but well-camouflaged and wary. Birds of prey must be boiled thoroughly.

Traps: Cage traps, deadfalls and spring snares can be used for birds that take bait. Nooses on branches may catch roosting birds. In woods, site traps in clearings or by banks. Small birds are easy to catch, or lime and bait works. A crude dummy owl will lure small birds.

FOOD

Tracks and signs: In desert and on snow, tracks help locate birds in close cover. Droppings indicate a night roost. Alarm calls may help locate other animals.

Autumn moult: Birds moult completely in autumn and are unable to fly more than short distances. Ducks, geese and game birds are easy to catch at this time.

Nests: Eggs can be found in ground nesters. Approach colonies warily to get within clubbing or stone-throwing distance. Some guard tenaciously. Expect an attack.

Flightless birds: Large birds such as ostriches should be treated with caution: they can deliver powerful kicks.

INSECTS

Rich in fat, protein and carbohydrates. Look in nooks of trees and in moist shady spots. Beetle grubs rest on peeling bark and decaying stumps. Avoid any that look sick or dead, smell bad, or cause a rash. Take care: scorpions, spiders and snakes also shelter in nooks and crannies. Most are edible raw, but more palatable cooked. Boiling is safest. Or roast on hot stones and the embers of a fire. Remove legs and wings from larger insects – fine hairs can irritate the digestive tract. Squeeze a hairy caterpillar to extract its innards. Do not eat skin. Take armour casing off beetles.

SURVIVAL SCENARIO
If you have no food supplies, which are the most important to hunt or forage for?
No one food source is more important than another. In fact, it is vital in any situation that a mixed diet is achieved. Otherwise, you will actually feel more tired or unwell if you just eat, say, fat or protein. However, if you are injured you will need more proteins to help repair the damage. In general, eat little and often.

FOOD

Small insects can be mashed to a paste and cooked, or dried to a powder then used to thicken other foods such as soups or stews.

 Do not gather insects feeding on carrion, refuse or dung – they may carry infection. Avoid grubs found on the underside of leaves, they often secrete toxins. Use as fish bait.
Brightly coloured insects and caterpillars are usually poisonous. Large beetles often have powerful jaws.

TERMITES

Found in warm climates. Most eat only vegetation but big ones have sharp jaws and will bite anything. Termites build mounds up to several feet high. Break off pieces and dunk in water to force termites out. A piece of the nest placed on embers will produce a fragrant smoke that will keep mosquitoes away. When fishing, suspend a piece of nest above a pool; termites falling from it will be good bait. Alternatively, insert a twig into the nest and gently withdraw it. Termites will bite it and hang on – but you won't catch very many.

Remove wings from large termites before boiling, frying or roasting. The eggs are nutritious too.

BEES, WASPS AND HORNETS

Bees are edible throughout life cycle. Honey is easily digestible and highly nutritious, but difficult to collect. Nests are found in hollow trees or caves, or under an overhanging rock. Strike at night: make a torch from a bundle of grass and hold it close to the entrance so nest fills with smoke. Then seal hole. That kills bees, providing an immediate meal and a supply of honey.

FOOD

Remove wings, legs and sting, before eating. Boiling or roasting improves flavour. Comb may be eaten, and wax used to waterproof clothing or make candles. In some places, there is a slight risk that honey may contain concentrations of plant poisons. Smell will be one guide, but use edibility test given for plants.

Wasps and hornets are dangerous. Hornets sting on sight and the pain is extreme. Search for a safer meal.

ANTS

Most ants have a stinging bite. Some fire formic acid. They must be cooked for at least six minutes to destroy the poison. They are then quite safe to eat.

LOCUSTS, CRICKETS AND GRASSHOPPERS

All have plump bodies and muscled legs. Swat with a leafy branch or clothing. Remove wings, antennae and legs. Eat raw or roast to kill parasites.

SNAILS, SLUGS AND WORMS

Must be eaten fresh after special preparation.

Snails are found in freshwater, saltwater and on land. Rich in proteins and minerals. Ones with brightly coloured shells may be poisonous. Sea snails should be left alone unless positively identified. Starve snails or slugs for a few days, or feed only on herbs and safe greens so they can excrete poisons. Place in a saltwater solution to clear out guts. Boil for 10 minutes, adding herbs for flavour.

Worms are high in protein, with essential amino acids. Starve them for a day, or allow them to purge themselves. Can be sun- or force-dried – left on a hot stone – then ground into powder to thicken other food.

FOOD

DANGERS

Diseases carried by mosquitoes, ticks and other insects, the unseen dangers of parasites one picks up from food or water, and various waterborne diseases, are much more serious than attacks by animals.

Dangerous confrontations

• Attacks by animals are rare, but large animals can be dangerous. Keep out of their way. Use self-control, do not unintentionally provoke the animal to attack.

• Avoid eye contact, act submissively, but don't run.

• If you come face to face with a large animal, FREEZE. Slowly back off and talk in a calm manner. Avoid sudden movements and remember animals can smell fear – many a hunter has fouled his breeches and given himself away. Do your best to calm yourself.

• If an animal appears to charge it may be that you are blocking its escape route. Move out of the way.

• If an animal gives chase (or you haven't the nerve to freeze or sidestep), zig-zag when you run. Some animals such as rhinos charge in a straight line and have poor eyesight.

• Nocturnal predators have excellent night vision but their colour vision is poor. They cannot see stationary objects well. Freeze if it hasn't already seen you.

• Shouting and making a commotion *may* put off a predator.

• Taking to a tree is the last resort, you may be 'treed' for a long time. Avoid a thorn tree if possible.

• If chased, drop your pack, clothing or food to confuse the animal.

FOOD

TRAPS AND TRAPPING

It is easier to trap than to hunt small prey. Choice of baits and site is important. Food may be scarce, but a little used as bait may bring rewards. Be patient and give the traps time. Animals will be wary until they get used to them – that is when they will run into them.

> Regular checking is essential. Leaving a trap line unchecked will prolong an animal's pain and increase the risk of your catch struggling free – animals will bite off a limb to escape – or being poached by predators.

Establish as large a trap line as you can. Collect game and reset traps, repairing as necessary and removing any that are repeatedly unfruitful. Accept a proportion of failures, but if the bait has gone without the trap being fired it is an indication that the trigger mechanism is too tight or the bait insecurely fixed. Check both when you reset the trap.

Set traps on game trails or runs. Look for natural bottlenecks, e.g. where the track passes under an obstruction. Do not place a trap close to an animal's lair – it will be alert to anything unusual close to home.

When alarmed, animals panic and take the shortest route to cover. That is when the crudest and most obvious traps will be successful.

> **MANGLE STRANGLE DANGLE TANGLE**
> Deadfalls mangle. Snares strangle. Saplings can take the prey in the air – it dangles. The higher the sapling the more effectively it lifts the animal. A net tangles. Some traps combine two or more of these principles.

FOOD

RULES FOR TRAPS

Avoid disturbing environment: Don't tread on game trail, leave no sign that you have been there.

Hide scent: Handle traps as little as possible and wear gloves if you can. Do not set a trap of pinewood in a wood of hazel. Mask human scents by exposing snare to campfire smoke.

Camouflage: Hide freshly cut ends of wood with mud. Cover ground snares to blend in naturally.

Make them strong: An ensnared animal will fight for its life. Any weakness in the traps will soon be exposed.

Snares

Snares can be improvised from string, rope, twine or, ideally, non-ferrous wire with a running eye at one end through which the other end passes before being anchored to a stake, rock or tree. A snare is a free-running noose which catches small game by the throat and large game round the legs.

A wire snare (as big as your fist) can be supported off the ground on twigs, which can also be used to keep a suspended string noose open. Set it a hand's length from an obstruction to trap rabbits.

length of your hand

FOOD

> **USING A SIMPLE SNARE FOR SMALL ANIMALS**
> Make the loop a fist-width wide.
> Set it four fingers above the ground and
> a hand's width from an obstruction.
> Anchor securely. Support loop with twigs if necessary.

When constructing a snare under tension, use a sapling to lift the game off the ground. The trap is then more effective: the animal is less able to struggle and predators can't get at it. Hazel is ideal for this.

SPRING SNARE: Good for rabbits and foxes. Situate on trail by a natural bottleneck caused by deadfall or rock.

Cut notch in trigger bar (a) to fit notch in upright (b). Drive upright into ground. Attach snare to trigger bar and use cord to sapling to keep tension. Bar disengages, lifting game in air.

BAITED SPRING SNARE: ideal for medium-sized prey.

Bait support stake should be lightly driven into ground as it must fly away with noose.

FOOD

BAITED SPRING LEG SNARE: Push prongs of a natural fork of wood (or two sticks tied together) into the ground. The line from a bent sapling is tied to a toggle and to the snare; toggle is then passed under fork. Bait is attached to a separate bar. Ideal for large game: deer, big cats, bear. For deer, bait with blood or scent glands to arouse its curiosity.

Upper end of toggle presses against fork; lower end is prevented from pulling back through by the bait bar between it and the fork.

SPRING TENSION SNARE: For small animals. Site on trail. *Switch line secures one end of snare arm (b) while the other rests on keeper stick (a). Keep switch line near end of snare arm (c). When game becomes ensnared, snare arm is dislodged from keeper stick and switch line slips off other end.*

FOOD

TRAPEZE SPRING SNARE: Use to cover two game trails in open country.

Once ensnared, the prey's struggles disengage snare arm, regardless of direction from which it approached.

ROLLER SPRING SNARE: Good for rabbits and foxes.

A rounded grip holds the snare arm. Pull switch line back at a slight angle to keep it in place.

A wide area can be covered using several snares on long horizontal bar. Use where game trail widens.

FOOD

PLATFORM TRAP: Site in a small depression on game trail. Place snares on platforms on either side. When platform is depressed, trigger bar is released and game held by the leg. Ideal for deer, big cats, bear.

Platform of sticks or stiff bark rests on bottom bar. Upper bar fits in the notches.

STEPPED-BAIT RELEASE SNARE: Site in clearings. Will catch small carnivores and pigs.

Two forked sticks hold down a cross-bar engaging with baited notch upright (attached to a line in tension), holding it in place and carrying snares.

Retaining bar should be squared off to fit square-cut notch on the bait stick.

Deadfall traps

These traps work on the principle that when the bait is taken a weight falls on the prey.

> Large versions of traps can be dangerous for humans. Toggle release and deadfall traps are easily set off accidentally.
> In a survival situation ensure that everyone knows where the traps are. In survival practice keep people away from them and never leave a trap set up at the end of an exercise.

Setting a deadfall trap is risky. You cannot do it on your own. Keep the mechanism to the side of the trail, away from the dropping weight. Balance is critical – you are unlikely to get it right the first time.

TOGGLE TRIP-RELEASE DEADFALL: A mechanism similar to the toggle-release snare, but here the release bar keeping the toggle in position presses one end of the toggle upwards. A line from the toggle passes over a tree limb to support a weight (e.g. logs) above the trail. A trip-line runs above ground beneath the suspended weight to a securing point.

Run trip-line under a forked stick so that it will pull the trigger bar sideways when operated.

FOOD

FOOD

BALANCE LOG: A forked stick, its ends sharpened to dislodge easily, one fork baited, supports one end of a cross-bar. The other end rests on a fixed support, held there by the heavy logs or rock with rests on the bar. The trap collapses when the bait is taken.

Angle bait beneath trap.

DEADFALL TRAP: A weight suspended over the trail pulls the line carrying it against a retaining bar held by short pegs secured in a tree trunk at slightly downward angle. Make sure the line is long enough and the anchor weak enough to allow weight to reach ground.

FOOD

'*FIGURE 4' DEADFALL TRAP:* Balance a horizontal bait bar at right-angles to an upright with a locking bar which supports a weight, positioned over bait, pivoted on sharpened tip of upright.

Bait bar notched on top to engage locking arm, square cut on side to fit upright. Locking arm sharpened at end for quick release, notched at centre to pivot on upright.

Spear traps

> These traps can be lethal to humans. Always stand behind the spear when setting and mark with signs to warn humans the trap is there. Except in a survival situation, never leave spear traps set and unsupervised.

DEADFALL SPEAR TRAP:
Same mechanism as deadfall trap (p. 128), but rocks add weight and sharpened sticks deliver a stabbing blow.

FOOD

SPRING SPEAR TRAP: A springy shaft with a spear attached is held taut over the trail. A slip-ring made of smooth material attached to a trip-wire acts as release.

Toggle (a) and short line to fixed upright hold spear shaft in tension. A further rod through the ring is tensed between near side of spear shaft and far face of upright, securing the trap.

Bird traps

NETS: Stretch a fine net between trees where birds roost. Alternatively, a fine twine criss-crossed between trees across their flight path will damage birds which fly into it.

BIRD LIME: Boil holly leaves and any starchy grain in water; simmer until you have a gooey mess. Spread this on branches and perching places. Birds will get stuck in it when they alight.

SUSPENDED SNARES: Hang a line of snares across a stream a little above water level. This works best among reeds and rushes.

FOOD

BAITED HOOKS: Bury fish hooks in fruit or other food. The hook gets caught in the bird's throat.

NOOSE STICKS: Tie fine nooses 1.25–2.5cm (½–1in) in diameter in horsehair. Place stick in roosting or nesting spot with nooses uppermost. Do not remove as soon as the first bird becomes entangled – it will attract others into the trap.

'FIGURE 4' TRAP: This mechanism (see *'Figure 4' Deadfall Trap p. 129*) can be used with a cage made from a pyramid of sticks tied together and balanced over the bait. For small birds, lay all sticks in position, then lay another two sticks, the same length as the bottom ones, on top and tie them tightly to the bottom layer, tight enough to keep all the others in place. Larger animals are stronger; for them each stick must be individually tied.

FOOD

RUNNING NOOSE: Use a noose attached to a long pole to pull down roosting birds. Go to roosting site on a bright night. Slip noose over bird, tighten as you pull.

STALKING WATERFOWL: Get up close by getting into water and camouflaging your head with reeds or vegetation. Cautiously approach the nesting area, bearing in mind that birds can be ferocious in self-defence.

Where large gourds are available, make holes on one side to see and breathe through, then place over head. Throw several other gourds into water to prepare birds. The hunter then floats with current among birds, grabs them from below and strangles them underwater.

PIT TRAP: Find or dig a hole 90cm (36in) deep in an area where ground-feeding birds are common. The pit's width depends on the type of birds. Spread grain or bait round the hole and more concentratedly inside it. First taking the bait round the hole, birds will enter it to get more. Rush them: in their panic they are unable to spread their wings sufficiently to take off from inside the hole.

SEAGULLS

Seagulls can be caught by wrapping food round a stone and throwing it in the air. The gull swallows the bait while still on the wing, gulps down the stone with it, and the weight change causes it to crash. Obviously this is a technique for use over land rather than at sea. Be ready to dispatch the bird as soon as it hits the ground.

FOOD

HUNTING

Keen observation and a knowledge of animals make it easier to find prey and to take advantage of terrain.

Proceed quietly. Move slowly and stop regularly. To avoid stumbles and reduce noise, carry your weight on the rear foot, testing the next step with the toes before transferring your weight. Hunt against the wind.

> If an animal catches a glimpse of you, freeze. It may be more curious than frightened. Remain still until the animal looks away or continues feeding.

Hunt at first light, moving uphill, and return to camp in the afternoon. Tracks are easier to read moving uphill; thermal currents build up with the heat of day and carry scents upwards, so by returning downhill the scent of game reaches you before yours reaches them. If you must hunt in the evening, go out at least an hour before dusk so your eyes can develop night vision, but your prey will probably see better than you do.

Get as close as you can to your prey and take steady aim at a point just to the back of the front shoulder. A hit here will drop most animals instantly.

If an animal drops, wait five minutes before moving in. Stand back and observe. If hurt, loss of blood will weaken it and when you do approach it will be unable to bolt. If a wounded animal moves away, wait 15 minutes before following, otherwise it will run all day.

> Avoid large animals unless really confident of a first-shot kill – or you could end up becoming the hunted and not the hunter.

FOOD

WEAPONS

Bow and arrow

The most effective of improvised weapons: easy to make, it takes only a short time to become proficient.

A well-seasoned wood is best for the bow. Long-term survivors should put wood aside to season. Tension in unseasoned wood is short-lived, so make several bows and change as soon as one loses its spring.

Yew is ideal, but hickory, juniper, oak, white elm, cedar, ironwood, birch, willow and hemlock (the tree) are good alternatives.

MAKING THE STAVE: *Select a supple wand. To determine correct length: hold one end of stave at the hip with right hand, reach sideways with left hand and mark extent of your reach as length of bow.*

SHAPING THE BOW: *Stave must be 5cm (2in) wide at centre, tapering to 1.5cm (⅝in) at ends. Make notch about 1.25cm (½in) from ends (a) to take bowstring. Remove bark if you wish. Once whittled into shape, rub bow with oil or animal fat.*

FOOD

FITTING THE STRING: Cut rawhide to 3mm (⅛in) wide or use string, or twisted fibres from nettle stems to make bowstring. If bow has lots of give, use shorter string. String should be under only slight tension – the main tension is added when you pull it back to shoot.

Secure string to bow with round turn and two half hitches at each end. If wood is unseasoned, release one end when bow not in use to relax its tension.

MAKING ARROWS: Use straight wood – birch is best. Make arrows 60cm (24in) long, 6mm (¼in) wide. They must be as straight and smooth as possible.

At one end make a notch wide enough to fit bowstring and 6mm (¼in) deep.

FLIGHTING ARROWS:
a. split feathers, from top, down centre of quill
b. leave 20mm (¾in) quill at each end to tie to arrow
c. tie 3 flights, equally spaced, round shaft.
Flights increase accuracy. Paper, cloth or leaves can also be used as flights.

FOOD

ARROWHEADS: The arrow itself can be sharpened and hardened in fire, but a tip of tin or flint is better. Split end of shaft, insert arrowhead and bind tightly with wet sinews – they dry hard, securing head firmly.

Flint   *Tin*   *Burnt*   *Bone*

For details of how to make flint arrowheads see p. 198.

ARCHERY TECHNIQUE: Fit arrow into bowstring. Raise centre of bow to eyelevel. Hold bow just below arrow, extending arm forwards. Keep bow arm locked and draw string smoothly back across the front of your body, with arrow at eyelevel and lined up with target. Sight along arrow. Release string.

ARROW BURNS: *Arrow flights rubbing against hand and cheek can cause friction burns. Protect the cheek with a piece of cloth pulled tight to the face. Wear a leather mitten or fit a leather guard between fingers and wrist to protect hand.*

FOOD

Sling and shot

A sling is a simple leather pouch in the middle of a length of thong or rope (any strong fabric will do if you have no leather). Attach pouch as one piece threaded through, or two tied or sewn on.

SLINGSHOT TECHNIQUE: Use round smooth pebbles 2cm (¾in) across. Swing the sling above the head in a circle lined up on your target. Release one end of rope and ammunition should fly at target. Experiment with sling length to achieve accuracy and distance.

Catapult

Take a strong, pliable forked twig (hazel is ideal) and a piece of elastic material (inner tube from a tyre or elastic from clothing). Place a pouch in the centre of the elastic — a boot tongue works — and sew into position. Tie ends to each side of fork. Use stones as missiles.

Load several pebbles at a time when using sling or catapult against birds.

FOOD

Spears

A straight staff 1.80m (6ft) is ideal for a jabbing spear; 90cm (36in) is best for throwing. Make a spear thrower from a piece of wood half that length to improve accuracy.

Add a sharp point of flint or a flattened cone of tin to the spear tip. Or securely bind on a knife — but do not risk this if you have only one knife.

SPEAR THROWER: *Take a tree limb twice the width of spear, with branch stump to serve as handle. Split down centre, using knife as wedge. Gouge out a cleanly cut groove along most of upper face of thrower. Leave a solid portion as a buffer to add thrust.*

Hold spear at shoulder-level and aim at target, bringing holder sharply forwards then downwards.

FOOD

THE DANGERS OF HUNTING

Few animals will attack except in self-defence, but don't camp on a trail or near an animal watering spot.

Don't provoke a bear encounter

Bears are scavengers and will come to camps in search of food. Don't get close or try to catch them. A bear can easily kill a human. Use noise to drive them off – the same goes for other scavengers, e.g. hyenas.

Injured and cornered animals

Most animals try to escape when hurt. By preventing them from doing so you are forcing them to fight.

Keep well clear

Crocodiles and alligators should be given a wide berth. Large-horned animals may wound you before you can reach your weapon. Many animals, not just those with hooves, have deadly kicks – including ostriches.

Bites

Many small animals have sharp teeth and will attack ferociously. Chimpanzees and other monkeys can be very bad-tempered. Thoroughly cleanse any bites: they may cause tetanus. Some animals carry rabies.

Snakes and stinging insects

Get used to checking clothing, bedding and equipment for reptiles and insects.

If you awake to find one in your sleeping bag, move gently and calmly to get rid of them or to free yourself.

FOOD

HANDLING THE KILL

Before approaching, check that your prey is dead. Use a spear or tie your knife to a long stick and stab a large animal in its main muscles and neck. Loss of blood will weaken it, allowing you to move in and club the head.

Two people can carry a large animal tied to a bough. Place pole along belly and use clove-hitch round each pair of legs. Lash animal to pole and finish with clove-hitch round pole. If it has horns, tie these up out of the way or cut off head.

    Butcher game on the trap line. Other meat-eaters will be attracted and may become trapped. Use entrails to bait traps. Only carry to camp what you can manage without exertion: in camp it will only attract flies and scavengers. Cache remainder for collection later.

HIDING THE KILL

Suspend a carcass from a bough, out of reach from the branch. A cache in the crook of a tree will keep meat away from ground predators but will still be accessible to climbing predators. Where vultures are present the cache will be impossible to protect.

FOOD

> ☠ **HEALTH HAZARDS – DISEASED ANIMALS**
> All animals have lymph glands in their cheeks.
> If large and discoloured, the animal is ill. Any
> animal that is distorted or discoloured about the head
> should be boiled and care taken in preparation: cover
> cuts or sores in your skin when handling meat.

PREPARING THE KILL

Waste nothing: make use of parts you cannot eat.
Set about preparing the kill in four stages:

Bleeding: Essential if meat is to keep.
Blood is valuable food, rich in vitamins and minerals,
including salt, that are essential to survival.
Keep cool in covered vessel.

Skinning: Hide or fur can be used.

Gutting: To remove gut and recover offal.

Jointing: Produces suitable cuts for cooking.

BLEEDING: Hang animal head-down. Tie ropes round
hock (not ankle) and hoist it up to a branch or build a
frame, placing receptacle below to catch blood.

For a frame: drive strong posts into ground and lash
firmly to make A-frames. Rest horizontal bar on top.

Bleed animal by cutting jugular vein or carotid artery
in its neck. When animal is hanging, these will bulge
clearly. Make cut either behind ears – stab in line with
ears to pierce vein on both sides of head at same time –
or lower down in V of neck, before artery branches.
Unless you have a stiletto knife, the latter is best. Cutting

FOOD

throat from ear to ear risks contamination of blood with contents of stomach. It is important to bleed pigs thoroughly if the meat is to be saved.

SKINNING: While flesh is still warm, remove any scent

glands (deer have them behind knee of rear legs; felines on either side of anus). Remove testicles of males. To remove hide, cut through skin as shown by broken lines on illustration above.

1   Make ring round rear legs just above knee.
2   Cut round forelegs in same place.
3   Cut down inside of rear legs to crotch; cut circle round genitals.
4   Extend cut down centre of body to neck. Do not cut into stomach and digestive organs. Lift skin as you go, slip in the knife, sharp edge outwards, and cut along. Draw knife slowly down, cutting away from body.
5   Cut down inside of forelegs.

FOOD

Now ease skin of rear legs from the flesh. Use the knife as little as possible. Roll skin outwards, fur inside itself, and pull down. When back legs are clear, cut round tail. Insert hand down back of carcass and use fingers to separate flesh from skin. Next, peel skin from front legs. Separate the single piece of hide from the neck with a strong twist of the head. Cut through remaining tissues.

If working alone, lay carcass down a slope, scoop an impression in the ground to hold the collecting vessel.

Skin small animals by making incision over stomach (do not pierce organs). Insert thumbs and pull out. Free legs and twist head off. If you have no knife, snap off lower part of leg and use the sharp edge to cut skin.

GUTTING: Remove gut and offal from suspended carcass by pinching abdomen as high as possible and making a slit big enough to take two fingers in the pinched flesh. Insert fingers and use them as a guide for the knife to cut upwards then downwards, using hand to prevent gut from spilling. Cut down as far as breastbone. Then let gut spill out, hanging down. Remove kidneys and liver. Cut through membrane to chest cavity and remove heart, lungs and windpipe. You should be able to see daylight through anus – check it is clear.

JOINTING MEAT: Large animals can be quartered by first splitting down backbone, then cutting each side between tenth and eleventh rib. Hindquarters contain steaks (rump and fillet) and choicer cuts. Forequarter meat is more stringy and needs slow cooking to make it tender. Cuts vary according to the kind of animal.

FOOD

OFFAL

Liver: Eat as soon as possible. Little cooking is required. Remove bile bladder in the centre with care, don't allow it to taint meat. Avoid mottled or white-spotted liver.

Stomach: Tripe is easy to digest. Remove stomach contents (good invalid food, as it is already broken down, so boil lightly), wash tripe and simmer slowly with herbs.

Kidneys: Boil with herbs. White fat surrounding them (suet) can be rendered down to use in pemmican; see p. 192.

Lungs (lights): Do not eat if mottled with black and white spots. If pink and blemish-free, boil, or use for bait.

Heart: Roast, or use to liven up a stew.

Intestines: Ideal sausage skins: turn inside out and wash. Then boil well. Mix equal proportions of fat and meat, then stir in blood. Stuff the skins with this mixture and boil well. If smoked, sausages keep for a long time.

Sweetbreads (pancreas): Boil or roast.

Tail: Skin and boil to make soup.

Feet: Clean well, then boil to make stew.

Head: Large animal heads are meaty. Boil tongue to make it tender and skin before eating. Brain will make brawn and provide a solution to cure hides. Boil whatever is left, or the whole head with small animals.

Bones: Boil for soup – marrow is rich in vitamins. They can also be made into tools.

HANGING: Eat offal as soon as possible, but rest of meat is better hung to make it tender and to kill parasites. In moderate temperatures, leave carcass hanging for 2–3 days. In hot climates, preserve or cook at once.

PREPARING SHEEP-LIKE ANIMALS: Follow instructions for large animals, then split in two down centre of spine. Remove rear leg (cut through joint) and front leg. Cut off neck and loose flesh below ribs. Cut between ribs and vertebrae. Preserve fillet, found in small of back.

PREPARING PIG: Do not skin. Gut, then place over hot embers and scrape hair off (loosen it with water just hotter than your hand can bear). Boil to kill parasites.

PREPARING REPTILES: Discard internal organs, which may carry salmonella. Cook in skin. Cut off head well down, behind poison sacs; open vent to neck, keeping blade turned outwards – don't pierce innards. Skewer to suspend. Ease the skin down towards the tail. Skin of reptiles is useful for clothing.

PREPARING BIRDS: To kill, stretch the neck and cut throat, or cut just under the tongue to sever main artery. Hang head-down to bleed. Meat-eaters harbour parasites, so handle them as little as possible. Pluck while body is still warm. Hot water will loosen the feathers (except those of waterfowl). Make incision from vent to tail, insert hand and draw out guts. Retain heart and kidneys. Cut off head and feet. Boil meat-eaters and old birds; young ones can be roasted on spit or in oven. Leave skins on and eat them.

FOOD

FISH AND FISHING

Fish contain protein, vitamins and fats. They differ widely in size, eating habits and diet, but all can be attracted and caught with appropriate bait. Angling is not the most effective method of catching fish – the night line and gill net will give better results – but if you have plenty of time it is a pleasurable pastime.

WHERE TO FISH: If it is hot and the water is low, fish retreat to deep, shaded waters. In cold weather, they seek shallow spots where the sun warms the water. At any time, fish like to shelter under banks and rocks.

When a river is in flood, fish in slack water, e.g. on the outside of a bend or in a small tributary.

WHEN TO FISH: Leave lines out overnight and check them just before first light. If a storm is imminent, fish before it breaks. Fishing is poor after heavy rain.

IMAGE REFRACTION: Fish can see more on the bank than you think. Sit or kneel when fishing, so you are less likely to be in vision. Keep back from the edge and try to keep your shadow off the water.

INDICATIONS OF FISH FEEDING: Fish are likely to take bait when you see them jumping out of the water. Clear ring ripples breaking on the surface are another sign. Where lots of little fish are darting about, they may avoiding pursuit by a larger predatory fish.

FOOD

ANGLING

You can improvise hooks from all kinds of materials. Here (from left to right) are a pin, a thorn, a bunch of thorns, nails, bone and wood.

Large hooks will catch large fish, but small ones catch large and small fish. A rod is not essential (you can fish with a handline) but it makes it easier to land fish and cast away from the bank.

ANGLING WITHOUT HOOKS: Eels and catfish swallow without biting. To catch them, tie a blob of worms on a line (a) and pull them out as soon as bait is taken.

A small sharp piece of wood attached to the end of the line, and held flat along it by the bait (b) will, when the bait is swallowed, open out across the gullet of the fish (c).

BAIT: Fish are more likely to take bait native to their water: berries that overhang it, insects that breed in it. Examine stomach contents of your first catch for clues.

FOOD

USING FLOATS AND WEIGHTS

*A small floating object attached to the line, visible from the
bank, will show you when you have a bite. Its position will
help control where the line descends.*

*Small weights between float and hook stop the line trailing
along the water or too near the surface, while leaving
the hook itself in movement. Your survival kit includes a
small split-lead shot. Slip the groove along the line and
squeeze to fit tightly.*

*To get a deeper hook position, extend line to a weight below
the hook.*

FOOD

> Any suitable bait, scattered on water, will attract fish. Put the same bait on your hook to catch them. Suspend a termite or ant nest over water and the falling insects will prove an irresistible draw to fish.

SPINNING: Fish will attack a shiny object drawn through water: try coins, buttons, tin, or buckles. Thread a propeller shape to a piece of wire and it will spin with the current. Attach your hook to the end of the spindle.

ARTIFICIAL BAIT: *Feathers tied to a hook with thread can simulate a fly. Try to make lures move like live bait: carve a small jointed fish out of wood (hazel is best for cutting through), thread the segments and decorate with colour or glitter.*

LIVE BAIT: Cover hook completely with worms, insects, maggots, or small fish. A hook can be placed through a small fish or grasshopper without killing it. The distressed movement of the bait will attract fish.

FOOD

NIGHT LINES: Weight one end of a line and attach worm-baited hooks at intervals. Anchor free end securely on bank. Put this out overnight — use in daytime too, but change worms regularly because fresh wriggling ones attract more attention.

OTTER BOARD: To fish further than you can cast a line, make a board with a moveable pivoted rudder. Set a bar at front end of rudder and attach two control lines. Suspend baited hooks below. Float board out into lake. If winds are favourable, mount a sail, but first add a keel: gouge holes to fix dowel supports and tie on a flat stone (not so big as to conflict with the rudder). Undue movement of the board indicates a bite.

FOOD

JIGGING OR SNAGGING: When you can
see fish but they are not taking bait, tie
several hooks to a pole and lower it into
water. Suspend a bright object 20cm
(8in) above the pole, and when fish
go to inspect it, pull hooks up sharply to
catch them.

FISH TRAPS

In shallow streams build a
channel of sticks or rocks that fish can swim into but not turn
round in (arrows here indicate the current).

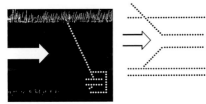

BOTTLE TRAP: Cut a plastic bottle off just below the neck.
Invert neck inside bottle. Use bait to entice them in. Once in,
fish cannot get out.

FOOD

A similar trap can be made for larger fish using a hollow log. Make a lattice cone of twigs for the entrance and block the other end of the log.

WICKERWORK TRAPS: Hazel or other pliant twigs can be used to make a trap which allows the current to flow through it and to a fish looks like stream-bottom debris.

Torpedo shape is made by weaving and tying wicker in position. Entrance starts wide but inside, the angle of the struts makes escape difficult. Place opening downstream, against current.

The lobster-pot trap utilises holes in a circle of board to make it easier to shape. This trap sits on the bottom. Bait will attract eels and crayfish.

FOOD

OTHER TECHNIQUES

Fish snares: Large fish can be caught in a noose-line fixed to a pole, or through a length of bamboo. Pass loop over fish from tail end. Pull sharply to trap fish.

Eel bag: Tie fresh offal and straw or bracken in a cloth (not plastic) bag. Attach line and weight to end of bag and allow it to sink. Leave overnight. By morning, eels that chewed their way in will be wriggling in the straw.

Gill net: If you have a net, set floats at the top and weight the bottom, then stretch it across a river. It will soon empty a stretch of water, so do not use for long.

Attracting and driving: A torch held above water at night draws fish. Trap fish using nets. A mirror on the riverbed reflects sun or moonlight to attract fish.

Spearing: Sharpen a long stick to make a spear. Try to get above the fish and strike down swiftly. Make sure you are not casting a shadow over the fish. Aim slightly below it, to allow for the refraction of its image.

Muddying: Receding flood water leaves isolated pools. Stir up the mud at the bottom of the pool with a stick, or by stamping in the water. Fish will try to escape to clearer water. Scoop them out.

Explosives: Explosives kill nearby fish and force to the surface those which are further away.

Guns: Fish can be shot in the water, but do not submerge the gun barrel – it will explode and the detonation will blow back at you.

Fish narcotics: Some plants stupefy fish, bringing them to the surface. This works best in slack, warm waters. Do not use in closed pools. Toxic only to the cold-blooded, but should not be eaten by humans.

FOOD

SURVIVAL CASE STUDY

Monsoon weather is always bad, but in 1963 it broke all records. In this year I was deployed in Borneo to gather topographical information and intelligence. We were coming to the end of a long operation when our base camp was washed away by torrential rains.

Most of our personal kit and equipment was lost, except for what we were wearing. Low clouds made air re-supply impossible and the tropical storms affected our radio communication. We had to seek higher ground as the whole area became flooded. Moving was extremely difficult because of the swollen rivers and resultant landslides. It took us five days to reach a safe landing zone (LZ) where we awaited a helicopter to lift us to safety.

During these five days, the only food we had were our meagre survival rations: a hard biscuit, nuts and raisins, a tube of honey and a 56.7g (2oz) meat block. We shared everything between the four of us. Even under normal conditions wild food is scarce in the jungle. Fishing is probably best, and collecting various palms, roots and shoots is next best. But the weather had washed all these sources away, and most animals had fled the area before we did, so we were unable to pick any food up on our route. What we found at the LZ were large white snails. We baked,

FOOD

steamed, poached, and even ate them raw, but however we ate them they still tasted the same. Nevertheless, they were an excellent source of nourishment. We had come to the stage of eyeing each other up – and I think these snails even prevented cannibalism!

Water was not a problem in this case, in fact we had too much. Caught rain is the only water we don't treat. But if at all unsure of water quality, then boil it. Also boil all meat, insects and roots until tender, then reduce to a simmer before adding herbs or plants as constant boiling destroys their Vitamin C content, which is essential to good health.

For instance, if using spruce needles which are rich in Vitamin C to make an infusion, do not boil them. Simply steep in hot water.

LESSONS LEARNT:
- **Carry survival kit at all times**
- **Eat anything you can find**
- **Pool your resources**
- **Know and practise your survival skills**

FOOD

ARCTIC FISHING

The technique of fishing through ice is effective on any frozen lake or river where the ice is thick enough to bear your weight but not so solid it cannot be penetrated.

PREPARING FISH

All freshwater fish are edible. Those under 5cm (2in) need no preparation: eat them whole. Gut larger fish.

As soon as it is caught, cut its throat to bleed it, and remove gills. Slit from the anal orifice to the throat. Remove offal (use for hook bait). Keep roe, which runs down side of fish. To scrape scales off, draw knife from

tail to head (a). Fish skin retains moisture and can be eaten. To skin eels and catfish, pass stake through fish, lodge across two up-rights, skin it and draw it down (b).

CRUSTACEANS: Eat as soon as possible. Boil for 20 minutes. Crabs have poisonous parts. Twist off claws and legs. With crab on its back, your thumbs under flap at tail, push up. Pull flap up, away from body, and lift to prevent stomach contents tainting flesh. Discard lungs.

CAMP CRAFT

In a survival situation it is vital to know where to set up camp, how to build a shelter with the materials available, how to make fire, to cook and preserve food, and to improvise tools, clothing and equipment.

SHELTER AND MAKING CAMP

An accident, exhaustion, or sudden fog may leave you stranded. Local conditions and materials will determine the type of shelter you build. While there is still daylight to see by, scour the vicinity for the best natural shelter from wind, rain and cold before night sets in.

A wrecked plane or vehicle may provide shelter or materials from which one can be built, but if there is a risk of fire or fuel tanks exploding, wait until it has burned out before attempting salvage.

BAD PLACES TO CAMP

- Exposed hilltops (go down, seek shelter on lee side).

- Valley bottoms and deep hollows – damp and more liable to frost at night.

- Hillside terraces where the ground holds moisture.

- Spurs that are on a game trail – they often lead to watering places.

- Too close to water: you will be troubled by insects and heavy rainfall may cause rivers to swell and flash floods to occur. Even old, dry watercourses are at risk.

- Near solitary trees, which attract lightning.

- Near bees' or hornets' nests.

CAMP CRAFT

WHERE TO CAMP

You should be sheltered from the wind, near water —
but clear of any risk of flooding — with a plentiful
supply of wood near at hand (in forest areas, keep to the
edges where you can see and be seen). Check above
your head for dead wood in trees that could crash down
in a high wind. Don't camp across a game trail. Bear in
mind that the sound of running water can drown out
other noises which might indicate danger, or the sound
of search parties.

TYPES OF SHELTER

For immediate protection, rig up a makeshift shelter
while you construct something more permanent. If
walking to safety, build temporary shelters at each halt;
if sufficiently light, they can be carried with you.

HASTY SHELTERS: Where no materials are available for
constructing a shelter, make use of natural cover. In
completely open plains, sit with your back to the wind
and pile any equipment behind you as a windbreak.

BOUGH SHELTERS: Branches that sweep down to the
ground or partly broken boughs can provide shelter,
but make sure they are not likely to fall off the tree.

*Make a similar shelter by lashing a broken-off bough to the
base of another branch where it forks from the trunk (a).*

CAMP CRAFT

ROOT SHELTER: The spreading roots and trapped earth at the base of a fallen tree make a good windbreak. Fill in the sides between extended roots for added shelter.

NATURAL HOLLOWS: Even a shallow depression will provide protection from the wind, but you must deflect any downhill flow of water if it is a hollow on a slope.

Make a roof to keep rain off and warmth in. A few sturdy branches laid across the hollow can support a light log laid over them, against which shorter sticks can be stacked to give pitch to the roof and so allow water to run off. Consolidate with turf, twigs and leaves.

FALLEN TRUNKS: A log makes a useful windbreak if it is at a right angle to the wind. With a small trunk, scoop out a hollow in the ground on the leeward side.

A log also makes an excellent support for a lean-to of boughs.

DRAINAGE AND VENTILATION: A run-off channel dug around any shelter in which you are below, or lying directly on, ground level will help keep you dry. Do not try to seal all gaps: ventilation is essential.

Stone Barriers: A shelter is more comfortable if it is high enough to sit in, so increase its height by building a low wall of stones round your hollow. Caulk between the stones with turf and foliage mixed with mud.

Sapling shelter: If suitable growth is available, select two lines of saplings, clear the ground between them of obstructions and lash the tops together to form a frame for sheeting. Weigh down the edges of the sheeting with rocks or timber. A similar shelter can be made from pliable branches driven into the ground.

If you lack sheeting, choose or place saplings closer together, weave branches between them and consolidate with ferns and turf.

CAMP CRAFT

SHELTER SHEET: With a waterproof poncho, groundsheet, plastic sheeting or canvas, a number of shelters can be made.

Use a natural shelter (a) or make a triangular one with the apex pointing to the wind (b). Stake or weigh down edges. If it is long enough, curl sheeting below you, running downhill (c). If short on material, attach it to shield from wind (d). Use dry grass or bracken as bedding. Do not lie on cold or damp ground.

A closely woven fabric will keep out most rain if set at a steep angle. Fit one shelter within another (e) — rain will rarely penetrate both layers. Avoid touching the inner surface of woven fabric during rain — this draws water through.

TEPEES: The quickest type to erect has three or more angled support poles, tied where they cross to make a cone. They can be tied on the ground and lifted into place before covering with hides, birch bark, or sheeting. Leave an opening at the top for ventilation.

Wider angles will give greater area but shed rain less easily.

A parachute, suspended by its centre, makes an instant tepee. Peg out bottom edge.

Even simpler, suspend a parachute tepee from a tree. Steep-angled sides will allow water to run off. Fold a segment of the chute double for a door flap, slit along a seam and make a tie fastening to close it.

Stick walls and screens

Build walls by piling sticks between uprights driven into the ground and (if possible) tied at the top. Use to make one side of a shelter, to block an opening, or for a heat reflector behind a fire. Can be used in place of large rocks to dam a stream.

To make a very sturdy stick wall, increase the space between the uprights, use two stacks of sticks and fill the gap with earth.

COVERINGS: Use springy saplings, plant stems, grasses and long leaves to make wattle and woven coverings for roofs and walls. First make a framework from less pliable materials, either *in situ* or as a separate panel to attach later. Tie the main struts in position. Weave in the more pliant materials.

   If no ties are available, drive vertical stakes into the ground and weave saplings between them. Caulk with earth and grass.

   If suitable firm cross-pieces are scarce, weave creepers between the uprights. Very large leaves, lashed or weighted down, can be overlapped like tiles or shingles to keep out rain.

Long grass can be bunched and woven, or use birch bark to make tiles. Ring a birch tree with even 60cm (24in) cuts and remove bark (a). Fix pairs of canes and creepers across a frame (b). Upper ends of tiles are gripped between the canes; lower ends rest on those below (c).

OPEN LEAN-TO SHELTER:

If there is nothing to lean a roof against (and no need to keep out heavy rain or blizzards) use panels of wattle or grass-covered frames.

Erect horizontal cross-piece between trees or on supports. On the windward side lean panel of wattle, or saplings, at 45 ° as roof (a). Site fire leeward side and build reflector (b) to conserve heat. Adding to either side of shelter makes it secure and gives you space for fire wood and supplies (c & d). A canopy (e) may also be added.

TROPICAL SHELTERS

In rainforests and jungle where the ground is damp and crawling with insects a raised bed is preferable. Unless the nights are cold, the number one priority will be to keep reasonably dry. The following are useful materials.

BAMBOO: A very versatile building material found in damp places from India through to China, parts of Africa, Australia and the southern USA, which can be used for supports, flooring, roofing and walls.

Split bamboo vertically to make roofing and guttering to collect rainwater. Split stems, laid alternately to interlock with one another, to form waterproof pantiles.

Flatten split bamboo for walls, floors or shelving by cutting vertically through the joints every 1.25cm (½in) round the circumference. It can then be smoothed out.

The paper-like sheaths formed at the nodes can be used as roofing material.

 Take great care when collecting bamboo. Some stems are under tension and when cut explode into sharp slivers. Split bamboo can be razor-sharp and cause serious injury. The husks at the base of bamboo stems carry small stinging hairs which cause severe skin irritations.

THATCH OF LEAVES: Atap and other large leaves when thatched make the best roofs and walls for jungle shelters. Look for any plant similarly structured, the bigger and broader the better.

a

Atap (a) is best used horizontally, splitting each leaf in two from the tip (b) and tearing it into two halves down its length. Do not try to split from the thick end as it will break. There are barbs at each leaf tip, so handle it carefully.

b

Closely layer halves of atap on a roof frame (c). Walls can be less dense.

c

Another method involves not splitting down the leaf but folding the leaflets on one side across to the other and interweaving them (d). This is easiest if you work from one side then the other, but requires practice.

d

Three-lobed leaves or leaves cut in this fashion (e) can be locked over a thatching frame without any other fixing being necessary to hold them in place (f).

Elephant grass and other large leaves can be woven between the cross-pieces (g). Only a small number are needed to produce a shelter very quickly.

Long, broad leaves can be sown along the thatching battens with vines (h).

Palm and other long-stemmed leaves can be secured by carrying the stem round the batten and over the front of the leaf, where it is held by the next leaf (i). Leaves must overlap those below on the outside of the shelter.

CAMP CRAFT

ARCTIC SHELTERS

In polar areas caves and hollows form simple shelters. If you carry a bivouac, increase its protection by piling up loose snow around and over it, so long as it can support the weight. At very low temperatures snow is solid and you need spades and ice saws to cut into it or make blocks of it.

Snow or rock caves are easily recognisable, but look also for spaces left beneath conifers when snow has built up round them. A medium-sized tree may have a space right round the trunk (a) or a large one may have pockets in the snow beneath a branch (b). Try digging under any tree with spreading branches on the lee side.

Even soft snow can be built into a windbreak. Cut and stack blocks (c). Use another course of blocks to anchor a ground sheet or poncho along the top, use others to secure the bottom edge and more to close the sides.

CAMP CRAFT

> ### BUILDING IN SNOW
> Cut compacted snow – using a saw, knife, shovel or machete – into blocks 45 x 50cm (18 x 20in) and 10–20cm (4–8in) thick. These will provide good insulation while allowing the sun's rays to penetrate.

SNOW TRENCH: This is a one-person shelter for short-term use only. Mark out an area the size of a sleeping bag; cut out blocks the whole width of the trench. Dig down at least 60cm (24in). Along the top of the sides cut a ledge c. 15cm (6in) wide and the same depth.

Rest snow bricks on each side of the ledge and lean them in against each other to form a roof (a).

Put equipment under sleeping bag as insulation. Block windward end with a block or piled snow. At the downwind end, dig an entrance, or have a removable block as a door. Fill gaps with snow. This shelter is best built on a slight slope with entrance at lower end.

SNOW CAVE: Dig into a drift of firm snow. Create three levels inside: build a fire on the highest, sleep on the centre one and keep off the lower level which will trap the cold. Drive two holes through the roof: one for a chimney and one to ensure adequate ventilation.

CAMP CRAFT

Use a block of snow as a door, keeping it loose-fitting and on the inside so it won't jam. Smooth inside surfaces to discourage drips, and make a channel round the internal perimeter for melt.

IGLOO: An efficient snow house. Make sure entrance does not face wind (erect windbreak if necessary).
To construct an igloo by the circular method, mark out a circle 4m (13ft) in diameter and tramp it down to consolidate the floor. Cut and lay circle of blocks on perimeter. Dig a tunnel (a), leaving space for an entrance (b). Add a layer, centring new blocks over previous vertical joint.

Each new layer should be placed halfway over lower tier, so igloo forms a dome shape. Shape entrance arch as you go. Seal top with flat block. Make ventilation holes near top and bottom (not on side of prevailing wind, or so low that snow blocks the hole). Fill other gaps with snow. Smooth off the inside to remove drip-points.

Inside the igloo, build a sleeping level higher than the floor and create a lower cold level for storage.

- Sweating is to be avoided, so take your time over building a complex structure and rest frequently.

- Adequate ventilation is essential to prevent carbon monoxide poisoning and to allow moisture to escape.

- The smaller the shelter, the warmer it will be, but it will not be possible to heat it much above freezing.

CAMP CRAFT

LIVING IN A SNOW HOUSE

- Make sure you have a supply of fuel in the shelter.
- Knock snow off boots and clothing before entering.
- Mark the entrance so that it is easily found.
- Keep shovels and tools inside to dig yourself out.
- Stop drips by placing a piece of snow on the source.
- Relieve yourself indoors in containers.

> No matter how low the external temperature, inside a well-constructed snow house the temperature will not drop below -10°C (0°F). An oil burner or fat on bones are good alternatives where there is no wood.

LONG-TERM SHELTERS

If you decide that there is no hope of rescue and it is impractical to make your own way to safety due to distance, time of year, lack of equipment or physical condition, make a comfortable, permanent shelter.

CAVES: Those situated above a valley will be dry even if water seeps through in some places from above. They are weather-proof and require little aside from a barrier of rocks or wattle to close off the entrance. Caves may be inhabited by wild animals, so approach with caution. Dry plant matter on the ground will provide insulation. A good fire will make animals leave (allow them an escape route). Build the fire at the back of the cave so smoke goes up to the roof – smoke from a fire near the open mouth of a cave will be blown in. If you seal the entrance, make sure to leave a gap for smoke to escape.

CAMP CRAFT

 Check for the possibility of a rock-fall inside or outside the cave. You could be trapped or injured by falling rocks.

LIGHT STRUCTURES: Follow the methods outlined for the lean-to structure (p. 164). Extend it with a less angled roof and a front wall, or build vertical walls and roof them over with deep eaves to give extra shade and to ensure that rain runs off. In hot climates the walls can then be fairly open lattice to allow air to pass through. Grasses and mud will seal cracks. In climates with heavy rainfall, use leaves or bark-like tiles on top.

   If you have bamboo or other strong material to build a firm frame in tropical climates, raise the floor of your shelter off the ground to keep out other creatures.

LOG CABIN: Scale it to the number it will house, on a flat site. Size of logs will determine the length of walls. Place first layer of logs in the shape of hut – 2.5m (8ft) square is a good size, and easiest to roof. Cut logs to fit neatly on top. Build the front up higher than the back to give pitch to the roof. Make last log front and back project well beyond the walls. These will support the roof.

 SURVIVAL SCENARIO
Having built a shelter, where should you wash yourself and your clothes?
All ablutions should be carried out downstream. This will be at a lower point than where you are getting your drinking water from, thereby ensuring your supply remains clean and uncontaminated.

CAMP CRAFT

FIRE

Fire is essential to survival. You must learn to light a fire under any conditions, anywhere. Most important uses of fire are: boiling water – this counters 90 per cent of all waterborne diseases – signalling, cooking and protection from animals and flying insects. Fire can also help to make or fashion tools. Fire-lighting is a vital skill.

> **PRACTISE FIRE-LIGHTING**
> Fire provides warmth, protection, a means of signalling, boils water, and cooks and preserves food. It is not enough to know all the methods of lighting a fire – you have to be expert at them.

PREPARATION

Ensure adequate ventilation for your fire. The more oxygen introduced, the brighter the fire; by reducing ventilation the fire burns less fiercely, needing less fuel. Collect sufficient supplies of tinder, kindling and fuel. Prepare a fireplace so you can control the fire.

The fireplace

Choose a sheltered site. Except for signal purposes (see pp. 272–75), do not light a fire at the base of a tree. Clear away leaves, twigs, moss and dry grass from a circle 2m (6.5ft) across until you have a bare earth surface.

If the ground is wet or snow-covered, build a platform from a layer of green logs covered with a layer of earth, or a layer of stones.

TEMPLE FIRE: A raised platform of green timber. Four uprights support cross-pieces in their forks. Place a layer of green logs across them and cover this with several inches of earth. Light the fire on top of this. A pole across upper forks on diagonally opposite uprights can support cooking pots.

In windy conditions dig a trench and light your fire in it.

Alternatively, encircle your fire with rocks to retain heat and save fuel. They serve as heated pot-stands and can be used as bed-warmers.

☠ Avoid placing wet or porous rocks near fires, especially rocks which have been submerged in water – they may explode when heated, producing dangerous flying fragments which could take out an eye if you are close to the fire. Avoid slates and softer rocks. Test them by banging them together, and do not use any that crack or sound hollow.

CAMP CRAFT

Tinder

Tinder is any material that takes only a spark to ignite. Birch bark, dried grasses, wood shavings, bird down, waxed paper, cotton fluff, fir cones, pine needles, powdered dried fungi, scorched or charred cotton are excellent tinder, as is the fine dust produced by wood-burrowing insects and the inside of birds' nests.

Kindling

Kindling is the wood used to raise flames from tinder. Small dry twigs, resinous and softer woods are best.

> Tinder and kindling must be dry. Don't collect this straight from the earth. If the outside of kindling is damp, shave until you reach dry wood.

Make fire sticks

Shave sticks with shallow cuts to 'feather' them. This will make the wood catch light more quickly.

Fuel

Use dry wood to get a fire going. Once established, mix green and dried-out damp wood.

Hard woods such as hickory, beech and oak burn well, are long lasting, and give off great heat.

Soft woods burn fast and give off sparks: the worst culprits are alder, spruce, pine, chestnut and willow.

CAMP CRAFT

Dry wood across two supports high enough above a fire that they won't be set alight. Lay green logs beside fire, tapering away from the wind, so they shelter the fire while they dry.

A basic woodshed is vital

in wet weather. Position where fire will warm it, but clear of stray sparks.

Save energy: don't chop logs, break them over a rock (a).

Or feed them over the fire, letting them burn through in the middle (b).

Split logs without an axe by placing a knife on the end of a log and hitting it with a rock (c). Once begun, split can be widened with wooden wedge plugged in gap and driven downward. Don't do this if you have only one knife – it could get damaged.

CAMP CRAFT

OTHER FUELS

Animal droppings: These make excellent fuel. Dry well. You can mix them with grass and leaves.

Peat: This is often found on moors. Soft and springy underfoot, it looks black and fibrous. Dry it before burning. Needs ventilation when burning.

Coal: This is sometimes found in the northern tundra.

Shales: Rich in oil, these burn readily. Some sands contain oil and burn with a thick smoke – good signals.

Combustibles: These include petroleum, hydraulic fluid, engine oils, insect repellent. Soaked in oil, tyres, upholstery and rubber seals are inflammable.

Animal fats: Use a tin for a stove and burn with a wick.

BURNING OIL AND WATER: Pierce a small hole at the base of a tin can for each liquid and fit tapered sticks to govern the flow (a). The oil and water run down a trough to a metal plate. To increase flow pull out stick; push in to reduce.

Try 2–3 drops water: 1 drop oil. First light a small fire under plate to get it hot. Light the mixture itself on top of the plate. It is highly volatile and will burn almost anything.

CAMP CRAFT

Burning oils: *Mix petrol with sand and burn in ventilated tin, or dig fire pit. Burn oil by mixing in petrol or antifreeze. Do not set a light directly to any liquid fuels: make a wick for flame.*

FIRE-LIGHTING

Form a tepee of kindling round tinder bed. If windy, lean kindling against a log on the lee side. Ignite tinder. Add larger sticks once kindling has caught. Or light a bundle of dry match-thin twigs and place in tepee.

MATCHES

The easiest way to start a fire. Carry the non-safety type in waterproof containers, packed so they can't rub, rattle or ignite. Split in half to make them go further. To strike split matches, press inflammable end against the striking surface with a finger.

Strike a damp match by stabbing obliquely instead of drawing it along striker strip.

If your hair is dry and not too greasy, roll a damp match in it. Static electricity will dry out the match.

CAMP CRAFT

> Whenever you strike a match, light a candle. Many things can then be lit from it, saving matches. Even a small candle will last a long time if used carefully.

SUNLIGHT THROUGH A LENS: *This can ignite tinder. Use your survival kit magnifying glass, telescope or camera lens. Focus sun's rays to form a tiny, bright spot of light. Keep it steady and shield from wind. Blow it gently as it glows.*

POWDER FROM AMMUNITION: *Break open a round and pour gunpowder on tinder (a) and use flint. Or leave half the powder in cartridge case and stuff piece of cloth in (b). Chamber the round and fire into the ground. The smouldering cloth will be ejected. Place on tinder to ignite.*

FLINT: A stone found in many parts of the world. Strike with steel and hot sparks fly off (a). Or use saw-edged blade from survival kit (b) for more sparks.

CAMP CRAFT

BATTERY FIRE-LIGHTING: Attach two lengths of wire to battery. If you have no wire, use metal tools. If using a car battery, remove it from the vehicle first.

Slowly bring bare ends of two pieces of wire together. A spark will jump across just before they touch. Aim it at tinder. A small piece of cloth with a little petrol is best tinder for this.

FIRE BOW: The friction of a hardwood spindle rotated on a softwood base produces wood-dust tinder, then heat. Both spindle and base must be dry.

Gouge a small depression at near end of baseboard. Cut a cavity below for tinder. Shape the spindle evenly. Make a bow from a pliable shoot and twine, hide or a bootlace. Use hollow piece of stone/wood to steady top of the spindle and exert downward pressure. Wind bowstring once round spindle. Place spindle in the depression, hold steadying piece over its end and bear down lightly while moving bow backwards and forwards so spindle spins. Increase speed as spindle starts drilling. When it enters cavity, apply more pressure and bow vigorously.

Keep spindle upright and steady, and bow strokes even. It helps to kneel with one foot on baseboard. Carry on bowing until a glowing tip drops on to tinder. Blow on it gently to ignite.

HAND DRILL: A variation on the fire bow.

Cut a V-shaped notch in hardwood baseboard. Make a small depression. Use stem of hollow softwood with soft pith core for spindle. Roll the spindle between the palms of your hands, running hands down it as you go, to press it into depression.

When friction makes the spindle tip glow red, blow gently to ignite the tinder. Put a pinch of sand in spindle hole to increase friction.

FIRE PLOUGH: Cut a straight groove in a softwood base board and then plough the tip of a hardwood shaft up and down it. This produces tinder, then ignites it.

CAMP CRAFT

FIRE-LIGHTING WITH CHEMICALS

The following mixtures can be ignited by grinding with rocks or putting them under friction point in a fire drill. Mix carefully and avoid contact with metal. Keep dry.

Potassium chlorate and sugar in a 3:1 mix.

Potassium chlorate is found in some throat tablets.

Potassium permanganate and sugar in a 9:1 mix.

Potassium permanganate is part of your survival kit.

Sodium chlorate and sugar in a 3:1 mix.

Sodium chlorate is a weed-killer.

 Handle chemicals with care. Sodium chlorate ignites from percussion – DO NOT shake or spill (spillage can ignite when stepped on)!

TYPES OF FIRE

Fires for warmth

Only surfaces facing an outdoor fire are warmed by it.

A reflector not only reflects heat but makes smoke go upwards. Use one to reflect heat into a sleeping shelter.

Site fire near a rock. Sit between the two so that the rock reflects the heat and warms your back. Add a reflector.

If there is no rock to reflect heat, build a second reflector to go behind you.

CAMP CRAFT

SNAKE HOLE FIRE: On the side of a firm earth bank dig a chamber about 45cm (18in) deep. From above, drive a stick down into the chamber, manoeuvre it a little to make a chimney, removing the spoil that falls below.

The smoke from this fire is ideal for preserving meat and fish. Build the fire in the chamber. The entrance is best sited downwind in windy conditions.

Cooking fires

TRENCH FIRE: Dig a trench 30 x 90cm (12 x 36in) and 30cm (12in) deep plus the depth of a layer of rocks with which you now line the bottom. Build a fire on the rocks. Even when it dies down, they will remain hot

enough to make a grill. A spit placed across the embers is ideal for roasts.

HOBO STOVE: Punch holes in the bottom and round the bottom sides of a 5-gallon oil drum. Cut out a panel on one side, 5cm (2in) from the bottom, through which to stoke the fire. Set the drum on a ring of stones to allow ventilation beneath.

CAMP CRAFT

COOKING

Cooking makes food more appetising and easy to digest.
It destroys bacteria and parasites that may be present, and
neutralises poisons. But when heated, food loses
nutritional value. Never cook longer than necessary.

- Use the fire to boil water then let the flames die
  down and use embers and hot ash for cooking.

- Never leave your fire unattended when cooking.

- Having a fire, always have water boiling – unless
  in short supply – for drinks, sterilising wounds, etc.

- Do not just balance a can on the fire. Support
  vessels on rocks or suspend them over the fire,
  for stability.

COOKING METHODS

BOILING: Cans and metal boxes are ideal for boiling
water. Make a handle, hang them from a pot support or
use tongs to move them. Punctures can be repaired by
hammering in small plugs of wood – when wet they will
expand and stop leaks. Improvise pots from a
thick length of bamboo or sections of birch
bark – but do not let them boil dry.

*To cook in a bamboo stem, angle it across
the heat of the fire, supporting it on a
forked stick driven into the ground.*

Boiling conserves natural juices – always drink the
liquid unless boiling out toxic substances.

CAMP CRAFT

Any dead animal that is not actually decomposing can be eaten if you use only the large muscle areas. Cut into 2.5cm (1in) cubes and boil for 30 minutes. Eat only a little, and wait half-hour – most toxins act in that time or less. If there are no ill effects, tuck in.

ROASTING: Skewer the meat on a spit and turn it over hot embers or beside a blazing fire. Continually turn meat to keep the fat moving over the surface.

A spit should be set to one side of fire to allow for a drip tray to catch fat for basting. Fierce heat cooks the outside, leaving the inside undercooked, so a slow roast is best. Cut off outer meat, then continue roasting to cook the inner flesh.

GRILLING: Wastes fat – use only when food is plentiful.

Rest a wire mesh or a grid of green sticks on rocks over the embers. Or use a long stick on a forked support to hold food over the fire. Wrap the food round the stick.

BAKING: This requires an oven. Cook the meat on a dish and baste it with its own fat. Slow cooking on a steady heat tenderises meat. Baking is also ideal for root vegetables.

A large metal box with a hinged lid and a catch you can use as a handle, can be set up to open sideways. If it has no catch let it open downwards. Place a support in front, to rest lid on. Prop it closed and avoid a tight fit which could build up dangerous pressure inside. If no box is available, make a clay dome, set a fire inside and scrape this out before cooking. Leave a small aperture which can be easily sealed while baking.

Stand the box on rocks so a fire can be lit under it. Build up rocks and earth or clay around the back, sides and top, but leave a space behind and make a chimney hole from above leading to this space.

STEAMING: Is a good way to cook fish and vegetables. Punch holes in a can and suspend it inside a larger can, or put something in the bottom of the large can to keep the inner one above water. Cover the outer can, but do not seal it or the pressure could cause it to explode.

Improvise a steamer of bamboo: between the inner compartments make a hole just big enough to let water through to fill the bottom section. Make a lid (not too tight) for the top. Water boiled in the lowest section will produce steam to cook food in the top one.

CAMP CRAFT

FRYING: A good way to vary diet, if fat is available. Any sheet of metal that can be fashioned into a curve will serve to fry in. Some large leaves (e.g. banana) contain enough oil not to dry out before the cooking is done. Try the leaves out first before cooking food on them and fry only over embers.

COOKING IN CLAY: This requires no utensils. Wrap food in a ball of clay and place in the embers. Heat radiates through the clay, which protects against food scorching.

Animals must be cleaned and gutted first but need not be otherwise prepared: when the clay is removed spines, scales or feathers from small birds come away with it, but big birds should be plucked. Not advisable for root vegetables – skins are too nutritious to lose.

HANGI: Another way of cooking without utensils. It requires kindling, logs and round rocks the size of a fist. Do not use stones which may explode (see p. 174).

Dig an oval hole with rounded sides 45–60cm deep (18–24in); place kindling at the bottom. Lay logs across the hole, place another layer at right angles, interspersed with stones. Build up 5 or 6 more alternating layers, and top off with stones. When the kindling is set alight the logs will burn, heating the stones above them, until, eventually, all falls into the pit.

Remove embers and ash, place food on top of the hot rocks, meat in centre and vegetables to the edge. There must be a gap between the food and earth. Lay saplings across the pit and cover with sacking, leaves and earth. Uncover after 1½ hours; your meal is ready.

    The hangi can be used to boil water collected in a waterproof sack, provided the fabric won't melt. Place tied-up sack in the hangi. Takes about 1½ hours to boil.

USEFUL UTENSILS

Tongs: *Lash two branches so they spring apart at the ends — use a tapering piece of wood between them under the lashings. Grip is improved if one has forked end. Use for holding hot pots.*

Pot rod: *Drive a sturdy forked stick into ground near fire. Rest a longer stick across it with one end over fire. Drive bottom of long stick in ground and weight with rocks. Cut a groove near the tip to prevent pots slipping off, or tie on a strong hook.*

Swinging pot holder: *Bind two forked sticks together so forks fit in opposite directions on a firm upright. The cantilever action will maintain the height you set it at, and a push sideways will swing the pot away from the flames.*

CAMP CRAFT

VARIABLE POT HOOK: *Cut a strong piece with several branches from a small tree or bush and trim branches to 10–12cm (4–5in). Strip off the bark, which may hide rotten wood.*

CUP: *Cut a section of bamboo just below a joint, then cut just below the next joint up. Smooth the edges to prevent splinters.*

SPOON: *Scribe a spoon shape on a flattish piece of wood with a knife point. Whittle to required shape. Never cut towards yourself.*

BIRCH BARK CONTAINERS: *Use the inner layer of bark to make cooking vessels. Sew or tie them near the top to prevent unfolding. Make a second vessel with a larger base for a lid.*

A circle, folded into quarters, will make a cone-shaped cup or a boiling vessel if suspended.

CAMP CRAFT

COOKING TIPS

MEAT: Cut into cubes and boil. Venison is prone to worms, pork to worms and liver fluke. Marinade tough meat in citric juice for 24 hours before cooking.

OFFAL: Check liver: only if firm, odourless, free from spots and hard lumps can it be eaten. Boil, then fry if you wish. Hearts: par-boil then bake. Brains: skin head and boil, simmering for 90 minutes. Strip all flesh from the skull, including the eyes, tongue and ears. Blood: collect in a container and leave covered until a clear liquid comes to the top. When separation seems complete, drain it off. Dry the residue by the fire to form a firm cake. Use to enrich soups and stews.

FISH: Stew or wrap in leaves and place in hot embers (avoid toxic leaves).

BIRDS: Boil all carrion. Old birds are tough and best boiled. Stuff young ones with herbs or fruits and then roast.

REPTILES: Gut, then cook in their skins. Place in hot embers, turning continually. When skin splits meat can be removed and boiled. Some snakes have poisonous secretions on the skin and others have venom glands in their head, so cut this off before cooking. If you are not sure they are safe, take care in handling them. Skin frogs (many have poisonous skins) then roast on a stick.

SHARK: Cut into small cubes and soak overnight in freshwater. Boil in several changes of water to get rid of the ammonia flavour.

CAMP CRAFT

SHELLFISH: Safest boiled. All seafood spoils quickly. Drop into boiling salted water and boil for 10 minutes.

INSECTS & WORMS: Best boiled. Cook and mince them by crushing in a can. Or dry on hot rocks then grind into a powder with which to enrich soups and stews.

EGGS: Boil, or roast after first using a sharp stick or knifepoint to pierce a small hole in one end. Place on warm embers to cook slowly. If a boiled egg contains an embryo chick remove the embryo and roast it.

GREEN VEGETABLES: Wash and boil until tender. Can be steamed if you are sure they are safe. Add to stew after the meat is cooked. Eat fresh greens raw as salad.

ROOTS: Any toxins are destroyed by heat. Try boiling for five minutes then place in a hole dug beneath the fire, cover with ash and embers and leave until tender.

LICHENS & MOSSES: Soak overnight. Add to stews.

SAGO: Fell a sago palm at base of the trunk and trim the tip just below last flowering line. Divide the trunk into sections cut lengthwise. Using each section as a trough, pound pith into a mash, then knead in a container of water and strain through a cloth. A starchy paste will form in the water. Roll this into sticky balls and cook.

PALM SAP: Choose a fat stalk carrying a flowering head (at the base of the crown on trunk). Bruise with a club then cut off head. Sweet juice will flow from end of stalk. Bruise and cut daily to stimulate flow. Drink raw or boil, then cool to produce lumps of pure sugar.

CAMP CRAFT

PRESERVING FOOD

If food is not plentiful or is limited by season, ensure that stores keep safely.

• Do not store food in direct sunlight, near excessive warmth or moisture, nor where scavengers may ruin it.

• Wrap in airtight and waterproof materials – or store in containers with a good seal. Label stores and separate different foods to avoid cross-flavouring.

• Check occasionally to see all is well.

DRYING

Wind and sun can dry food but it is easier to force-dry over a fire. Dried foods are less vulnerable to moulds and maggots. Meat with a high fat content is difficult to preserve. Cut off most of the fat and rub salt into the flesh. Hang the salted meat in a cool airy place.

SMOKING: This dehydrates meat and coats it with a protective layer. Smoking can be carried out in a smoke tepee. Get a fire going to produce hot embers. Have a pile of green leaves ready.

To build a smoke tepee, drive three sticks into the ground to form a triangle and tie the tops together. Build a platform between them and set a fire beneath.

CAMP CRAFT

Hardwood leaves are ideal, but avoid holly and other toxic leaves, and conifers which may burst into flame. Do not use grass. Make sure there are no flames left, and pile leaves over the embers.

Cut meat into fat-free strips, 2.5cm (1in) by 6mm (¼in), gut and fillet fish. Cover the tepee with a cloth to keep in the smoke. If you don't have a cloth, pile boughs and turfs on the frame and seal it. Leave for 18 hours and ensure little or no smoke escapes.

To avoid risk of embers setting the tepee alight, build a snake hole fire (see p. 183); erect tepee over chimney.

BILTONG: Cut strips, as for smoking; hang them in sun, out of reach of animals, 2–3m (6–10ft) above ground. They can take 2 weeks to dry. Protect them from rain and dew. Turn the strips to ensure all surfaces are dried, and keep flies off so they don't lay eggs.

To dry fish, cut off the head, tail and gut. Split open, remove the backbone and score inner flesh. Lay on hot, sun-baked rocks. Fish less than 7.5cm- (3in-) long need not be gutted.

Fish can also be smoked. They will be easier to hang if cleaned and gutted without removing the backbone, head or tail. Suspend by one side of the head.

CAMP CRAFT

PEMMICAN: This is concentrated food made from biltong, ideal for provisions to carry on treks. Before setting out, take equal quantities, by weight, of biltong and rendered fat. Shred and pound the meat. Melt the animal fat over the shredded meat and mix together well. When cold pack in a waterproof bag. It will keep for a long time, especially in cold climates.

Nuts and cereals

Place on hot rocks from the fire, turning frequently until dried. Store in damp-proof containers.

Fruit, fungi and lichens

Fruit and berries can be dried whole or cut into slices and dried by sun, smoke or heat. Fungi also dry easily. Fruit can be eaten dry. Add fungi to soups or soak in water for several hours to regain their texture.

To store lichens, soak overnight, boil well and allow to dry. Grind to a powder then boil again to form a thick syrup, which adds body to other foods.

PICKLING AND SALTING

Citric acid from limes and lemons can be used to pickle fish and meat. Dilute juice and water 2:1, mix well and soak the flesh for at least 12 hours. Transfer it to an airtight container with enough solution to cover meat.

Vegetables can be preserved by boiling and then keeping in saltwater. To make sure a brine solution is strong enough, add salt until a potato or root vegetable will float in it. Another method of using salt is to tightly pack layers of salt and vegetables. Wash off the salt when you need to use them.

CAMP CRAFT

ORGANISING THE CAMP

If no command structure exists between a group of survivors, establish an organising committee with particular responsibilities. A roster is essential for daily chores. Everyone who is fit should take their turn at unpleasant tasks, unless their skills are in such demand that it would be a waste of their abilities.

> Keeping busy eliminates boredom and keeps up morale. Invalids should get light jobs. At all times there must be someone in camp able to operate the signals should a search aircraft appear. If numbers permit, avoid venturing from the camp without a partner.

A nightly gathering will provide discipline, and an opportunity to debrief and to discuss new strategies.

Boredom is dangerous for a lone survivor and objectives should be set each day, whether practical or for amusement. A regular routine helps morale.

CAMP HYGIENE

Strict hygiene should be practised in the camp.

CAMP LAYOUT

• Latrines must be downhill of camp and away from the water supply to avoid risk of seepage.

• Establish a collection point for drinking water. Ensure no-one washes upstream of it. Downstream choose a point for ablutions and laundry, and downstream of that a place for cleaning cooking utensils.

• Latrines and rubbish disposal should be well away from camp – preferably downwind – but not so far as to be inconvenient. Cut a track to make access easier.

CAMP CRAFT

Never urinate or defecate near your water supply. Latrines must be established, even for a lone survivor. Do not use disinfectant – after defecating, cover faeces with earth. Make a latrine cover to keep out flies and always replace it. If a latrine starts to smell, dig a new one. Fill in the old latrine and burn old timbers.

DEEP TRENCH LATRINE:
Dig a trench 1.25m (4ft) deep and 45cm (18in) wide. Build up sides with logs, rocks or earth to sitting height. Seal gaps. Lay logs across to leave only a hole for use. Pour wood ash on logs to make a seal and deter flies.

Cover opening with wooden lid, flat rock or a large leaf weighted with stones.

URINAL: *Dig a pit 60cm (24in) deep. Fill it three-quarters full with large stones and top up with earth, with a bark cone set into it as a funnel.*

CAMP CRAFT

Incinerator: Rubbish should be burned. Make a fire in the latrine area using a large can as an incinerator. Bury unburned refuse in a pit.

CAMP DISCIPLINE

• Do not prepare game in camp: bleed, gut and skin on the trap line to attract game to traps, not to the camp.

• Keep food covered and off the ground.

• Replace lids on containers immediately after use.

• Stow clothing and equipment where it cannot get wet or burned. Keep things tidy: hook mess tins and cooking utensils on twigs and branches.

• Never leave the fire unattended.

Soap: Washing with soap leaves skin less waterproof and more prone to attack by germs. However, soap is an antiseptic, better than many others, such as iodine, which destroy body tissue as well as germs. It is ideal for scrubbing hands before administering first aid. Save supplies for this.

Soap-making: Two ingredients – an oil and alkali – are needed. The oil can be animal fat or vegetable, but not mineral. The alkali can be produced by burning wood or seaweed to produce ash.

To make soap, wash the ash with water then strain and boil it with the oil. Simmer until excess liquid is evaporated and allow to cool. This soap is not antiseptic. Add horseradish root or pine resin to make it antiseptic. Too much alkali in the mix will dry the skin, leaving it sore.

CAMP CRAFT

TOOLS

STONE TOOLS

Split a cobble with a blow at an angle
of less than 90° from a hard,
smooth pebble to form a flat
face. Shape by hitting edge-on
with another stone (a), then
create a platform on one side
(b) from which a series of flakes can
be struck vertically down (c). Then
strike with softer stones, and hit
and press small flakes away with
a piece of antler or hard wood.
Flakes may be used as scrapers,
to cut edges, and as arrowheads.

BONE TOOLS

Bones, antlers and horns make useful
digging implements, gougers and
hammers. Cut them with stone tools or
grind with coarse stones. A shoulder blade
is a good shape for a saw (a). Split in half,
then cut teeth along it with a knife. A
small bone scraper (b) could also be
made, the edge ground sharp. Ribs are
ideal for shaping into points (c). For a
bone needle, sharpen a suitably sized bone to a point.
Burn an eye with a piece of hot wire, or scrape
with a knife point or piece of flint.
Don't heat the knife in the fire.

AXES

To improvise a handle for an axehead use any straight, knot-free hardwood. The flukes of a buttress tree (a) are ideal; slightly curved, straight-grained and easy to work. Cut two notches into the fluke of a buttress, spaced to the desired length (b to c).

Hit along side of fluke close to the cuts. It will split away at their depth.

FITTING THE HEAD: Whittle the handle into shape with one end cut to fit the hole in the axehead, cutting a notch in that end. Make a wedge to fit the notch. With the head in place drive in the notch, then soak the axe in water overnight to tighten the head on the shaft. Always check axeheads for tightness before using.

CAMP CRAFT

To FIT A STONE AXEHEAD: Select a hardwood handle. Tie a band of cord round it 23cm (9in) from one end. Split end as far as this band (use a knife and a wedge or the axehead flint). Insert flint and tie end.

SHARPENING AN AXE: Use a file to get rid of burrs, and a whetstone to impart the sharp edge. A file is a one-way tool – it works when pushed, not pulled.

Prop axehead between a log and a peg (a). Always sharpen inwards from cutting edge to avoid producing burrs.
Use a file or rougher stone first to remove rucks and burrs (b).
Finish with a smooth stone, in a circular motion. Don't drag stone off cutting edge. Push on to blade (see pp. 23–25). Turn axe over. Repeat process circling in opposite direction (c).

USING AN AXE: Swing an axe in an arc that feels natural with a firm grip and always away from your body, hands, and legs. Make sure that, if you miss your target and follow through the axe will not strike you or anyone else. Never throw an axe on the ground. Sheathe it or bury the blade in a log.

Tree felling

Check overhead for dead branches and hornets' nests.
Clear creepers and branches which could deflect blows.
Cut branches off from the outside of the join.

*Cut from both sides of the tree, first
chopping out a notch at an angle of
45 ° and another on the opposite
side at a lower level, on the side to
which you want the tree to fall (a).
Do not cut more than
halfway before starting
the other notch.*

A tree with most of its branches on one side will fall
in that direction regardless of the placing of the cuts.

Use a steady rhythm of blows. Put too much effort
behind the axe and your aim will suffer. Alternating the
angle of stroke will prevent the axe from jamming. Too
steep an angle will cause the axe to glance off; dead-on

will make it jam or be
inefficient. Aim for 45 °.

SPLITTING LOGS: *Stand
behind log with feet apart.
Swing down to cut the side
away from you (a). Do not chop
downwards (b). To split a small
log, angle it against another log
(c). Do not put your foot on it.*

CAMP CRAFT

CAMP CRAFT

BROKEN HANDLES: Axe handles break when the head misses the target and the handle takes the impact (a). To remove a broken handle, put it in a fire, burying metal in the earth to prevent it losing temper – single-headed (b), double-headed (c).

USING A FLEXIBLE SAW: *Always use a flexible saw so the cut opens (a) rather than closes (b), causing it to jam. Don't pull too hard or the saw will break. Keep the wire taut (c), pulling straight, never at angles (d). Maintain the rhythm when 2 people saw. A kink may break (e) the saw.*

It is usually easier for a single person to cut a log by pulling it upwards (f). Keep the log off the ground and give it an angle to keep cut open. Alternatively, to remove a branch, pull down from above (g). This could be dangerous. High branches can be removed by attaching strings to the saw toggles for extra reach. Be ready to jump clear of the branch.

CAMP CRAFT

FURNISHING THE CAMP

BEDS

Avoid lying on cold, damp ground. In the tropics raise the bed to provide a current of air. In cold climates, keep a fire going through the night and build a screen to reflect heat back on your sleeping area. On dry ground, stones heated in the fire and then buried under a thin layer of soil beneath the bedding will keep you warm.

A-FRAME BEDS: Drive two pairs of posts into the ground at an angle, leaving a little more than your height between the pairs. Lash tops together. On hard ground cross-members will be needed between the feet of each A-frame and between the two A-frames.

TUBE BED: Make a tube of strong material, sewn or thonged together. A large heavy-duty plastic bag is suitable. Do not use any fabric that might give under your weight or seams that might come apart.

Make A-frame supports, choose two straight poles, slightly longer than the distance between the frames, and pass them through the tube of fabric. Place them over the frames so they rest on the sides, the tube preventing them from slipping lower.

BOUGH BED: Fir-tree branches arranged in alternate layers make a comfortable and fragrant bed.

CAMP CRAFT

LADDER BED: Make A-frame supports and select poles as for the tube bed, and add a number of cross-pieces. Strong, springy saplings are best. Lash end rungs to the A-frame, jutting out either side. Make these of strong timber and lash them securely. Fit ladder over frames and lash in place. Lay bedding of ferns or leaves.

SEATS: Never sit on damp ground. Use a log, or lash together a couple of low A-frame supports and rest a bough across them.

LADDER: Lash cross-pieces to two long poles set at an angle, not parallel, so rungs won't slip down.

TRAVOIS: Choose two boughs with some spring to them and lash cross-pieces, as for the ladder. Use additional struts to provide closer support. Pull the load on its runners like a sled. (See also p. 245.)

ANIMAL PRODUCTS

SKINS AND FURS

Properly prepared skins are supple, strong, and resist tearing. They have good thermal insulation, and are permeable to air and water vapour. For moccasins, shelters, laces, thongs, water bags or canoes, the fur is removed, but for warm clothing, bedding or a good insulating groundsheet should be left on.

Remove fat and flesh by scraping the skin, using an edge of bone, flint or wood. Take care not to cut it. Remove every trace of flesh. Ants and other insects may help if you lay skin on the ground. Keep watch that they do not start to consume the skin itself.

To cure, stretch the skin as tight as possible and leave it in the sun to dry. Rubbing in salt or wood ash will aid the process. Do not let it get damp until the process is complete. If little or no sun is available, force-dry over a fire, but use only the heat and smoke and keep it away from the steam of any cooking pots.

LACES AND LASHINGS: Cut short laces straight from the skin, along its length. To obtain greater length cut in a spiral, keeping width consistent to avoid weak points.

SINEW AS THREAD: The hamstring and the main sinews of the legs can be dried and used as thread, bowstrings, short ropes, and arrowhead bindings. They look like strong white cords. Sticky when wet, they dry hard.

BLADDER: The bladder of a large animal can be used as a water carrier, as can the stomach. Tie off the openings to seal them.

CAMP CRAFT

CLOTHING

• Salvage towels, blankets, seat-covers, curtains, sacking from the wreckage – any fabric can be used for garments, bedding or shelter.

• Improve insulation by adding layers. Wear one sock on top of another and stuff dry grass or moss between them. Grass, paper, feathers, animal hair, etc. can be stuffed between other layers of clothing.

• Use plastic bags and sheets to improvise waterproofs or cut off large sections of birch bark. Discard the outer bark and insert the inner layer under outer clothing.

• Improve water-repellent qualities by rubbing animal fat or the tallow from suet into your clothing. Do not do this in situations of intense cold, where the reduction in insulation would be too great a loss.

• Cut shoe soles from rubber tyres, make holes round edges for thongs to tie them over wrapped feet, or to sew on to fabric uppers.

• Tie on several layers of foot-wrappings with thongs or use a triangular shape. Fold one point back over toes, make slits in front. Bring other points from behind the heel, through slits and tie round ankle.

• Tie long leaf strips and fibres round a belt or neck band to hang down as a grass skirt or cape.

• Cut a head hole in a blanket or carpet and use as a poncho. Tie at waist or thong sides.

• Sew together small skins. Fur on the inside will give greater insulation but on outer garments the suede side sheds snow better.

CAMP CRAFT

ROPES AND LINES

Match the type, thickness and length of rope you carry to the demands you expect to make on it. Nylon has advantages in very damp climates and when weight is critical but can melt and is slippery when wet.

Rope of about 9–10mm (⅜in) is recommended for lashings, throwing and mountaineering. It can be used for safety lines and for climbing, provided belay and abseiling techniques are used – it is not thick enough for a hand over hand and foot grip.

Climbing rope must be elastic, to absorb shock without putting strain on anyone who falls.

ROPE CARE

• Rope should be protected from exposure to damp or strong sunlight and, if made from natural fibres, from attack by rodents and insects.

• If rope does get wet, do not force-dry it in front of a fire. Do not drag it or leave it on the ground. Dirt can penetrate and work away at the fibres.

• Try to keep rope for the job for which it was intended – do not use clothesline for climbing, or climbing rope for lashing – though in a survival situation you may have to use the same length of rope for many purposes.

THROWING A ROPE

A coil of rope is easier to throw than a loose end. Have a large knot or weight on the throwing end. Make sure that you keep hold of the other end! Always over-throw a lifeline so that the recipient stands a chance of catching part of the rope, even if they miss the end.

CAMP CRAFT

TO THROW A ROPE: Coil half the rope on fingers and palm of right hand, raise index finger and coil remainder on other fingers only. Pass second coil back to left hand. As you throw, release right-hand coil a split second before the left.

FOR A LONG THROW: Tie a suitable missile to the end of the rope. Coil rope carefully on the ground or loop it loosely over the other hand so it will pay out freely.

Don't risk losing your end. Tie it to an anchor such as a heavy stone. Use a killick hitch (see p. 219).

If throwing a weighted rope over a branch, keep out of its path as it swings back towards the throwing point. If throwing a lifeline, make sure you don't knock out the person you're trying to help.

ROPE-MAKING

Vines, grasses, rushes, barks, palms and animal hairs can all be used to make rope or line.

The stems of nettles make first-class ropes and those of honeysuckle can be twisted together to make tight lashings. The stronger the fibre, the stronger the rope. Some stiff fibres can be made flexible by steaming or warming. While pliable vines and other long plant stems can be used for short-term purposes, they may become brittle as they dry out. A rope made from plant fibres that are twisted ('spun') or plaited together will be more durable.

The tendons from animals' legs also make good strings, but they tend to dry hard. (They are also very useful as binding on arrow and spear heads; see pp. 135–37.)

CAMP CRAFT

KNOTS

It is important to select the right knot for the task in hand.
You never know when you may need to tie a knot, so learn
their uses and how to tie – and untie – each one.

> In the instructions for individual knots that follow the
> end of the rope or cord being used to tie the knot is
> referred to as the 'live end' to distinguish it from the
> other end of the rope, or 'standing part'.

REEF KNOT: Use to tie ropes of
the same thickness. Holds firm
under strain, yet is easily untied.
It is not reliable for ropes of
different diameters, nor for
nylon. Can be tied in other
materials. Use in first aid – it
will lie flat against the patient.

Pass right end over left (a) and
then under it (b). Take left over
right (c) and under it (d).

Check – the 2 loops should
slide on each other. Tighten by
pulling both strands on each
side (e). To be doubly sure, finish
by making a half-hitch with the
live ends on
either side of the
knot (f).

a

b

c

d

e

f

CAMP CRAFT

SIMPLE KNOTS

These knots are quickly made and will help you understand the more complicated knots that follow.

OVERHAND KNOT: Make a loop and pass the live end back through it.

OVERHAND LOOP: Fixed loop for throwing over a projection. Double the end of rope and tie overhand knot with the loop.

FIGURE-OF-EIGHT: An end-stop. Make a loop. Carry live end first behind, then round, the standing part. Bring it forward through the loop.

FIGURE-OF-EIGHT LOOP: Made in the same way as the figure-of-eight, but with line doubled, using loop as the live end. Can be used over a spike anchor for a belaying rope.

REWOVEN FIGURE-OF-EIGHT: Use when top end of a projection is out of reach. Make loose figure-of-eight along the rope. Pass live end round anchor and feed it back round the figure-of-eight, following exactly. Ease tight.

JOINING ROPES

SHEET BEND: If correctly made and strain is not erratic this won't slip. **1** Make a loop in one rope. Take live end of the other (a) right round behind loop to the front, carry it over itself and then tuck down through loop. **2** Draw it tight and ease into shape as strain is increased.

DOUBLE SHEET BEND: More secure variation of sheet bend – use on wet ropes and where strain is not constant.
1 Make a loop in the thicker rope. Take live end of thinner rope (a) through loop, beneath thicker live end and then forward on outside of loop and right round it. Bring thin live end back between itself and outside of thick loop. **2** Take thin live end completely round the loop again and back through same place on outside of thick loop.
3 Draw tight and ease into shape.

If not tightened these knots tend to work loose. Do not use with smooth lines, e.g. nylon fishing line.

CAMP CRAFT

CAMP CRAFT

FISHERMAN'S KNOT: Ideal for joining springy vines, wires, slippery lines and gut fishing line (soak gut first to make it pliable). Very secure but hard to untie. Not recommended for bulky ropes or nylon line.

1 Lay lines beside each other, the ends in opposite directions. Carry live end of one line round the other and make a simple overhand knot. **2** Repeat with live end of other line.

3 Partially tighten knots and slide towards each other. Ease them to rest against one another, completing tightening process.

DOUBLE FISHERMAN'S: Stronger version of the above. Do not use for nylon fishing lines, nylon ropes, or bulky ropes.

1 Carry live end of one line round the other, then round both.

2 Carry live end back through the two loops. **3** Repeat with the end of the other line. **4** Slide the 2 knots together and tighten, easing them to rest well against each other. Apply strain gradually.

TAPE KNOT: Use to join flat materials, e.g. leather, webbing, tape and sheets or other fabrics. **1** Make an overhand knot in the end of one tape. Do not pull it tight. **2** Feed the other tape through it so it follows exactly the shape of the first knot. **3** Live ends should be well clear of the knot so that they will not slip back when you tighten it.

LOOP-MAKING

BOWLINE: A fixed loop that will neither tighten nor slip under strain. Use at the end of a lifeline. **1** Make a small loop a little way along the rope. **2** Bring live end up through it, round standing part and back down through loop. **3** Pull on live end to tighten, easing knot into shape. Finish with a half-hitch.

RUNNING BOWLINE: A loop which tightens easily. Make a small bowline and pass long end of rope through loop.
Never tie a running bowline round the waist, it acts like a hangman's noose and could kill.

CAMP CRAFT

Triple bowline: A bowline made with a double line. Form a loop, pass doubled live end through loop, behind standing part and back through loop. This produces 3 loops which can be used for equipment haulage, or as a sit-sling or lifting harness with one loop round each thigh and the other round the chest. It takes practice – learn it before you need to use it.

Bowline-on-the-bight: To support or lift someone from a crevasse. The loops will neither tighten nor jam, forming a bosun's chair, one loop fitting round buttocks, the other round upper body. Practise before you need to use it.

1 Using doubled line, form a loop and pass the live end through it. Bring this end down (a) and over the end (b) of the larger double loop now formed. Ease it back up to behind the standing part (c). Pull on the large double loop to tighten (d).

MANHARNESS HITCH: A non-slip loop. It can be made along the length of the rope, but does not require access to an end. Several loops can be put on a rope for harnessing people together. Also a good way of preparing a rope for climbing. Toes and wrists can be put into the loops to carry weight, allowing you to take a rest.
1 Make a loop in rope.
2 Allow left side of rope to cross over loop. **3** Twist loop.
4 Pass it over left part of rope and through upper part of original loop. **5** Pull knot gently into shape, ease tight and test carefully.

Note: If not eased tight correctly loop may slip.

Different ways of making this knot may be found where the loop is not twisted at **3**. The final strength of the loop does not appear to be affected either by making this twist or not, nor if the twist should straighten out in use.

CAMP CRAFT

CAMP CRAFT

LADDERS

Tie as many manharness hitches in a rope as you need hand and foot holds. Rungs may be added, using strong sticks or pieces of wreckage.

Use 2 ropes or a long rope, doubled, with manharness hitches placed equally along both sides to make a rope ladder. As you make loops, pass sticks through the corresponding loops and ease tight to hold sticks firmly. Allow sticks to project a few inches on either side of the ropes and test for strength.

LADDER OF KNOTS: A series of overhand knots tied at intervals along a smooth rope will make climbing it much easier.
1 Leaving a reasonably long free end, make a half-hitch near the end of a short piece of log. **2** Continue making loose half-hitches along the log – the diameter of which will fix the spacing of the knots. **3** Pass start end back through all the loops and then slide them all off the end of the log. **4** As each turn of rope comes through, the centre of the half-hitch loops to the other end. Shape and tighten each knot.

CAMP CRAFT

HONDA KNOT: A free-running noose with a circular loop which is ideal for lassoing. If you have only one rope, don't use it as a lasso – this causes wear and damage to rope.

a Start with an overhand knot.
b Form a loop further down the rope.
c Double rope into a bight between loop and knot.
d Pass bight through loop.
e Tighten loop round bight.
f Pass long end of rope through new eye formed by bight.

Before lassoing an animal, consider its strength. A big animal may wrench the rope away, depriving you of a meal and a rope. If the rope is anchored to you, you may be dragged along and injured. Instead, use a firm anchor – a tree or rock – to take the strain.

CAMP CRAFT

HITCHES
Use to attach ropes to posts, bars and poles.

ROUND TURN AND TWO HALF-HITCHES: The best way to secure a rope to a post. Can take strain from any direction. Carry rope behind post, then round again. Bring live end over and back under standing end and through loop thus formed. Tighten and repeat half-hitch to make knot secure.

CLOVE HITCH: Effective when strain is perpendicular to the horizontal. Not so good when the strain comes at an angle or is erratic.
1 Pass live end over and round bar. **2** Bring it across itself and round the bar again. **3** Carry the live end up and under itself, moving in the opposite direction to standing end.
4 Close up and pull tight.

CAMP CRAFT

TIMBER HITCH: Use as a start knot for lashings and for hoisting and dragging or towing heavy logs.
1 Bring live end round bar and loosely round standing end.
2 Carry forward and tuck beneath rope encircling bar. Twist round as many times as will comfortably fit. Tighten knot by gently pulling on standing end until a firm grip is achieved.

KILLICK HITCH: To secure a line to an anchoring weight, make a timber hitch round one end of weight and tighten. Carry line along weight and make a half-hitch.

MARLIN SPIKE HITCH: A temporary knot for securing a mooring line to a post, or for dragging over the top of an upright peg. By attaching a short, stout stick to the line it is possible to gain extra purchase for a firmer pull.
1 Form a loop in the rope – study drawing carefully. 2 Bring one side of loop back up over standing end. 3 Drop this over the pole – the pole coming between the extended loop and standing part. Pull live end to tighten.

CAMP CRAFT

QUICK-RELEASE KNOT: A secure knot, but will come untied with a single sharp tug on the live end. Recommended for temporarily anchoring lines. **1** Carry a bight round a post or rail. **2** Bring a bight from the standing end through the first bight. **3** Form live end into a further bight and push doubled end through loop of second bight. Pull on standing end to tighten knot. **4** To release pull sharply on live end.

SHORTENING ROPE

SHEEPSHANK:
Treble the line.
Form half-hitches

in outer lengths and slip over adjoining bends. Or, instead of half-hitches, when a loop is formed in the standing part, pull a bight through it and slip this over bend in rope. Tighten as you gradually increase tension.

CAMP CRAFT

Make a sheep-shank more secure by passing a stick through

the bend and behind the standing part (a). Or, if you have access to the rope's end, pass that through the bight (b). A stick would make this more secure.

> Never cut a rope unnecessarily: a joined rope has only half the strength of a continuous one. Use sheepshank to shorten it or to exclude a damaged section.

SECURING LOADS

WAKOS TRANSPORT KNOT: Use to secure a high load or to tie down a roof. For maximum purchase, pull down with all your weight then secure with 2 half-hitches. If it comes loose, undo the hitches, retighten and secure.
1 Make a loop in rope. Further down, towards end of rope, make a bight. **2** Pass bight through loop. **3** Make a twist in the new lower loop. Pass end of rope round securing point and up through this twist. **4** Pull end to tighten. **5** With the end make two half-hitches round lower ropes to secure. Undo these to adjust and retighten.

CAMP CRAFT

PRUSIK KNOT: A sliding loop. It will not slip under tension, but will slide along when tension is released. A pair of Prusiks provide hand and foot holds for climbing or for swinging along a horizontal line. Slide them along main rope as you proceed. Also good for tent guylines.

1 Pass a bight round main rope, pull ends through. Keep loose.
2 Take ends over again and back down through loop. Ease tight. Do not allow circuits to overlap.
3 This gives the appearance of four turns on the main rope (a). Mountaineers take ends round and back through loop to give the appearance of six turns on main rope (b). **4** A Prusik knot can be made using a fixed spliced loop: pass bight over main rope and back through itself, and repeat.
5 For use as a tensioning line attach along the guy rope etc., and secure ends (a) to an anchor.

> When used for climbing, or travelling along a rope, a spliced loop (4) is safest. If you have no spliced loop, join ends after knot is made. Test joins rigorously before use.

LASHINGS

Methods of lashing differ
according to the position of the
components. These techniques
are invaluable in making rafts,
shelters, etc.

SQUARE LASHING: For lashing
spars which cross at right angles.
1 Make a timber hitch carrying
line alternately above and below
both spars in a complete circuit
before securing it. Then carry
rope anti-clockwise over and
under both spars. **2** After three
or four circuits make a full turn
round a spar and circuit in the
opposite direction. **3** Complete
circuits with a half-hitch round
one spar and secure with a clove
hitch on a spar at right angles.

ROUND LASHING: Use to lash
spars alongside each other or to
extend length of a spar.
Begin with a clove
hitch round
both spars
(a), then bind rope
round them. Finish knot with a clove hitch at other end
(b). Force a wedge under lashings to make them really
tight. If spars are vertical bang the wedge in downwards.

CAMP CRAFT

DIAGONAL LASHING: Use when spars do not cross at right angles, or when spars need to be pulled towards one another for tying. **1** Begin with a timber hitch round both spars, placed diagonally. **2** Frap (lash) both spars with a few turns of rope over a timber hitch, then make a full turn under the bottom spar. **3** Frap across other diagonal, then bring rope back over one spar and make two or three circuits above upper spar and below lower. **4** Finish with a clove hitch on a convenient spar.

SHEAR LASHING: To tie ends of two spars at an angle, e.g. for an A-frame. Begin with a clove hitch (a) round one spar. Bind, not very tightly, round both. Bring rope between spars and frap a few times round binding. Finish with a clove hitch round other spar (b). Tighten by opening up shears (c). A similar method can be used round three poles to make a tripod. Make turns round all

three legs and frappings in the two gaps. The feet of A-frames and tripods should be anchored to stop them spreading.

FISHING KNOTS

HOOK ON TO GUT: Turl knot. Soak gut. Thread through eye of hook. Make overhand loop and pass a bight through it (a) to form a simple slip knot (b). Pass hook through slip knot (c) and pull tight round shank.

HOOK ON TO NYLON I: Half-blood knot. Thread end through eye. Make 4 turns round standing part. Pass live end through loop formed next to hook (i). Pull taut and snip off fairly close to end (ii).

HOOK ON TO NYLON II: Two-turn turl knot. Thread hook. Pass live end round standing part to form a loop and through it. Twist live end twice round side of loop. Hold loop and pull twists tight. Pass hook through loop (1). Pull on standing part to tighten loop on hook (2).

JAM KNOTS: To secure improvised hooks to gut or cord. With an eye: thread gut. Make two turns round hook and bring live end up through turns (a). Ease tight and test for strength. Without an eye: make loop round lower part of shaft. Make two half-hitches from upper end downwards and pass live end through lower loop (b). Pull on standing part to tighten.

CAMP CRAFT

CAMP CRAFT

LOOP IN NYLON I: Double overhand loop. Double line to make a bight. Tie an overhand in it (a). Twist end through again (b). Pull tight (c) and snip off end.

LOOP IN NYLON II: Blood bight. Form a bight. Twist the end of it back round the standing part (i). Bring end back through new loop (ii). Pull tight and snip off loose end.

JOINING LOOPS: With free ends: pass each line through the other loop (1) and pull tight (2). With only one end free: make loop on one line. Take live end of other line through loop, round it and back through and then tie off with either of the knots for hooks on to nylon.

JOINING NYLON: Double three-fold blood-knots. Place ends alongside and twist one three times round the other. Bring live end back and pass it through the space where the two lines cross over the other line and under its own standing end (a). Repeat in the opposite direction with the other line. Live ends then point in opposite directions (b). Ease tight.

READING THE SIGNS

In addition to being able to read and make a map, your survival depends on interpreting natural signs to help you find your way and to anticipate the weather.

MAPS

Choose maps carefully. Make sure scale is appropriate to your needs and that you can interpret the information.

INTERPRETING MAPS

ALTITUDE: Since height cannot be reproduced on paper, altitude is recorded as contour lines, representing a series of points at the same distance above sea level. However, they do not record what happens in between.

Closely grouped contours indicate a steep slope (a). Greater spaces indicate gentler inclines (b). The rise in the ground is not comparable to the scale of the distance between them (contours at 5mm, on a 1:50,000 map, indicate a gradient of 1 in 25).

SCALE: The scale of a typical walker's map is 1:50,000 – each measure representing a distance 50,000 times

READING THE SIGNS

greater. Not all features can be shown to scale: roads, paths, streams and rivers are usually given standardised widths. Master which symbols stand for which features.

COORDINATES: Map grids are based either on degrees of latitude and longitude or on ground measurements. On British Ordnance Survey maps, grids indicate areas 1km apart with a diagonal of 1.5km. Position is described by coordinate line references from two adjoining sides. Thus you can fix your location for rescuers or a meeting point.

The point marked with a dot can be described as 15.5 x 62.8 using the coordinates from the sides of this grid. The map reference is usually expressed as 6 digits: 155628. Any letter area codes on the map should be included.

?   SURVIVAL SCENARIO
When navigating across unfamiliar terrain, what's the most important thing to watch out for?
One of the most common errors is to overestimate how much ground one has covered. One way around this is to fit the ground where you are to the map rather than the map to where you think you are.

NORTH ON MAPS: Unless they are lines of longitude, grids do not indicate north and south. A compass points not to true north but magnetic north. If a map doesn't indicate the latter, you can find it by the Pole Star (see p. 235).

In the northern hemisphere point the compass at the Pole Star. Note the difference between the pointer and indicated north. Line the compass up with the grid lines on the map to discover their variation. If you propose to walk on magnetic bearings you must compensate for the variation. If unable to make appropriate corrections, continually check your position against visible features.

MEASURING DISTANCES: As-the-crow-flies distances can be measured using a straight edge, which is then matched against the scale. Gradients make a difference. For example, a gradient of 45 ° will add another 82m (270ft) to a horizontal map distance of 200m (500ft to 725ft).

YOUR OWN MAPS: If you do not have a map, make one. Find the best vantage point and study the terrain. Note the number and direction of ridges – you won't be able to see what lies between them, so leave gaps to be filled in as you gain information from other vantage points.

> Mark anything of interest on your map: watercourses, rocky outcrops, landmarks, areas of vegetation. Plot positions of your traps, animal lairs, and places for foraging for food, fuel and stones for implements. It will be much easier than relying on your memory.

DIRECTION FINDING

The sun rises in the east and sets in the west, roughly speaking. In the northern hemisphere, at noon, the sun will be due south; in the southern hemisphere it will be due north. The hemisphere is indicated by the way shadows move: clockwise in the north, anti-clockwise in the south.

READING THE SIGNS

SHADOW STICK METHOD 1:
Place a 1m (3ft) stick upright on a patch of flat ground. Mark where tip of shadow falls (a). Wait 15 minutes and mark new shadow tip (b). Join the two for the directions of east and west – first mark is west. North–south are at right angles to line.

SHADOW STICK METHOD 2:
Mark first shadow tip in morning. Draw an arc at exactly this distance from the tip, using stick as centre point. Shadow shrinks at midday. In the afternoon, as shadow lengthens, mark the exact spot where it touches arc. Join to give east and west – west is the morning mark.

DIRECTION BY WATCH: A traditional analogue watch with two hands can tell direction, provided it is set to true local time (ignoring daylight saving and conventional time zones). The nearer the Equator you are, the less accurate this method is.

In northern hemisphere, hold watch horizontal. Point hour hand at sun. Bisect angle between hour hand and 12 mark to give north–south line.

In southern hemisphere, hold watch horizontal. Point 12 towards sun. Mid-point between 12 and hour hand will give a north–south line.

IMPROVED COMPASSES:

A piece of ferrous metal wire (a sewing needle is ideal) stroked repeatedly in one direction against silk will become magnetised and can be suspended so it points north.

Stroking with a magnet will be better than using silk – stroke the metal smoothly from one end to the other in one direction only.

Suspend the needle in a loop of thread so balance is not affected. Kinks or twists in thread must be avoided.

A floating needle can be used in the same way as the suspended one on p. 231. Lay the needle on a piece of paper, bark or grass and float it on the surface of water.

A power source of 2 volts or more, e.g. a battery, can be used with a short length of insulated wire to magnetise metal. Coil wire round needle. If the wire is uninsulated, wrap needle with paper or cardboard. Attach ends of wire to battery terminals for 5 minutes.

A razor blade can also be used as a compass needle. Magnetise the blade by stropping with care against palm of hand, then suspend.

Use other methods to establish the general direction of north, then mark the relevant end of your new 'compass' to indicate north. Top up your needle's magnetism from time to time, and always check readings against the sun.

PLANT POINTERS

Plants can give an indication of north and south. They tend to grow towards the sun, so flowers and most abundant growth will be to the south in the northern hemisphere, to the north in the southern. Moss on tree trunks will be greener and more profuse on that side.

If trees have been felled, the pattern of the rings is more widely spaced on the side towards the Equator.

A South African plant, the north pole plant, leans towards the north.

The compass plant is North American and directs its leaves in a north—south alignment so that profile from east or west is quite different from that of north or south.

WIND DIRECTION: If the direction of the prevailing wind is known it can be used to maintain direction.

Where a strong wind always comes from the same direction, plants and trees may be bent that way. Birds and insects will usually build nests on the lee side.

DIRECTION BY THE HEAVENS

Using the moon

As the moon orbits the earth over 28 days, the shape varies according to its position. When it is on the same side of the earth as the sun, no light is reflected from the sun (a): this is the new moon. Then it reflects light on its apparent right-hand side in a gradually increasing area as it waxes. At the full moon it is on the opposite side of the earth from the sun (b) and then it wanes, the reflecting area reducing to a narrow sliver on the apparent left-hand side.

If the moon rises before the sun has set, the illuminated side will be on the west. If it rises after midnight the illuminated side will be the east. Thus the moon gives a rough east–west reference in the night.

Using the stars

The stars stay in the same relation to one another. Their passage over the horizon starts 4 minutes earlier each night – a 2-hour difference over a month.

In the northern hemisphere groups of stars remain visible throughout the night, wheeling round the only star that does not seem to move: the Pole Star (a useful navigation aid, located almost above polar north).

THE NORTHERN SKY: The Plough or Big Dipper (a), Cassiopeia (b) and Orion (c) all circle the Pole Star, but (a) and (b) are recognisable groups that do not set. Use them to find the Pole Star.

Of the seven stars which form the **Plough** *(a), the two lowest ones point to the Pole Star, about four times further away than the distance between them.*

Cassiopeia *(b) is W-shaped, on the opposite side of the Pole Star and the same distance away as the Plough. On clear, dark nights this overlays the Milky Way. The centre star points towards the Plough. A line can be drawn connecting Cassiopeia and the Plough through the Pole Star.*

Orion *(c) rises above the Equator and can be seen in both hemispheres. It rises on its side, due east and sets due west. It is further from the Pole Star than Cassiopeia and the Plough.*

Other stars that rise and set can be used to indicate direction. Set 2 stakes in the ground, one shorter than the other. Sight along them at any star except the Pole Star. From the star's apparent movement you can deduce the direction in which you are facing:

*(vertical text, right margin)* READING THE SIGNS

READING THE SIGNS

Apparently rising = facing east
Apparently falling = facing west
Looping flatly to right = facing south
Looping flatly to left = facing north

These are only approximate directions. They will be reversed in the southern hemisphere.

THE SOUTHERN SKY: There is no equivalent of the Pole Star near the South Celestial Pole, but the Southern Cross, a constellation of five stars, provides a signpost to south. It can be distinguished from two other cross-shaped groups by its smaller size and its two pointer stars. Look along the Milky Way for a dark patch (the Coal Sack); the Southern Cross is on one side of it.

To locate south, project an imaginary line along the cross, four and a half times longer, then drop vertically down to the horizon. Fix, if you can, a prominent landmark on the horizon, or drive two sticks into the ground, to help you find the position again by day.

WEATHER SIGNS

Weather is much more localised than climate and there can be marked variations between one small area and the next.

COASTAL AREAS

A regular pattern of day–night change in wind direction suggests a large body of water – whether an ocean, inland sea or a lake – in the direction from which the day wind blows (during the day breezes blow from the sea to the land; at night the wind changes and blows off the land).

WINDS

Certain scents – the smell of the sea or of vegetation – carried on the wind can provide information about the place from which they blow.

Study wind and weather patterns: wind from a certain direction is likely to bring similar weather each time it blows. Where winds maintain direction, they can be an aid in keeping to a course – but verify your course by other means at regular intervals.

If a wind is strong and dry the weather should remain constant until the wind drops or veers, then it may rain.

If it is foggy and misty you may get condensation but you will not get rain. However, if a wind rises and blows away the fog, it may turn to rain.

On a fine day a noticeable increase in the strength of the wind indicates an imminent weather change (see pp. 370–73).

READING THE SIGNS

CLOUDS

Clouds are the most reliable of weather signs. There are ten main types of cloud formation. Approximate altitudes are given for each type. The same shapes occur at lower altitudes in polar regions. The higher the clouds, the finer the weather. The figures given at the end of the following entries indicate cloud heights.

 CIRROCUMULUS CLOUDS: *Look like rippled sand. An omen of fair weather, they usually follow a storm and dissipate to leave a clear blue sky.*

 ALTOCUMULUS CLOUDS: *Fair-weather clouds, on a larger scale than cirrocumulus, thicker, not so white and with shadows in them. Usually appear after a storm.*

 CUMULONIMBUS CLOUDS: *Low thunder clouds. Dark and menacing, with the top flattening out in an anvil shape. Brings hail, a strong wind, thunder and lightning. False cirrus appear above them, false nimbostratus below.*

CUMULUS CLOUDS: *Easily recognisable: fluffy white clouds. Usually indicate fair weather when widely separated, but if large and many-headed, they are capable of producing sudden heavy showers.*
    When seen at sea in an otherwise cloudless sky, they are often an indication that land lies beneath them.

CIRRUS CLOUDS: *High, wispy clouds formed from ice crystals which give them a white appearance. Seen in fine weather. 5–9km (3.1–5.5 miles).*

CIRROSTRATUS CLOUDS: *Made up of ice particles and look like white veins. These produce a halo round the sun or moon.*

If a cirrus-filled sky darkens and the clouds change to cirrostratus it is an indication that rain or snow is on the way. 5–9km (3.1–5.5 miles).

ALTOSTRATUS CLOUDS: *Form a greyish veil over the sun or moon. If wet weather is approaching the cloud will darken and thicken, obscuring the sun or moon until it begins to rain. 2.5–6km (1.6–3.7 miles).*

NIMBOSTRATUS CLOUDS: *Form low, dark blankets, which signal rain or snow within 4–5 hours, usually lasting several hours. 1.5–5km (0.9–3.1 miles).*

STRATOCUMULUS CLOUDS: *Form a low, lumpy, rolling mass, usually covering the whole sky, though often thin enough for the sun to filter through. Light showers may precipitate from them, but these clouds usually dissipate in the afternoon, leaving a clear night sky. Below 2.5km (1.6 miles).*

STRATUS CLOUDS: *The lowest of clouds, they form a uniform layer like fog in the air and are often described as hill fog. Although not a normal rain cloud, they can produce drizzle. When they form thickly overnight and cover the morning sky they will usually be followed by a fine day. Below 2.5km (1.6 miles).*

SURVIVAL CASE STUDY

This is a case study that I use when I do talks about survival situations. It has nothing to do with any personal experience that I have had, although it is a true story.

In this documented account from the 1950s, a family of three — a father, mother and child — set off by small plane from the east coast of the United States to get to California. After various stops for fuel and rest the family arrived safely at their destination, although the father, who was the pilot, reported a minor fault when the plane landed for the final time. When the family was ready to head back east they went up for a test flight to make sure that the repairs he had requested were successful.

However, what they failed to do was to register a flight plan, and this proved to be a fatal error. You should always tell someone where you are going and how long you expect to be, otherwise no one will realise you are missing or think to look for you. I suspect that that there were a number of failures on this occasion and the airport should have insisted on some sort of flight plan. Nonetheless, when the plane crashed in the Trinity Mountains in northern California, nobody knew that the family was missing. Despite their initial error in failing to alert the authorities about their route, this family was trained in survival techniques and, having survived the impact, remained alive for the next ten days. They then made the decision to leave the wreckage in search of civilisation. And this is where they finally fell down; they didn't know how to navigate effectively and they left the security of the wreckage. Stay where you are for as long as possible, but if you really feel that you must leave the area (and I don't recommend this) try to leave behind a message indicating your future movements. In this case the family had left a diary that was found by rescuers, revealing their whereabouts.

Survival skills are very important but you also need to know the best possible way to get to safety. The family was eventually discovered only a number of days after they had died, about 50km (30 miles) from the nearest road.

LESSONS LEARNT:
• **Always tell someone where you are going**
• **Inform them how long you expect to be**
• **Stay where you are for as long as possible**
• **If you have to move, leave indication of the direction in which you might be moving**

READING THE SIGNS

WEATHER PREDICTION

• To be caught in bad weather could prove fatal. Before setting out, take note of the weather conditions. Observe wind and pressure changes. Keep a record of the weather, the conditions which precede it, and what they develop into.

• Animals are sensitive to atmospheric pressure and are good for short-term weather predictions. Insect-eating birds feed higher in good weather, lower when a storm is approaching. Unusual rodent activity during the day may be a prelude to bad weather.

• Humans can sometimes sense a change in the weather, too. Curly-haired people find their hair becomes tight and unmanageable as bad weather approaches. Those with rheumatism, corns or similar ailments suffer discomfort in wet weather.

• If camp fire smoke rises steadily, the weather is likely to remain fine. If it starts swirling, or is beaten down after rising a short way, a storm or shower is coming.

• Sounds carry further when wet weather is on the way and the smell of vegetation becomes more distinctive before the arrival of rain.

• A red sky at night means that there is little moisture in the atmosphere and rain is unlikely within the next two hours. A red sky in the morning indicates a storm is approaching. A grey morning heralds a dry day, and a grey evening sky means that rain is imminent.

• A *corona*, a coloured circle visible around the sun or moon, will enlarge if fair weather lies ahead and shrink if rain is likely. A rainbow in the late afternoon is another sign of good weather.

ON THE MOVE

This section deals with skills needed on the move. It should be read in conjunction with the techniques described in *Climate and Terrain* (p. 37 ff).

THE DECISION TO MOVE

In the short term, unless local dangers or a lack of food and water make it imperative to leave the site of your accident, stay close in the hope of rescue. If you have injured persons and limited resources, send a party to contact help while others stay to care for the sick.

In the long term, if no rescue comes, resources may become exhausted and there is an increased risk of disease from staying too long in one place. Such factors will make a move advisable.

Where to go next will be determined by the information you have been able to gather, by the fitness and endurance of the group and the nature of the terrain. Remember: the most direct route may not be the easiest to travel.

If you have a clear idea of your location, make for the nearest settlement. If you have no idea where you are, follow waterways downstream – they generally lead to populated areas. Move at least three days' journey from the old camp so that fuel, flora and fauna will be undisturbed in the new location.

Before you abandon camp, leave signs to show you have moved on (see p. 283), and where you are heading. Rescuers can then follow you.

ON THE MOVE

• Stock up preserved food, and make water containers.

• Make foot-coverings and clothing, and packs to carry equipment and supplies. Build a sledge or raft or other form of transport.

• Take signalling gear and shelter materials with you. If shelter can be quickly erected on arrival you will then be free to gather food and fuel.

• Study weather patterns. Set off in settled weather.

HUDSON BAY PACK: A comfortable and simple way to carry equipment, this needs strong, waterproof material c. 90cm

(36in) square, two small stones and cord or thong long enough to loop across the body.

Place stones in diagonally opposite corners of the cloth. Fold ends of cloth over stones. Tie cord below stones to secure them in position — they will prevent cord slipping off. Lay cloth on ground and roll possessions up tightly. Wrap pack round body, either across the back or round the waist.

Carry babies papoose-style on your back or front. Tie lower corners of a rectangle of cloth round the waist, pop in baby and tie upper corners round your neck.

Sit small children on a back-pack frame. For adults and heavy equipment make a travois (see p. 204) or sledge.

MAKING A SLEDGE

Ideal for snow and ice, sledges may also be used on smooth ground. Use doors and cowlings from a crashed vehicle or plane in construction. Tie lines to front runners with a bowline to the people hauling – ideally two at the front and two at the rear. Test before use.

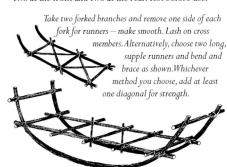

Take two forked branches and remove one side of each fork for runners – make smooth. Lash on cross members. Alternatively, choose two long, supple runners and bend and brace as shown. Whichever method you choose, add at least one diagonal for strength.

PLANNING THE ROUTE

Visibility will often be restricted and you must guess what lies ahead. Things you can see may be misleading: what looks like an easy slope may prove to be a barrier when you get close. If you have them, use binoculars.

Climbing a tree may help you see further, but keep close to the trunk and test each branch before risking your weight on it. This is no time to risk a fall.

FOLLOWING RIVERS

Watercourses offer a route to civilisation and a life-support system on the way. Apart from rare occasions when they suddenly disappear underground, rivers offer a clearly defined route. Where they cut through gorges it may be impossible to follow their banks – take to high ground and cut off the bends.

In tropical conditions, vegetation may be densest by the river and the banks hard to negotiate. If the river is wide enough, build a raft of bamboo or fallen trees.

When a river meanders widely on a plain the inside of loops may be swampy and prone to flooding. Avoid these marshy areas if you can – cut across the loop.

MAINTAINING DIRECTION

• Choose a distant landmark and head towards it.

• Try to skirt dense vegetation: orientation is difficult in forests. A compass becomes a valuable asset.

• In featureless territory, if in a group of three or more, to maintain a straight line separate and follow at intervals in each other's tracks. Look back frequently: those behind should be directly behind each other in a straight line. Move in relay: the one who went ahead can rest while everyone else moves up from the rear.

• If travelling alone, align yourself by looking back at your own tracks, if visible, or set up markers (sticks, piles of stones) at intervals in alignment with each other so you can check that you are not deviating from your route.

• Once on high ground, stick to it until certain that you have found the spur down which will allow you to make the best progress in the desired direction.

MOVING IN GROUPS

Always move in formation. This will make it easy to check that no stragglers have been left behind. Have a briefing before setting out to discuss the route and to designate rallying points at which to regroup.

DIVIDING RESPONSIBILITIES

Appoint a scout to select the best route and find ways to skirt obstacles. A number two should make sure the scout maintains correct overall direction. Both will need to be relieved frequently as it is tiring work.

The others should travel in pairs to ensure that no one drops by the wayside. A head count is vital after negotiating difficult terrain (check equipment regularly too). Nominate prominent landmarks as rallying points so that everyone knows what to head for if separated.

PACE AND PROGRESS

• A large group can send an advance party to clear the route and set up camp. A clear trail will make carrying baggage and injured people much easier.

• The scout must not go too fast. Frequent rests – a 10-minute break every 30–45 minutes – are vital. After an obstacle wait and allow everyone to catch up and check and adjust loads.

• Try to maintain an even pace. A smooth, pendulum-like movement is easiest. Keep arms free to aid balance. On steep ground the pace should be shortened, on easy ground lengthened. Avoid overstepping on descents. Use ropes to provide handholds on slippery terrain. Attach Prusik knots (see p. 222) for extra safety.

ON THE MOVE

WALKING AT NIGHT

Negotiating territory at night can be dangerous, but may be necessary. Because it is difficult to see clearly you are easily disorientated. It is always darker among trees, so keep to open country if you can. When looking at an object at night, look at one side rather than directly at it. It is hard to distinguish anything in a dark mass, but edges show clearly.

> It takes 30–40 minutes for the eyes to get accustomed to darkness. Once this is achieved, protect eyes from bright light or night vision will be impaired. If a light must be used, cover one eye so that vision in that eye will be retained. A red filter over a torch will also help.

Ears are good sensors. The sound of a river indicates how fast it flows. Smells can aid identification.

Walk slowly. Test each step before putting your weight forward. Use a shuffling step to descend slopes.

UPLAND TRAVEL

In mountainous country keep to high ground – it makes navigation easier. Rivers in steep-sided gullies are difficult to negotiate on foot: climb up and follow the ridges. Drop down to collect water and to seek shelter, but don't go right to the valley bottom if you can find what you need on the way. Pockets of cold air get trapped in valley bottoms: you may be warmer and less tired if you choose a sheltered spot higher up. If you carry water and shelter materials, stay on the high ground and make camp in a sheltered spot. When the river gets larger and the valley opens out, drop down to follow the river banks once more.

STEEP SLOPES

Traverse slopes in a zigzag. As you change direction always set off with the uphill foot to avoid crossing your legs over and losing balance. When climbing steep slopes, lock your knees together after each step to rest the muscles.

To descend slopes, keep your knees bent and try to go straight down (sit back and dig in the heels if you find you are picking up too much speed). Avoid loose rock and scree. When climbing, test every foothold before putting your weight on it. Avoid stepping on stones or logs that may dislodge.

Jump down loose ground provided there are no sudden drops. Keep feet square and shoulder-width apart, dig in heels and slide. You will lose control as speed increases – jump again. Abseil down steep slopes (see p. 47).

JUNGLE TRAVEL

You may have to cut through dense jungle if there is no way round. Chop downwards and as low as possible at the stems on both sides so they fall away from the path, not across it. Avoid leaving bamboo spikes – they can be lethal if stumbled on. Atap and rattan have thorns like fish hooks at the end of the leaf. When snared, back off and untangle. Rushing only makes it worse.

> Keep feet covered to protect them from sapling spikes, snakes and chigoes (chiggers), burrowing parasites. Stop frequently to remove parasites. Chigoes ignored for more than an hour will cause infection.

ON THE MOVE

WATERWAYS

A wide river will be easier to float on than to walk beside. Long-term survivors should experiment with making canoes by burning out the centre of a tree trunk or covering a frame of willow with birch bark or skins.

RAFTS

A raft, even if the structure is not perfect, will not readily capsize.

Use bamboo, uprooted trees which are sound and unrotted, or the tops of the trunks of dead falls. Oil drums or floating objects will support a raft. If there is no supply of timber a sheet of waterproof material can be used as a man-carrying coracle.

> Never take chances. Only a really tough structure will survive rapids, and on wide reaches you face a long swim to the bank if your raft breaks up. Test all rafts in safe water near camp before setting off on a journey.

Tie all equipment securely to the raft or safety line. Make sure that nothing trails over the edges – it could snag in shallows.

Everyone aboard should have a bowline round the waist securing them to a safety line or to the raft. Lifelines should be long enough to allow free movement, but no so long as to trail in the water. In swift-flowing rivers with rapids and falls it is better not to tie on. Head for the bank if the raft is out of control.

In shallow water, control the raft with two long poles like a punt – one person poling at the front corner, another at the diagonally opposite back corner.

Bamboo raft: Cut thickish bamboo in 3m (10ft) lengths. Make holes through canes near ends and half way along. Pass stakes through holes to connect canes. Lash each cane to the stakes with twine or vines. Make a second layer to fit on top of the first and lash them together.

Gripper bar raft: Place two thickish, pliable stakes on the ground – they should be long enough to overlap the width of the deck. Lay logs over them. Place two stakes on top. Tie each pair of stakes on one side. Then, with a helper standing on top to force the other ends together, tie these so the logs are gripped between. Notching the ends of the gripper bars will stop ropes slipping.

Steering: Make a paddle rudder and mount it on an A-frame near one end of raft. Secure A-frame with guylines to the corners of the raft. Tie the rudder on so it does not slip. You may need to notch the raft for the A-frame base.

ON THE MOVE

TRAVELLING BY RAFT

• A large group will need several rafts. The first should carry no equipment or provisions, just the fittest group members to act as lookouts and warn of hazards.

• Waterfalls and rapids are often indicated by spray or mist. They can also be heard for some distance. If in doubt, moor the raft and reconnoitre on foot.

• Unload the raft when you reach a dangerous stretch. Carry equipment overland downstream and post someone at the point where the river becomes safe to recover the raft. Then go back and release the raft to drift down. It may need repairs, but you will be safe.

• Never raft in the dark. At night secure the raft firmly and make shelter on high ground away from the river.

BOGS, MARSHES AND QUICKSAND
Avoid crossing a marsh if possible. If unavoidable, jump from tuft to tuft. Should you sink into a bog, swim with a breast-stroke to firm ground. Don't try to jump. Spreading your body distributes your weight.

CROSSING RIVERS

River headwaters are narrow and swift-flowing. Find a place where water is shallow enough to wade across – test for hidden depths with a pole. Look for stepping stones, but mind you don't slip and sprain an ankle.

Estuaries have strong currents and are subject to tides. Avoid crossing there unless equipped with a boat or raft. Head upstream to find a safer spot. Do not set off right opposite the point you hope to reach – make allowances for where the current will take you.

STUDY THE WATER:

Surface movement can indicate what lies beneath. The main flow of the current is evident from a chevron shape of smoother water round any projection (a), the V widening downstream.

Waves that seem to stay in one position (b) are evidence of a boulder on the bottom.

An obstruction close to the surface creates an eddy downstream where surface water appears to run back against the main flow. If a large boulder coincides with a steep drop (c) these eddies can produce a powerful backward pull downstream of the obstruction. They are very dangerous.

☠ ICE-COLD WATER CAN BE FATAL
Do not swim or wade through deep water at very low temperatures, it could prove fatal. Make a raft. Wade only if no more than your feet will get wet, and dry them vigorously as soon as you reach the other bank.

ON THE MOVE

Wading across

Never underestimate a stretch of water, however shallow. Use a stick to aid balance. Roll trousers up or take them off so you have them dry for the other side. Keep boots on – they give a better grip than bare feet. Undo the belt fastening of a backpack so you can slip it off if you get swept over, but don't let go of it: use it to help you right yourself.

Turn at a slight angle, sideways on to your destination. The current will then take you there. Do not stride: shuffle sideways, using the stick to test for depth and trying each foothold before using it.

A group wading across together should line up behind the strongest, each holding the one in front at the waist and moving in step. Alternatively, link arms side-by-side, holding on to a branch or pole to keep in alignment. Cross facing the bank and moving forwards. Only the side of the first person opposes the current and the group provides stability for everyone.

 Look out for submerged branches. You could get tangled and lose your balance. When forced against an obstruction by the current you will feel its full force and may be unable to move.

Crossing with ropes

You need a loop of rope three times as long as the width of the stream and at least three people in the party – the fittest person crosses while two control the rope to keep it out of the water as much as possible, and stand by to haul the crosser to safety if difficulties are encountered.

The person crossing (**1**) is secured round the chest to the loop. The other two (**2** & **3**) are not tied on. They pay out rope as it is needed. The strongest should cross first.

When he reaches the bank, **1** unties himself and **2** ties on and crosses, controlled by the others. Any number can be sent across this way.

When **2** has reached the bank, **3** ties on and crosses. **1** takes most of the strain; **2** stands by in case anything goes wrong.

ON THE MOVE

RIVERS ARE DANGEROUS

Never enter the water unless there is no other way of getting across. Choose a crossing point carefully.

Avoid high banks on to which it is difficult to climb out.

Avoid obstructions in the water.

Current is likely to be fastest on the outside of bends, and steep banks may be undercut, making landing impossible.

Look for an even section of river bed – shingle is the best surface for wading.

ON THE MOVE

Swimming across

If you can't swim, don't try – rely on others and use a float. Even strong swimmers should use flotation aids to save energy and keep kit dry. Don't swim fully clothed, you need something warm to put on at the other end.

Make sure your landing point has a beach or something to haul yourself out with. Avoid tangled branches in the water where you might get trapped. Enter well upstream and let the current carry you.

Check the strength of the current by watching floating logs and flotsam. Look for obstructions and eddies. If you hit weed in the water, adopt a crawl stroke to cut through it. Once a strong swimmer has cleared a passage, others may follow in that channel.

FLOTATION AIDS

• Use anything that floats: fuel cans, plastic bottles, logs.

• Put your clothes in a waterproof bag, leaving plenty of air space. Tie the neck, bend it over and tie again. Hold on to it, using just your legs to propel yourself.

• Pile twigs and straw into the centre of a waterproof sheet to create air pockets, then pile your clothes and equipment on top and tie securely. Do not attempt to sit on the bundles or place your weight on them.

• A group should split into fours, each lashing their bags together and using them as a support for an injured person or a non-swimmer.

• If no waterproof material is available, make a small raft or coracle to float your things on. Bundle your belongings and, if heavy, make the raft two-layered so only the lower layer sinks and your kit stays dry.

SURVIVAL AT SEA

Four-fifths of the earth's surface is open water – the most difficult environment in which to survive. Water and wind rapidly chill the body. Alone in cold water your chances are not good without equipment. If you know your location you may be able to predict where the currents will carry you. Warm currents, e.g. the Gulf Stream, are often rich in sea foods, as are coastal waters. Your main problem is likely to be a shortage of freshwater if you have no means of distilling sea water.

ABANDONING SHIP

When you are on board a ship, lifeboat drill should be a well-rehearsed procedure. Even in small boats everyone on board should be acquainted with safety equipment and procedures.

If the signal is given to abandon ship, put on warm, preferably woollen, clothing, including hat and gloves, and wrap a towel round your neck. Take a torch, chocolates and boiled sweets if you can. Don't panic. An orderly embarkation will be faster and will establish a calmer attitude. Take what equipment you can with you. A life-jacket or life-belt will make it easier to float.

Don't inflate your life-jacket until you leave ship. On small boats life-jackets should be worn all the time. If you have to jump overboard, first throw something that floats and jump close to it. Without a life-jacket or belt, air trapped in clothing will aid buoyancy – a good reason to keep your clothes on despite the frequent advice to strip off before entering the water.

SURVIVAL AT SEA

If you are swept overboard keep afloat and try to attract attention. Sound travels well over water – shout and splash. Wave with one arm above water (not both, you will go under). Movement makes you more noticeable. Most life-jackets are equipped with a whistle and light.

IN THE WATER

Swim slowly and steadily. If abandoning a sinking boat or aircraft get upwind and stay clear of it. Keep away from any fuel slick. If forced to swim through flames, jump in feet first and up wind. Swim into the wind using breast stroke. Splash flames away from your head to make breathing holes. Swim underwater until clear of danger. If an underwater explosion is likely, reduce the risk of injury by swimming on your back.

If within sight of land, relax and float until the ebb turns and helps carry you to land.

1 In rough seas, float upright and take a deep breath. 2 Lower face into water (keeping mouth closed) and bring arms forward to rest at water level. 3 Relax in this position until you need to take in more air. 4 Raise head above surface, tread water, and exhale. Take a breath and return to the relaxed position.

FLOTATION 'BAGS': Improvise a short-term float from a pair of trousers. Knot bottoms of legs, sweep them over the head to fill with air, then hold the waist below water to trap the air, making legs into water wings.

IMMEDIATE ACTION: Once clear of the wreck, inflate your dinghy. If there is no dinghy, grab as much flotsam as possible to use as a raft. Tie it together with belts, shoelaces, spare clothing. Salvage floating equipment.

Inflating a dinghy

Many dinghies are self-inflating. If not, a pump is provided. Dinghies are built in sections, so there are several inflation points.

BOARDING AN INFLATABLE DINGHY: If already in the water move to the end (not the side) of the dinghy, place one leg over the edge and roll into the vessel. Do not jump in from above, you may damage it. Large dinghies have a righting line attached to one side. Grab it from the opposite side, brace your feet against the dinghy and pull. The dinghy should rise up and over, pulling

you out of the water momentarily. In heavy seas, or high winds, this can be very difficult.

To haul someone else aboard, hold their shoulders and lift one leg over the end, then roll them in. Discourage them from putting their arms round your neck – they could pull you into the water. Then tie yourself and others to the dinghy.

Ensure the dinghy is fully inflated. It should be firm but not rock-hard. If not, inflate it with your own breath or a pump. The valves are one-way and air will not escape when you take off the protective cap.

Check for leaks. Escaping air causes bubbles under water and a hissing sound above water. Seal holes with screw-in conical plugs in the dinghy kit. There should also be a supply of rubber patches and adhesive.

Make daily checks for inflation and leaks. To repair a leak on the underside, swim under and insert a plug.

SURVIVAL AFLOAT

• Rafts, boats and dinghies are built to carry a limited number. These numbers should not be exceeded.

• Place infants and the infirm aboard, and as many able-bodied as can be accommodated. The rest must hang on in the water, frequently swapping places with fit survivors in the raft.

• Stow gear in stowage places and tie securely. Check that no sharp objects will damage the inflatable. Put items that will spoil if wet in a waterproof container.

• Check signalling equipment: heliographs, flares, etc.

• If distress signals have been sent giving your position, try to maintain location. A sea anchor streamed out from the boat will keep it into the weather and slow down drift. Improvise a sea anchor from any weighted object securely tied to a line. Use clothing tied to a paddle with reef knots.

• If you can see the shore head towards it.

> **SURVIVAL PRIORITIES**
> PROTECTION from weather and effects of exposure.
> LOCATION Try to establish where you are and the
> best way of attracting rescue.
> WATER Take stock. Ration at once. Collect rain.
> FOOD Don't eat, unless you have sufficient water.
> Check all rations, stow them securely. Start fishing.

PROTECTION

Keep a log: record names of survivors; date, time, and
position of accident; weather conditions; equipment
salvaged. Record sightings and circumstances daily.

IN A COLD CLIMATE: Get out of cold water as soon as
possible. Keep the dinghy as dry as you can. Bail out
water. If it doesn't have a built-in shelter, rig up a spray
shield and windbreak using any available material.

Dry all wet clothing. If there is no dry clothing,
squeeze out as much water as possible and put it back on.
Maintain body heat by wrapping up in any available
material, e.g. parachute or canvas. If in a group, huddle
together. To keep circulation going, do mild exercises but
do not disturb the balance of the raft.

IN A HOT CLIMATE: Keep covered in strong sun. Cover
head and neck to avoid sunstroke. Protect eyes from glare
(see p. 60). Damp down clothes to cool the body, but
make sure you are dry by evening, for nights can be very
cold and darkness comes quickly in the tropics.
Prolonged contact with sea water causes sores.

Air expands with heat, so if it is very hot let some air
out of an inflatable. Re-inflate in the evening cool.

SURVIVAL AT SEA

TRAVELLING

If an SOS has been sent, or you are in or near regular shipping lanes, stay in the same vicinity for 72 hours. If none of these circumstances hold, get underway at once to take advantage of initial energy. Assess the nearest shipping lane and head in that direction. Your craft will move with the wind and current – seldom more than 9–13km (6–8 miles) per day. Take in the sea anchor. Use a paddle as a rudder. If the wind is against your chosen direction stream, sea anchor to maintain position.

> **FACTORS TO CONSIDER WHEN DECIDING WHETHER TO STAY OR TRAVEL**
> Has an SOS been sent? Is your position known to rescuers? Do you know it? Is the weather favourable for a search? Are other vessels likely to pass you? How many days' supply of food and water have you?

TO USE THE WIND: Inflate dinghy fully and sit high. Improvise a sail if necessary. Do not secure its lower edges. Hold lower lines or bottom of sail, then release them in sudden gusts of wind so the raft is not capsized.

IN ROUGH WATER: Stream sea anchor out from the bow to keep it into the wind and prevent capsizing. Keep low. Do not sit on the sides, stand up, or make sudden movements. Tie several rafts or dinghies together.

> Assign lookouts, even in darkness, to watch for shipping, aircraft, signs of land, seaweed, fish, birds and flotsam. They should also inspect the raft for signs of leakage or chafing. Watches should be kept short to avoid exhaustion and lack of concentration.

SURVIVAL AT SEA

INDICATORS OF LAND NEARBY

• Cumulus clouds in an otherwise clear sky are likely to have formed over land. In tropical waters the reflection of sunlight from shallow water over coral reefs produces a green tint on the underside of clouds.

• Lone birds may have been blown off course by rough weather, but few seabirds sleep on the water or fly more than 100 miles from land. Their direction of flight is usually outwards from land before noon and inwards in the late afternoon. The continuous sound of bird cries is usually an indication that land is not far away.

• Drifting vegetation, e.g. coconuts, may be a sign of land (but they can be carried right across an ocean).

• A change in the sea's direction may be caused by the tide pattern around an island. A constant wind with a decreasing swell suggests land to windward.

• Water that is muddy with silt is likely to have come from the mouth of a large river.

SIGNALLING AT SEA

Use flares, dye markers and movement of any kind to attract attention at sea.

If you have no signalling equipment, wave clothing or tarpaulins and churn the water if it is still. At night or in fog use a whistle to maintain contact with other survivors.

If a radio transmitter is part of the equipment aboard a life-raft, instructions for its operation will be found on its side (see p. 271).

Sea markers which release dye are only of use in daytime. They are usually conspicuous for three hours.

SURVIVAL AT SEA

Pyrotechnic equipment must be kept secure and dry. Read instructions and beware of fire hazards. When firing flares do not point them downwards or towards yourself or anyone else. Use flares only when certain they will be seen. Fire when a plane is flying towards you, not when it has gone past (see pp. 281–282).

HEALTH

• Exposure and severe hydration are major problems.

• Constipation, difficulty in urinating or concentrated urine are not unusual. Do not attempt to treat them or you could force further liquid loss.

• If feeling sick, try not to vomit. Never induce vomiting.

• Continued exposure to saltwater can cause boils. Do not prick or squeeze. Do not damp yourself down too often with saltwater. Stop damping yourself with seawater if there is any soreness.

• Protect eyes from glare. If eyes are sore moisten a cloth with sea water and place over the eyes and rest them. Do not do this for long, it can make skin sore.

• Trenchfoot (see p. 328) can occur when awash with water. Exercise will help protect you from it and from frostbite and exposure. Keep well covered when resting and, when on watch, gently exercise the limbs.

WATER

Even if you have a good water supply, ration it at once. Do not relax the ration until final rescue or until you can replenish it, for you have no idea how long you will have to last out.

SURVIVAL AT SEA

> **WATER RATIONS**
> DAY 1: NO WATER. The body is a reservoir.
> DAYS 2–4: 400cc (14fl oz) if available.
> DAY 5 onwards: 55-225cc (2-8fl oz) daily, depending
> on the climate and water available.
> **When drinking, moisten lips, tongue and throat
> before swallowing. Sip slowly – gulping will
> make you vomit.**

REDUCING WATER NEEDS: Reduce sweating. Make use of breezes and sea water to cool the body. If it is very hot and the waters are safe, take a dip over the side – but first check your safety line. You should always be tied on. Beware of dangerous fish and be sure that you can get back aboard.

Take anti-sickness pills, if available, as soon as you feel queasy, for vomiting will lose valuable fluids.

If you are low on water do not eat (see p. 27).

GATHERING FRESHWATER: Collect rainwater night and day – rig up a catchment from canvas or plastic. At night rig canvas with edges folded to catch dew. Stow as much in containers as you can. Drink up puddles in the boat first. But be careful in heavy seas as the water will be contaminated with salt.

Sea ice can produce drinking water (see p. 32). In summer, pools on old sea ice may be drinkable (if they are not wave splashes). Taste carefully before drinking.

You can also get water from fish (see p. 35).

TREATMENT OF SEA WATER: Life-raft equipment may include solar stills and desalination kits (see p. 32). Set solar stills out immediately, but use desalination tablets only when the weather is unfavourable for the stills, and dew or rain catchment is ineffective.

DO NOT drink sea water
DO NOT drink urine
DO NOT drink alcohol
DO NOT smoke
DO NOT eat, unless water is available

Sleep and rest are the best way of enduring periods of reduced water and food – but make sure that you have adequate shade during the day. If the sea is rough, tie yourself to the raft, close any cover and ride out the storm as best you can. Try to relax.

FOOD

Conserve emergency food supplies until needed. Try to live off sea life. There are dangerous fish (see p. 350 ff) but in the open sea, fish are generally safe to eat. Near the shore there are dangerous and poisonous species.

FISHING

• Never wrap fishing line round bare hands or tie it to an inflatable dinghy. Salt gives it a sharp cutting edge.

• Wear gloves if available or use a cloth to handle fish to avoid injury from sharp fins and gill covers.

• Fish and turtles attracted to the shelter provided by a dinghy will swim under it. Pass a net under the keel from end to end (it takes two to hold the ends).

• Improvise hooks (see p. 147). If using a metal spoon or spinner keep it moving by paying out and reeling in. Let the 'bait' sink and then retrieve it.

Fish flesh spoils easily and must be eaten fresh unless the air is dry, when it can be dried in the sun for future meals. Clean and gut before drying.

BIRDS: Will be attracted to a raft as a potential perching place. Keep still until they settle and try to grab them.

Wrap a diamond-shaped tin gorge with fish and trail to attract birds. When seized by a bird the gorge should lodge across its gullet.

SEAWEED: Occurs on shorelines and in floating forms. Raw seaweeds are tough and salty and hard to digest. They absorb fluids – do not eat when water is scarce.

Seaweeds also provide food in the form of small fish, crabs and shrimps living on them. These decapods are not easy to see, being mottled brown, like seaweed.

Make a grapple hook by lashing pieces of wood or metal wreckage together to form a multiple hook. Attach it to a line and trail it, or throw it out to rake in weed. Use it for gathering drifting wreckage to consolidate a raft.

SURVIVAL AT SEA

DANGEROUS FISH

POISONOUS FISH: Many reef fish have toxic flesh (avoid the liver, intestines and eggs). No amount of cooking neutralises the poison. They are tasteless, so standard edibility tests are useless. Do not assume that because a bird can eat a fish it is non-toxic. Cats and birds are less susceptible to the toxins than human beings.

Symptoms of poisoning include numbness of the lips, tongue, extremities, severe itching and a reversal of temperature sensations: cold things seem hot and hot things cold. Nausea, vomiting, loss of speech, dizziness and paralysis may follow. They can be fatal.

AGGRESSIVE FISH: These include the Barracuda, which charges at lights or shiny objects at night, the huge Sea Bass and the Moray Eel. Sea snakes are venomous.

SHARKS

The survivor at sea is vulnerable to shark attack. Ocean sharks are not usually ferocious when food is plentiful. Most are cowards and can be scared off by the jab of a stick, especially on the nose. However, making a commotion may attract sharks.

Sharks feed off the ocean bottom, but hungry sharks will follow fish to the surface and into shallow water; their hunger at such times makes them dangerous.

Sharks feed at night, dusk and dawn, locating prey by smell and vibration. They seek easy prey (wounded fish and stragglers) and are attracted to blood, bodily wastes and rubbish (they will scavenge refuse thrown overboard). Weak movements draw attention. Strong, regular movements and loud noises repel them. Human appearance is strange to a shark and clothing produces a confusing shape. A group of clothed humans bunched together will be safer than a lone individual. If a shark keeps its distance, it is only curious. If it circles inwards and makes sudden movements, attack is likely.

SURVIVAL AT SEA

PROTECTION AGAINST SHARKS: IN THE WATER

• Avoid passing body wastes. If you must urinate do it in short spurts and allow it to dissipate between spurts. Collect faeces and throw far away. Try to hold vomit in the mouth and re-swallow it (or throw it far away). If you must swim use strong strokes; avoid schools of fish.

• Sharks cannot stop or turn quickly. A good swimmer can evade a single shark by rapid changes of direction.

• If in a group, bunch together and face outwards. Kick and punch out with a stiff arm using heel of hand. Slap the water with cupped hands. Put your head under and shout. If you have a knife, let the shark take it in the snout, or go for the gills and eyes.

PROTECTION AGAINST SHARKS: ON A BOAT

• Don't fish when sharks are around. Don't throw waste overboard. Let go of baited hooks. Do not trail arms or legs in the water. To deter a shark from attacking, jab its snout with a paddle or pole. Beware: a large shark could take a bite out of a boat.

• If you catch a small shark, haul it to the side of the craft, pull the head clear, and club hard before approaching and finishing it off with more blows. Don't try this with a large shark. It could injure you and your craft. Cut your line and sacrifice part of it – the shark's threshing will soon attract its fellows.

MAKING A LANDFALL

When approaching land, select a landing point where it will be easy to beach or swim ashore. Take down the sail; the sea anchor will keep you pointing at the shore and will slow down your progress. Steer away from rocks. Try not to land with the sun in your eyes.

A sloping beach with a small surf is ideal. Try to ride the back of a breaker. To avoid being swamped by an oncoming wave paddle hard, but do not overshoot a breaker which is carrying you along. In heavy surf point vessel seawards and paddle into an approaching wave.

Note the lie of the land: high ground, vegetation, watercourses. If with companions, choose a rendezvous point in case you are separated. Do not try to land at night – it is too dangerous. Wait until morning.

If you float into an estuary try to reach a bank. The turning tide could carry you back out to sea. Take in the sea anchor and make the boat as light as possible. Bail out an inflatable and inflate it to the maximum to make the most of the incoming tide. If being swept back out to sea by the ebb, ballast the dinghy by part-filling it with water and stream the sea anchor.

> Tie yourself to the raft. Even if it is overturned or damaged and you are rendered unconscious, you stand a chance of surviving, whereas alone in the water and dashed on the rocks you will be killed.

If swimming ashore in a heavy sea, keep on clothing, shoes and life-jacket. Raise legs, knees bent, and take the shock of impact of the rocks on the soles of your feet.

RESCUE

The first requirement for rescue is to let others know of your situation and your location. Once contact has been made you can pass on other information.

SIGNALLING

SOS (Save Our Souls) is an internationally recognised distress signal. Mayday (from *m'aidez:* French for *help me*) is the signal used in radio-telecommunications.

Almost any signal repeated three times will serve as a distress signal: three fires, or columns of smoke; three whistles, or shots, or flashes of light. If using noises or lights, wait one minute between each group of three.

TRANSMITTERS: Dinghies, life-rafts and jackets are often equipped with transmitters which indicate position over a short range. To avoid wasting precious batteries, hold in reserve until there is a chance of their signals being picked up. With long-range transmitters, send distress signals at regular intervals. Frequencies are usually preset at 121.5 and 243 megacycles and the range is about 32km (20 miles). Portable VHF transceivers can communicate only with stations in a direct line of sight and without any intervening obstruction (though a relay station may be established on a high point). Such sets are usually tuned to a mountain rescue frequency but procedures should be established before departure.

If you have a transmitter, check the batteries. Can an engine be used to generate electricity or recharge the batteries? Conserve fuel and plan your transmissions to a pattern rather than attempting long periods on air.

RESCUE

The International Mountain Distress Signal is six whistles a minute (or six waves, light flashes, etc.) followed by a minute's silence, then repeated.

Siting signals

Take account of the terrain. Choose high points for light signals. Erect an unusual silhouette on a ridge to attract attention.

Planes fly over hilly territory from the lower to the higher ridges. Thus slopes behind ridges may be hidden as the plane approaches. Signals near tops of ridges should be seen from any direction. Lay out marks on level ground or on slopes that are not likely to be overlooked.

VEHICLE OR AIRCRAFT WRECKAGE: A stranded vehicle or downed aircraft provides useful signalling aids. Fuel, oil and hydraulic fluid can be burned. Tyres and electrical insulation generate smoke. Glass and chrome make good reflectors. Life-jackets, dinghies, and parachutes are eye-catching. Arrange colourful, shiny objects in a visible spot to attract attention to your location.

Switch lights on at night. If batteries are low, keep them in reserve to flash headlamps and sound the horn.

FIRE AND SMOKE: Establish signal fires once immediate needs for treatment of injury and provision of shelter have been met. Gather fuel for camp and signal fires.

Place three fires in a triangle at equal distances apart. Failing that, a group of clearly separated fires will serve. If fuel is scarce, use only your campfire.

Signal fires should be kept dry, and maintained, ready to be lit to attract attention of passing aircraft. Use tinder to get them going rapidly (see p. 173 ff).

RESCUE

Petrol can be used as a fire-lighter but don't just pour it on. Lay a piece of petrol-soaked rag among the tinder. Don't light it at once. Carry the fuel can off to a safe distance. Wait a few seconds, then light the wick. If a fire does not light first time pull tinder apart and check for sparks or embers, before adding extra petrol.

• Keep a stock of green boughs, oil or rubber close by to create smoke if needed.

• Among vegetation or close to trees, build an earth wall round each fire to contain it.

• Do not build fires among trees where the canopy will block out the signal. Place them in a clearing.

If by a lake or river, build rafts to place your fires on and anchor or tether them securely in position. Arrow indicates direction of current.

TORCH TREES: Use small, isolated trees for fire signals. Build a fire between the boughs using dry twigs or old bird's nests. This will ignite the foliage, producing lots of smoke. Fires at the base of dead trees burn for a long time, but don't risk starting a forest fire. Apart from the damage this will cause, your life will be in jeopardy.

LUMINOUS CONE FIRES: On a clear, open site make a tripod with a platform to support a fire. Use evergreen boughs as cover to keep the cone dry; they will burn

RESCUE

brightly and give off smoke. Cover the entire cone with bright-coloured material, e.g. a parachute, which will itself be noticeable by day. Whip it off when you ignite the fire – you may not attract attention the first time.

Keep tripods well maintained, ensuring wood is dry. Drive pole ends into ground to prevent tipping in strong winds. A flaming cone fire is visible for miles. In exposed locations make a tepee of fabric with smoke and heat outlet at top to keep fire under control. Add fuel from side so as not to mask firelight.

USE WRECKAGE TO HELP FIRE-SIGNALLING: Stand a fire on a piece of metal. When hot it increases convection and makes the fire burn brightly. If polished, it will act as a reflector, intensifying the brightness.

SMOKE INDICATORS

• By day smoke is a good locater. Have a supply of smoke-producing material ready to put on your fires. Smoke not only helps rescue aircraft find you, it also shows surface wind direction. Make sure smoke is downwind of landing site and of any panel codes you have laid so it does not obscure them from above.

• Light smoke stands out against dark earth or forest. Use green grass, leaves, moss and ferns. Wet materials produce a good smudge fire, e.g. damp seat covers smoulder for a long time. The smoke also keeps insects at bay.

• Dark smoke shows best against snow or desert sand. Use rubber or oil to produce it. If atmospheric conditions make the smoke hang in layers along the ground, build up the fire to increase its height. Thermal currents will then take the smoke to a good height.

BE IMAGINATIVE: On a river a noticeable floating object carrying a message may attract attention: a small raft with a bright sail labelled SOS, for instance.

> If rescue is unlikely and you start making your own way back, leave clear signs so that searchers have an indication of the route you have taken. Stay close to regular flight routes or keep to open territory.

CODES

GROUND-TO-AIR SIGNALLING

Attract attention during daylight, even if you are asleep or injured, with the following signals. Make them as large and as noticeable as possible. A recommended size is 10m long and 3m wide (33ft x 10ft) for each symbol, with 3m (10ft) between symbols.

Lay panel codes in the open; avoid steep gullies or ravines and do not make them on reverse slopes. Use the marker panels from your survival pouch (see p. 22), or improvise. Lay out wreckage or dig a shallow trench: banked up earth increases the depth of the shadow. Use rocks or boughs to accentuate it. On snow, trampled-out symbols will show clearly until the next snowfall.

RESCUE

GROUND-TO-AIR CODE

I　Serious injury – immediate casevac
(casualty evacuation) – (can also mean 'need doctor')

II　Need medical supplies

F　Need food and water

N　Negative *(No)*

Λ　Affirmative *(Yes)* – *(Y will also be understood)*

LL　All is well

X　Unable to move on

→　Am moving on this way

K　Indicate direction to proceed

⌐L　Do not understand

□　Need compass and map

△　Think safe to land here
(Broken at angles, means 'attempting take-off')

!　Need radio/signal lamp/battery

⌐|　Aircraft badly damaged

RESCUE

Once contact has been made, a message signalled by the aircraft can be answered with A or Y (affirmative) and N (negative) signals, or Morse Code or body signals.

NIGHT SIGNALS: Use inflammable substances to make signals which will work at night. Dig or scrape an SOS (or any symbol) in the earth, sand or snow and, when the signal is needed, pour petrol into it and ignite it.

MESSAGE SIGNALLING

International Morse Code can be transmitted by flashing lights on and off, by a heliograph, by waving a flag or a shirt tied to a stick. Always carry a copy of the code.

HELIOGRAPH: Use the sun and a reflector to flash light signals. Any shiny object will do – polished tin, glass, a piece of foil – but a hand-mirror is best. Long flashes are dashes and quick ones dots. If you do not know Morse Code, random flashes should attract attention. At least learn the code for SOS. A flash can be seen at a great distance and requires little energy. Sweep the horizon during the day. If a plane approaches make intermittent flashes or you may dazzle the pilot. Once you have been seen, stop signalling.

With an improvised single-sided reflector pick up sunlight to get an image on the ground or some other surface and lead it in the direction of the aircraft.

*Punch a hole in a double-sided
reflector to improvise a heliograph.
Sight target you wish to contact
through hole in heliograph (a) in the
direction of the sun, so sun shines
through hole (b). You will see a spot of
light on your face (c). Angle mirror so
dot of light on your face 'disappears'
back through hole in mirror — still
sighting your contact.*

If your attempts are unsuccessful, bring the mirror close
to your eyes with a hand lined up between you and the
contact. Angle the mirror to flash on to your hand, then
move hand away.

Practice this form of signalling, but unless in a survival
situation, do not signal to aircraft or transmit messages
which could cause alarm or danger to others.

RAG SIGNALS: Tie a flag or a piece of bright-coloured
clothing to a pole. Move it left for dashes and right for
dots. Exaggerate with a figure-of-eight movement.

*For a 'dot' swing to the right and
make a figure-of-eight; for a
'dash' swing to the left and
make a figure-of-eight.*

At close range,
this may work without
figure-of-eight
movements. Keep 'dash' pauses on the left, slightly longer
than 'dot' movements to the right.

RESCUE

MORSE CODE

A	▪ ▬	N	▬ ▪	1	▪ ▬ ▬ ▬ ▬
B	▬ ▪ ▪ ▪	O	▬ ▬ ▬	2	▪ ▪ ▬ ▬ ▬
C	▬ ▪ ▬ ▪	P	▪ ▬ ▬ ▪	3	▪ ▪ ▪ ▬ ▬
D	▬ ▪ ▪	Q	▬ ▬ ▪ ▬	4	▪ ▪ ▪ ▪ ▬
E	▪	R	▪ ▬ ▪	5	▪ ▪ ▪ ▪ ▪
F	▪ ▪ ▬ ▪	S	▪ ▪ ▪	6	▬ ▪ ▪ ▪ ▪
G	▬ ▬ ▪	T	▬	7	▬ ▬ ▪ ▪ ▪
H	▪ ▪ ▪ ▪	U	▪ ▪ ▬	8	▬ ▬ ▬ ▪ ▪
I	▪ ▪	V	▪ ▪ ▪ ▬	9	▬ ▬ ▬ ▬ ▪
J	▪ ▬ ▬ ▬	W	▪ ▬ ▬	0	▬ ▬ ▬ ▬ ▬
K	▬ ▪ ▬	X	▬ ▪ ▪ ▬		
L	▪ ▬ ▪ ▪	Y	▬ ▪ ▬ ▬		
M	▬ ▬	Z	▬ ▬ ▪ ▪		

SENDING SIGNALS (* SEND AS ONE WORD. NO PAUSES)

AAAAA* etc. – Call sign. *I have a message*

AAA* – End of sentence. *More follows*

Pause – End of word. *More follows*

EEEEE* etc. – Error. *Start from last correct word*

AR – End of message

RECEIVING SIGNALS

TTTTT* etc. I am receiving you

K – I am ready. *Start message*

T – Word received

IMI* – Repeat sign. *I do not understand*

R – Message received

USEFUL WORDS

SOS ▪ ▪ ▪ ▬ ▬ ▬ ▪ ▪ ▪

SEND ▪ ▪ ▪ | ▪ | ▬ ▪ | ▬ ▪ ▪

DOCTOR ▬ ▪ ▪ | ▬ ▬ ▬ | ▬ ▪ ▬ ▪ | ▬ | ▬ ▬ ▬ | ▪ ▬ ▪

HELP ▪ ▪ ▪ ▪ | ▪ | ▪ ▬ ▪ ▪ | ▪ ▬ ▬ ▪

INJURY ▪ ▪ | ▬ ▪ | ▪ ▬ ▬ ▬ | ▪ ▪ ▬ | ▪ ▬ ▪ | ▬ ▪ ▬ ▬

TRAPPED ▬ | ▪ ▬ ▪ | ▪ ▬ | ▪ ▬ ▬ ▪ | ▪ ▬ ▬ ▪ | ▪ | ▬ ▪ ▪

LOST ▪ ▬ ▪ ▪ | ▬ ▬ ▬ | ▪ ▪ ▪ | ▬

WATER ▪ ▬ ▬ | ▪ ▬ | ▬ | ▪ | ▪ ▬ ▪

BODY SIGNALS

Use these to signal to airmen. Make all signals in a clear and exaggerated manner. Note changes from frontal to sideways positions and use of leg and body posture as well as hand movements. Use a cloth in the hand to emphasise YES and NO signals.

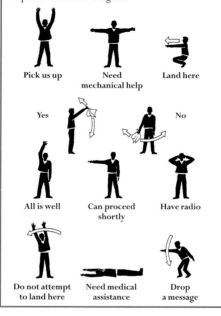

Pick us up

Need
mechanical help

Land here

Yes

No

All is well

Can proceed
shortly

Have radio

Do not attempt
to land here

Need medical
assistance

Drop
a message

Pilots will respond to body signals as follows:

Message received and understood

In daylight: tipping the plane's wings from side to side
At night: flashing green lights

Message received but not understood

In daylight: flying the plane in a right-handed circle
At night: flashing red lights

MOUNTAIN RESCUE CODE

* Repeat after 1-minute interval

Message: SOS

  Flare signal: Red
  Sound signal: 3 short blasts, 3 long, 3 short*
  Light signal: 3 short flashes, 3 long, 3 short*

Message: HELP NEEDED

  Flare signal: Red
  Sound signal: 6 blasts in quick succession*
  Light signal: 6 flashes in quick succession*

Message: MESSAGE UNDERSTOOD

  Flare signal: White
  Sound signal: 3 flashes in quick succession*
  Light signal: 3 flashes in quick succession*

Message: RETURN TO BASE

  Flare signal: Green
  Sound signal: Prolonged succession of blasts
  Light signal: Prolonged succession of flashes

FLARES

Any flare will be investigated in a search, but choose
one best fitted to the location. In closely wooded
country green does not stand out but red does. Over
snow, white merges – green and red are best.

RESCUE

Make sure you understand the instructions, as some flares eject a white-hot ball of magnesium that will burn a hole in anything it hits – your chest or dinghy.

Some flares are hand-held and reversible. One end produces smoke for daytime the other a flare for night. The higher these are held the easier they are to see. Flares fired into the air can be seen from afar.

Keep flares dry and away from naked flames and heat sources. Ensure safety pins are in position and secure, but may be easily removed when necessary.

HANDLING FLARES: Hand-held flares are cylindrical tubes with a cap at each end. The top cap is often embossed so it can be identified by touch. Remove it first. Then remove base cap, exposing a short string and safety pin, or other safety device. Point flare upwards and away from you and anyone else. Remove pin, or turn to the fire position. Hold flare at arm's length, shoulder-height, pointing up. Tug the firing string vertically downwards. Brace yourself for the kickback. Some flares have a spring-mechanism trigger.

To fire Very pistols, load, point skywards, cock the hammer and squeeze the trigger. Mini-flares are lighter than Very pistols but as effective. Handle with care. To use, screw a flare of the selected colour into the end of the discharger, aim skyward, pull back striker and fire!

> Hand-held flares get hot. When they burn down do not drop them into the bottom of a boat, where they could start a fire or burn straight through an inflatable.

INFORMATION SIGNALS

If you abandon camp leave clear direction markers to indicate your route. Continue to make them, not only for people to follow but to establish your own route as a guide if you start going back on your trail.

Place rocks or debris in arrow shape (a) to be visible from the air. Ground-level signs include: stick in crooked support, with the top indicating direction followed (b); grasses tied in an overhand knot with end hanging in direction followed (c); forked branches laid with fork pointing in direction followed (d); small rocks on larger rocks, with small rock beside (e); indicating a turn or arrow — notches cut in tree trunks (f). A cross of sticks or stones (g) means 'not this way'. Signal danger or emergency with three rocks, sticks or clumps of grass.

RESCUE

SEARCH

A search will start from the last known location and sweep on the proposed route. An assessment will be made of probable strategy adopted. The search will then be extended to cover the whole area. Ideally this will be done from the air but severe weather may mean it has to be done on foot.

Aerial search patterns will cover both sides of the intended flight path of missing aircraft or your known route. If weather conditions permit, a night search will be made, for lights will be visible from a great height and a wider area can thus be covered.

If you are signalling to an aircraft and it turns away, keep watching. It may be following a search pattern and you will be able to anticipate when to signal again. Most aerial searches involve parallel sweeps towards and away from the sun so any reflection from a missing aircraft or other wreckage and signals will be seen.

At sea, combined sea-and-air searches allow aircraft to locate survivors so that ships can pick them up.

HELICOPTER RESCUE

Helicopters are frequently used to carry out rescues. Where possible the pilot will land to take on survivors and fly them out. Survivors should check out suitable landing sites and create a site if necessary.

A helicopter requires an obstruction-free approach and exit path, both into prevailing winds. The ground should be level – a slope of no more than 7 ° (a gradient of 1 in 10) is acceptable. The touch-down surface must be firm and free of loose materials – no leaves, etc.

SELECTING AND PREPARING A LANDING SITE

• Find a natural clearing at least 26m (85ft) in diameter. A further 5m (16.5ft) is needed all around, cleared to a height of 60cm (24in). It must have a clear approach path into the prevailing wind with no obstructions within an angle of 15 ° of the landing pad (LP). In close country, seek a river bank on a large bend. On level high ground, fell trees so they fall downhill, clear of approach and exit paths. Don't cut an LP on flat ground.

• Mark touch-down point with an H made of rocks (keep surface smooth), or securely anchored clothing. Stamp snow down firmly to stop it swirling. Water dry surfaces to keep dust down. In mountains updraughts and downdraughts can be considerable. Select a site giving maximum lift in take-off direction.

• Use smoke to indicate direction and strength of wind, but make sure it doesn't obscure the touch-down area. If a fire is not practical make a T sign from contrasting material and place it at downwind edge of LP with horizontal bar of T placed upwind. Or stand on far downwind side of the LP with arms outstretched and back to the wind to signal. Don't do this too soon, and then only in the correct position. It is similar to the body signal 'need help'.

• For a night rescue use flares and fires to indicate your position. If using torches or other beams, shine them skyward to attract attention then shine them on to the touch-down or winching area. Don't dazzle the pilot.

• When helicopter touches down, do not approach from the rear. This is a blind spot for the crew and the tail rotor is unprotected. On sloping ground always approach up the slope, never down a slope.

RESCUE

Do not carry anything which could foul the main rotor. Keep sharp objects away from body panels of the helicopter. Sit in the seat allocated to you by crewman, fasten seat belt and keep fastened until told otherwise. Do not try to alight until engine has been shut down after you have landed – even then, wait for directions.

Non-landing rescue: If an LP is impossible you can be winched up while the helicopter hovers.

If survivors are being lifted from a ship place deck at 40 ° to the right of the eye of the wind. Try to give a wind speed over the deck of about 29kph (18mph).

WINCHING TECHNIQUES

Double lift: A crewman is lowered on the winch with another strop for the survivor. During the lift, the crewman supports the survivor with his legs and hands. After the strop has been put in place survivor keeps arms down by sides and does not lift them.

Single lift: Fit yourself into the strop. When you have placed it under your armpits and securely tightened the grommet give the 'thumbs up' sign. Make no further signals until on board. When you reach the cabin doorway, do exactly as the winchman directs.

If on a raft, disconnect yourself from lifeline. Fold down cover and lower sails. Stream the sea anchor to assist the pilot in trapping raft under rotor downwash.

Aircraft build up static electricity. This is discharged when the aircraft, or the cable, touches the ground. Allow the winch sling or cable to touch down before you approach it, or you'll get a substantial electric shock.

HEALTH

Take precautions to avoid illness and injury, but make sure that if medical problems do arise, everyone in the group knows first aid. If there is no hope of expert help, the survivor may have to take drastic measures to save a life. Some of the advice given in this section is intended only for such circumstances.

FIRST AID

PRIORITIES

Where there are many casualties, treat those with multiple injuries, bleeding, breathing and heart trouble first. Assess injuries and handle in this sequence:

1 **Restore and maintain breathing/heartbeat**
2 **Stop bleeding**
3 **Protect wounds and burns**
4 **Immobilise fractures**
5 **Treat shock**

 The possibility of AIDS infection demands care in dealing with blood and wounds. Cover your hands with gloves or plastic bags.

REDUCING DANGER

Before approaching a casualty, check for danger from falling debris, gas, traffic, etc. Switch current off before touching electrocution victims (see p. 292).

If possible, examine patient before moving, but if there is danger move patient to safety. Those with spinal injuries are at risk when moved (see p. 315).

HEALTH

UNCONSCIOUS CASUALTIES

Check whether they are breathing and begin artificial
respiration immediately if necessary. Check for external
bleeding and injury. Establish cause of unconsciousness.

UNCONSCIOUS BUT BREATHING

Check there is no spinal injury, clear obstructions in the
mouth, deal with any serious bleeding and place them in
recovery position. Turn patient on one side (by grasping
clothing at hip). Loosen tight clothing.

Move arm and leg on one
side outwards to stop patient lying flat. Bend elbow and knee.
Turn head in same direction. Lay other arm along other side of
patient. Allow other leg to bend slightly to produce a stable
position. Check airway is clear.

Do not place a casualty with a suspected spinal injury
in the recovery position. Use an artificial airway if
available to maintain respiration.

BREATHING AND PULSE

Loud breathing, froth around nose or lips, blueness of lips
and ears all indicate difficulty breathing. Check breathing
regularly: listen near the nose and mouth. Remove
obstructions. If breathing stops, give artificial respiration
(see p. 293).
Check at neck or wrist for pulse (see p. 296).

HEALTH

| CESSATION OF BREATHING |

This dire emergency may be caused by:

Choking, or blockage of air passages (see below).

Drowning or electric shock (see pp. 291–2).

Inhalation of smoke, gases or flame (see p. 291).

Lack of oxygen (see p. 291).

Compression of the chest (see p. 291).

CHOKING AND BLOCKAGES

If breathing has stopped, remove any obstruction in the airway, sweep mouth with a finger and ensure tongue has not fallen back. Give artificial respiration.

If a person can inhale and cough, encourage them to cough out blockage. If they cannot clear the airway, use the Heimlich manoeuvre with adults (see p. 290 for methods to use on infants and other special cases).

HEIMLICH MANOEUVRE: Stand behind a conscious casualty, arms around them. Make a fist of one hand and press it thumb inwards above navel but below breastbone. Clasp other hand round the fist. Pull sharply upwards and inwards four times.

If this does not work, give 4 sharp blows to the back between shoulder blades and repeat the manoeuvre. Check to see if the blockage is dislodged. Repeat – do not give up.

Place unconscious casualty on his or her back, head tilted back. Kneel astride or alongside, place your hands, one on top of the other, with heels of your hands resting above navel. Keep fingers clear. With arm straight, make quick thrusts upwards and inwards as if to dislodge blockage. Thrusts must be strong enough to dislodge blockage. If unsuccessful, roll patient on to side and strike

four times between shoulder blades. Repeat abdominal thrust as necessary.

Self-help
If alone, use Heimlich manoeuvre by pulling or pushing against a blunt projection (e.g. a tree or a chair back).

CHOKING: SPECIAL CASES

Children: Hold upside down by heels and strike 4 blows with heel of your hand between the shoulder-blades. Alternatively, lay child over your lap, head-down, supporting child under chest. Slap back with heel of hand. If blockage not dislodged, apply Heimlich manoeuvre with one hand. Use less pressure than for an adult, but it must be sufficient to clear blockage.

Babies: Use much less pressure for back slaps. If blockage not dislodged, put 2 fingers of one or both hands between navel and bottom of breastbone. Press down and forward quickly, repeat 4 times.

Pregnant women: Position fists against middle of breastbone and thrust upwards and inwards.

HEALTH

PREVENTING ASPHYXIATION

Pressure on chest can cause asphyxiation. In an avalanche or landslide, crouch with arms bent and elbows tucked well in to protect the chest. A climber who slips and is suspended by a rope round his chest will find it hard to breathe. Pass down a loop (see p. 49) to relieve the pressure.

   If wreckage cannot be lifted off a trapped person, use a lever to raise it and prop securely.

Smoke and gas can be prevented from entering lungs by placing a fine mesh over nose and mouth. Casualties must have fresh air. Get upwind or use a respirator.

Lack of oxygen is a danger in shelters with no ventilation. A fire adds the risk of carbon monoxide poisoning. Casualties must have fresh air.

Carbon monoxide poisoning is deadly in confined spaces, but is hard to detect. Symptoms resemble alcohol overdose: impaired memory and judgement, and a disregard of danger.

Ensure adequate ventilation when using stoves. To test whether there is sufficient oxygen, light a candle: if the flame gets longer and higher, there is a severe lack of oxygen: ventilate. Casualties must have fresh air.

NOT BREATHING/NO PULSE

DROWNING

Symptoms: Can occur through fluid blockages, but patient is often immersed. Face, especially lips and ears, livid and congested; fine froth at mouth, nostrils

(cont. over)

HEALTH

Treatment: Do not attempt to remove liquid from lungs. Begin artificial respiration (see p. 295) as soon as possible. If still in water, support body and begin mouth-to-mouth after removing any obstructions.

ELECTROCUTION

Symptoms: Heart may stop; muscle spasms may throw victim some distance. Electrical burns will be much deeper than they appear.

Treatment: Do not touch until current is off. It may be possible to break contact by pulling on insulated cable to disengage. But beware – liquids will conduct current (victims may urinate). Give artificial respiration and treat for cardiac arrest (see p. 297), then treat burns.

LIGHTNING

Symptoms: Victim usually stunned, or unconscious. Clothing may catch fire. Electrical burns will be most severe where metal objects (jewellery, etc.) are worn.

Treatment: Give artificial respiration (see p. 293) if necessary and treat burns (see pp. 304–5). Prolonged resuscitation may be needed. Recovery often delayed.

POISONING

Symptoms: Poisons which enter lungs or attack the nervous system can cause asphyxia (see p. 320–21).

HEART ATTACK

Symptoms: Severe chest pain, shortness of breath, giddiness, collapse, anxiety, heavy sweating, irregular pulse, blueness of lips or skin.

Treatment: If breathing fails give artificial respiration and, if pulse stops, cardiac compression (see p. 297).

HEALTH

ARTIFICIAL RESPIRATION (AR)

With any form of resuscitation the first five minutes are the most critical, but if breathing does not start, keep artificial respiration up for at least an hour. In a group, take turns. Don't give up!

MOUTH-TO-MOUTH ('KISS OF LIFE')

The fastest and most effective method. Begin as soon as airway is cleared. If face is injured, or poison or chemical burns are suspect, use Silvester method (see p. 294).

Lie patient on back, tilt head back, hold jaw well open and nostrils closed. Check mouth and throat clear. Loosen tight clothing. Take deep breath, place mouth over patient's mouth and blow.

Watch for chest to rise as you blow into patient's lungs (if it does not, airway may be blocked: treat for choking, see p. 289). Remove your mouth and chest will fall. Repeat quickly for first 6 inflations, then continue at 12 per minute until breathing is established.

FOR A CHILD: Do not blow. Exhale normally, or in gentle puffs for a baby. Cover nose and mouth for babies. Do not tilt child's head back too far. Give first four inflations as quickly as possible. Check pulse after two inflations.

HEALTH

> **AIDS** The danger of infection is small, but if you feel at risk, place a clean handkerchief or a thin polythene bag with a small slit in it between your mouth and that of the victim. Blow through the slit or handkerchief.

SILVESTER METHOD

Use when poisoning or facial injury prevent mouth-to-mouth, and when patient needs cardiac compression.

Lie casualty on back, raise shoulders with pad of folded material. Kneel astride casualty's head. Place hands flat over lower ribs and rock forward to press steadily downwards.
Lift casualty's arms upwards and outwards as far as possible.
Repeat 12 times a minute for adults. If there is no improvement, treat for choking to clear airway then resume cycle. Don't give up. This has saved lives after three hours without breathing.

AFTER BREATHING HAS BEEN RESTORED:
Place patient in recovery position – after all forms of resuscitation. But not in cases of spinal injury.

HEALTH

HOLGER NIELSEN METHOD

Use to resuscitate a drowning victim if mouth-to-mouth not possible. Face-down position allows liquids to flow freely from mouth without choking the patient.

Lay casualty face down, head turned to one side, arms bent, forehead resting on hands. Loosen tight garments, clear mouth of weed, mud, etc. and ensure tongue is brought forward.

Kneel at head, facing casualty. Place your hands over shoulder blades, thumbs touching and fingers spread. Perform the following procedure to a count of eight:

1-2-3 Rock forward with arms straight, producing gentle, even, increasing pressure (about 2 seconds)

4 Rock back, sliding hands to grasp patient's upper arms (½–1 second)

5-6-7 Pull and raise patient's arms gently by rocking further backwards (2 seconds). Avoid raising torso or disturbing head too much.

8 Lower patient's arms to ground and slide hands back to initial position (½–1 second).

Repeat 12 times a minute

If patient's arms are injured, place folded garment under forehead and lift under armpits. This is impractical if ribs or shoulders are badly damaged.

HEALTH

IS HEART BEATING?

Taking pulse at wrist
Rest fingers lightly at front of wrist, about 1cm (⅓in) from thumb side at lower end of forearm.

Taking pulse at neck
Turn face to one side. Slide fingers from Adam's apple into groove alongside and press gently.

In a relaxed adult the normal pulse rate is 60–80 beats per minute (average 72); in young children 90–140 per minute. The rate increases with excitement.

Count the beats in 30 seconds and multiply by two. Use a watch with a second hand to keep timing accurate; note the result.

> If you cannot feel a pulse and the pupils of the eyes are much larger than normal, start cardiac compression while artificial respiration is continued. Mouth-to-mouth and Silvester methods allow both activities to be carried out at same time.

CARDIAC COMPRESSION

Regardless of which method of resuscitation is used, if there is no pulse and no improvement after 10–12 breaths, cardiac compression (external heart massage) should be started.

Cardiac compression
Lay casualty on their back on
a firm surface and kneel
alongside. Place heel of one
hand on lower half of breastbone, about an inch above where the
ribs meet, not on the end of the breastbone or below it. Place heel
of other hand on top. Keep fingers off the casualty's chest. With
arms straight, rock forward and press down about 4cm (1½in)
15 times. Repeat about 60 times a minute – more than once per
second. Press smoothly and firmly. Erratic or rough pressure could
cause injury.

INFANTS AND CHILDREN: Use less pressure and more
compressions. For a baby or toddler, light pressure with
two fingers is enough at 100 compressions per minute.
Depress chest only 2.5cm (1in). For children up to 10
years, use heel of one hand only and push lightly 80–90
times per minute to depth of 3.5cm (1⅜in). Give five
compressions to one lung inflation.

Compression should only be carried out by a
trained first aider. Never give compression if the
heart is beating – even if only a very faint pulse
can be felt. You could stop the heart.

HEALTH

AR WITH COMPRESSION (CPR)

If alone, use mouth-to-mouth or Silvester methods. Give 2 lung inflations, 15 compressions, repeat. Check for pulse after a minute, then at 3-minute intervals. Don't give up.

If two first aiders are present, give 5 compressions, then one deep inflation on upstroke of fifth compression. Repeat. First aider should check pulse and pupils.

As soon as a pulse is detected, stop compressions but continue inflations until the casualty is breathing unaided. Place the victim in recovery position.

DANGEROUS BLEEDING

An adult has up to 6.25 litres (11 pints) of blood. Loss of 0.5 litre (¾ pint) causes mild faintness, 1 litre (1¾ pints) faintness, increased pulse rate, shallow breathing. 1.5 litres (2½ pints) leads to collapse, more than 2.24 litres (4 pints) can be fatal. Blood loss must be stopped. Internal bleeding may not be apparent. If severe, it can lead to shock or kill.

> When bleeding is coupled with cessation of breathing, treat both at the same time as a double emergency.

Bleeding veins and capillaries can be stemmed by pressure over the bleeding point, with or without a dressing. Keep up for 5 to 15 minutes to allow clotting. Preventing blood loss is a priority. If a sterile dressing is not available, use any clean, non-fluffy cloth. If not, use your hand. Join edges of wound together. If it is on a limb, raise it above level of heart – lay victim down and prop up head or limbs. If you are wounded and alone, use free hand to apply direct pressure. If anything is embedded in wound, do not remove it. Apply pressure beside the fragment.

HEALTH

ARTERIAL BLEEDING

Speed is vital in stopping blood spurting from an artery.
Compress artery at pressure points where it runs near the
surface over a bone. Watch wound: if flow does not lessen,
move fingers until it does. These figures and captions show
where to apply pressure to stem arterial bleeding.

Temple or scalp (a):
Forward of or above the ear
Face below eyes (b):
Side of jaw

Shoulder or upper arm (c):
Above clavicle
Elbow (d):
Underside of upper arm

Lower arm (e):
Crook of elbow
Hand (f): *Front of wrist*

Thigh (g): *Midway on groin / top of thigh*
Lower leg (h): *Upper sides of knee*
Foot (i): *Front of ankle*

Do not apply pressure for more than 15 minutes. You will
cut off the blood supply to the tissues.

HEALTH

With bleeding under control, apply dressing and bandage securely but not so tight as to cut off circulation. Do not lift dressing. If a clot is disturbed, bleeding is made worse.

 After bandaging a limb, check circulation frequently. Loosen a dressing if toes or fingers are blue, cold or numb; there's a risk of gangrene if dressings are too tight. Never use a tourniquet.

LESSER BLEEDING

Clean wound carefully and apply sterile dressing. To avoid risk of infection, do not touch it or allow anything non-sterile near it. Replace dressing only when it is very dirty.

For a nose bleed, sit patient up, head slightly forward, and pinch soft part of nostrils for 10 minutes. Patient must breathe through mouth and not sniff or blow the nose.

INTERNAL BLEEDING

This serious condition is common after a violent blow, broken bones or penetrating wounds. Hard to detect.

SYMPTOMS

- Victim feels light-headed, restless and faint; looks pale; skin cold, clammy to touch; pulse weak but very fast.
- Red/wine-coloured urine (injury to kidney/bladder).
- Blood passed with faeces (lower bowel injury).
- Blood vomited (stomach injury).
- Blood coughed up as red froth (damage to lungs).

Lie patient flat with legs elevated. Keep warm. Do not overheat. Serious internal bleeding requires expert care.

HEALTH

WOUNDS AND DRESSINGS

Open wounds are at risk of infection, especially from tetanus – immunisation is essential for adventurers.

Extract foreign bodies with sterile tweezers. Other than in a survival situation, leave this to medics. Cut away clothing, clean area, and irrigate wounds to wash out dirt. Clean from centre out, not from outside in. Dry and apply clean dressing. Change if they become wet, give off a bad smell, or if pain increases and throbs, indicating infection.

Treat local infection with hot salty water, or poultices to draw out pus. Anything that can be mashed can be used: rice, potatoes, shredded tree bark, clay. Boil up and wrap in a cloth. Apply to infected area as hot as can be tolerated.

STITCHING WOUNDS

Minor wounds, e.g. knife wounds, can be closed by suturing. Clean wound thoroughly, then stitch across it.

STITCHES: Use sterilised needle and thread or gut. Make stitches individually, beginning across mid-point. Draw edges together, tie off thread, work outwards.

ADHESIVE SUTURES: Use butterfly sutures or adhesive plasters cut in butterfly shape. Draw edges of wound together. Apply plaster to one side, close up as much as possible. Press down on other side.

If the wound becomes infected – red, swollen or tense – remove some or all stitches to let pus out. Leave to drain.

HEALTH

Soap is antiseptic: use to wash wounds. Wash hands and wounds in boiled water. If not available, use urine to sterilise wounds. This will not introduce infection.

OPEN TREATMENT

Survival wounds are safest covered with a dressing but not sutured. If unable to clean properly, let it heal from inside.

You may have to drain a deep wound or open an abscess and insert sterilised loose packing of a bandage. Leave a tail hanging out. Allow it to drain for a few days. As healing progresses, reduce packing until able to remove it all and apply a dressing. If lancing or reopening a wound, sterilise blade first. Do not use antiseptic on deep wounds, to avoid risk of tissue damage. Wash the wound with boiled water.

Chest wounds: One of the greatest dangers with this is having the chest collapse – a 'sucking chest wound' – when the chest sucks air through the wound into the space around the lung, rather than into it. This must be sealed to enable proper breathing. Waterproof wrapper (or plastic film from a cigarette packet or foil preferably coated with petroleum jelly) can be used, clean side against the wound and taped at the sides and top only.

Abdominal wounds: Avoid giving solids or liquids. Relieve thirst with damp cloth to wet lips and tongue. If gut extrudes, cover and keep damp. Do not push back in place. If no organs extrude, dress and bandage firmly.

Head injuries: Ensure airway is clear and tongue forward. Remove dentures. Control bleeding. Provided there are no spinal injuries, place in recovery position.

Traumatic amputation: Examine wound and tie off exposed arteries with sterile thread.

BURNS

Extinguish burning clothing without fanning flames. Roll victim on ground, covering with a blanket. Remove smouldering clothes, tight garments, jewellery, etc.

Drench burned tissues – hold under slow-running cold water for at least 10 minutes. Avoid antiseptic, ointments, or butter. Use dry, sterile dressing – place between fingers and toes to prevent sticking together. Hardwood barks – oak or beech – can be boiled and applied to soothe wound.

Give patient plenty of fluids – small cold drinks with ½ teaspoon of salt or bicarbonate of soda to a pint of water.

TYPES OF BURNS

Deep burns are charred or white. Bone may be visible. Superficial burns hurt more. Never burst blisters. If face or neck burnt, ensure airway clear. Treat scalds as for burns.

For mouth or throat burns, use sips of cold water. If breathing is affected, give artificial respiration. For eye burns, flush out chemicals with water. Tilt head to avoid washing chemicals in. Never neutralise acid with alkali or vice versa. For electrical and lightning burns, see p. 292.

FRACTURES

Examine for broken bones before swelling complicates the process of locating the fracture, and before moving casualty. Treat urgent injuries like asphyxia and bleeding first. Immobilise before moving, and finish treatment later.

Two types of fracture are: open (bone pushes through skin, or wound open to fracture) and closed. In former, infection is possible. Straighten limb, if distorted, before splinting. It will hurt – if patient unconscious, do it first.

HEALTH

SURVIVAL CASE STUDY

My medical training came in handy on many occasions, especially in remote areas. Everyone should have some knowledge of first aid so they can at least help in an emergency.

In the early days of the Borneo campaign, to win the confidence of the locals we set up a 'hearts and minds' campaign. This included medical treatment, which quickly helped form a bond with the local tribes, who came from many miles around with a variety of illnesses, fevers and trauma.

One day a fisherman was carried in with his left foot covered in rags. The smell got stronger as he got nearer, and when the foot was unwrapped I had to hold my breath. The whole foot was bloated and oozing pus. He was feverish and rambled on about being hit by a boat propeller. After trimming away the rotten flesh and administering a course of penicillin his recovery was amazing. Undoubtedly he would have died from septicaemia, but after seven days' treatment, he was walking again.

The locals were amazingly receptive to modern drugs, and so care had always to be taken when administering any drugs to them, as they had built up a natural and inherited immunity to illnesses such as tropical fevers which can be eradicated by taking just one pill. A single anti-malaria pill, for example, can wipe out thousands of years of the locals' natural immunity in seconds, leaving them open to the perils of the disease.

Our fame spread and our queue of patients got longer. Most days we treated cuts, fractures and other similar ailments. As their confidence in us grew so did the challenge of treating some cases. The locals carried out their own childbirth, relying on tried and tested methods, unless something went wrong – then they would come to me.

There was, and still is, a very fine line to be trodden – do I assist or not? If I assist and it goes wrong I will lose face, contradicting the reason for being there in the first place. But if I don't assist I still lose face, as well as the trust that has been built up. It's all down to training and the amount of knowledge you have. I was lucky enough to get involved with a difficult birth and it turned out fine.

LESSONS LEARNT:
- **Some knowledge of first aid is essential**
- **Administer drugs to locals prudently**
- **Locals have a natural, inherited immunity that can be compromised by drugs**
- **Be sympathetic to cultural differences**

HEALTH

If no medical help is expected, reduce closed fractures as soon as possible after injury by applying traction (a slow, strong pull until edges of fractured bone are brought together), then splint and immobilise the whole length of the limb. Splints can be pieces of wood, rolls of newspaper, ski sticks, etc. Separate the hard splint material from the skin with padding (moss is ideal) or pressure sores may develop.

If no splint is available, strap the injured limb to the body. Insert padding in natural hollows to keep in position. Secure above and below fracture and below nearest joints. Tie with soft materials, using reef knots. Do not tie splints directly over injury or let knots press against limb. Check the circulation periodically.

TYPES OF FRACTURE

FRACTURE OF ARM BELOW ELBOW, OF HAND OR
OF FINGERS: *Place the sling (e.g. long-sleeved sweater) between the arm and body. Immobilise from elbow to mid-fingers with padded splint. Take one arm of shirt behind head. Tie to other on opposite side to injury. Knot below the elbow to prevent slipping. The arm is thus elevated to prevent swelling.*

FRACTURE AT THE ELBOW: *If the elbow is bent, support it in a narrow sling. Bind it across upper arm and chest. Check the pulse to ensure the artery is not trapped. If there is no pulse, straighten the arm a little, and if there is still no pulse, urgent medical aid is required.*

If the elbow is straight, do not bend it. Place a pad in the armpit and strap the arm to the body, or place padded splints on either side of arm.

FRACTURE OF THE UPPER ARM:
Place a pad in the armpit, with a splint from shoulder to elbow on the outside of the arm and a narrow sling at the wrist. Bind the arm.

FRACTURE OF THE SHOULDER BLADE OR COLLARBONE: *Make a sling to take the weight off the injured part, and immobilise it with a bandage across the arm and body.*

HEALTH

For fractures of the thigh or lower leg, apply a figure-of-eight bandage, binding feet and ankles of both legs.

FRACTURE OF THE HIP OR UPPER LEG: *Place a splint on the inside of the leg and another from ankle to armpit. Use a stick to push tying bands under the hollows of the leg. If no splints are available, pad a folded blanket between the legs and tie the broken leg to the sound leg.*

FRACTURE TO THE KNEE:
If the leg is straight, place the splint behind the leg. Apply a cold compress to the knee.

If the leg is bent: bring both legs together, place padding between calves and thighs and strap in those places. This is a temporary measure only. If rescue is unlikely, the leg must be made as straight as possible.

FRACTURE TO THE LOWER LEG: *Splint from above the knee to beyond the heel, or pad between the legs and tie them both together (see fracture of the hip or upper leg, above).*

FRACTURE OF THE ANKLE OR FOOT:
A splint is not normally used. Elevate the foot to reduce swelling, and immobilise with a folded blanket strapped twice at ankle and once under the foot. If it is a closed fracture, a shoe or boot will provide stability. Do not put weight on the foot.

FRACTURE OF THE PELVIS: Symptoms are pain in groin or lower abdomen. Pad between the thighs and tie at the knees and ankles. Place a pillow support below bent legs and strap the patient to a flat support (e.g. a door, stretcher) at shoulder, waist and ankle. Alternatively, place the padding between the legs and bandage around feet, ankles and knees, with two overlapping bandages over the pelvis.

FRACTURE OF THE SKULL: Symptoms include blood or watery fluid seeping from ear or nose. Lay the victim in recovery position, leaking side down. Lightly cover the ear with a sterile dressing, check breathing and pulse. Immobilise.

FRACTURE OF THE SPINE: Symptoms include pain in back and loss of sensation in lower limbs. Ask casualty to move fingers and toes and gently test for feeling. The patient must be immobilised – place soft, solid objects around patient to prevent movement of head or body.

HEALTH

FRACTURE OF THE NECK:
Immobilisation is essential. Use a
cervical collar of rolled-up paper or a
towel folded to 10–14cm (4–5½in)
wide to fit from top of breastbone to
jaw. Fold the edges to make them
narrower at back than front. Overlap
round the neck and secure with belt or tie.

SPRAINS

Tearing of tissues connected to a joint. Symptoms: pain, swelling. Bathe with cold water, support with a bandage (not too tight), elevate limb and rest. Do not put under painful stress or you risk permanent damage. If you must walk on a sprained ankle, keep boot on for support. If in doubt whether a sprain or a break, treat as fracture.

DISLOCATIONS

Symptoms include pain and obvious deformity but no grating sound. Muscle spasms fix bone in position.

TYPES OF DISLOCATION

For a dislocated shoulder, take off your shoe, put your foot in casualty's armpit and pull on the arm.

A dislocated finger should be pulled then gently released so bone slips back. Be very gentle with the thumb. If it does not work first time, leave it alone.

If the jaw is dislocated, place a pad of cloth over lower teeth. Rest head on firm support and press down on pads with thumbs, rotating dislocated side of jaw backwards and upwards. It should snap into place. Bandage round head and under jaw. Feed soft foods.

SHOCK

Shock can kill. Act quickly to prevent it. Symptoms are:

- Cold and clammy skin.
- Casualty weak, dizzy or faint.
- Shallow and rapid pulse.
- Casualty may be thirsty.
- Vomiting or unconsciousness.
- Skin paler than normal, often greyish.
- Loss of colour in lips.

Severe bleeding, loss of body fluids from severe burns or prolonged vomiting or diarrhoea commonly lead to shock. Other causes are electrocution and heart attack.

Reassure the casualty and do not excite or move them more than necessary. If they are conscious, lay them flat, legs elevated about 30cm (12in). Loosen tight clothing. The priority is to encourage the supply of blood to the vital organs. Do not give anything to eat or drink. Cover them to keep warm, but do not add heat. Check breathing and pulse, and treat injuries. If there is loss of consciousness, impaired breathing or signs that vomiting may occur, place the casualty in the recovery position.

> Stand by to give mouth-to-mouth resuscitation and cardiac compression. Shock can take a long time to pass. Encourage rest and do not move the casualty unnecessarily. If you appear calm and in control, the casualty will feel cared for and will respond. Never leave a shock victim on his or her own.

HEALTH

BANDAGING

A triangular bandage, with short sides not less than 1m (or 3ft) is a versatile dressing for slings and bandages.

HEALTH

Bandages should be applied firmly enough to stop slipping, but not so tight as to cut into the flesh or interfere with circulation. Crepe bandages are best, but any fabric will do. Keep bandages rolled up; unrolling as you apply helps keep bandages smooth and even.

After applying a dressing (a pad of cotton wool covered with gauze in a sterile wrapping – if you must improvise, use very clean, non-fluffy material and do not touch the pad when applying), begin bandaging with a firm oblique turn to anchor it. Each turn should overlap the previous one by two-thirds, with the edges parallel. Tuck in the ends below the last layer and secure with safety pin or adhesive tape, or tie in reef knot away from the wound.

> Never join bandages with knots. Anchor separate strips by binding over a previously applied layer. Tie finishing knots over uninjured side or limb. Use knots which are easily untied and easily accessible.

MINOR AILMENTS

Even minor ailments can turn nasty if untreated. Wash friction blisters, sterilise a needle and pierce near the blister's edge. Gently press out fluid, cover with dressing and bandage. Earache can be relieved by pouring drops of warmed edible oil into the ear and plugging with cotton wool. Toothache is usually caused by an exposed nerve. Plug the cavity with pine-tree resin: scar the tree trunk, soak up the gum which oozes out on cotton wool and plug the hole in the tooth with it.

HEALTH

MOVING THE INJURED

Improvise a stretcher by passing two poles through pieces of sacking, heavy plastic or clothing, or use a door or tabletop. If no poles are available, roll in the sides of a blanket and use these rolls to get a grip. Test an improvised stretcher before using it.

LOADING A STRETCHER

A patient on a blanket can be lifted using the blanket. Other methods of lifting depend on the number of helpers. Agree signals for synchronised movements.

WITH 4 PERSONS: *C supports head and shoulders, D hooks fingers with adjoining hands of B and C to aid lift. A, B and C support while D places stretcher in position. D helps lower the patient.*

WITH 3 PERSONS: *Place stretcher at patient's head. C lifts at knees, A and B lock fingers under shoulders and hips. Move casualty from foot of stretcher to over it.*

WITH 2 PERSONS: *Both stand astride casualty. B links arms beneath shoulders, A lifts with one hand under thighs, the other under knees. Both move forward to above stretcher.*

HEALTH

> **CASUALTIES WITH SPINAL INJURIES**
> Move only if in danger. Three or four people are
> needed. Do not bend or twist. One person supports
> head and neck, another holds shoulders. In absence
> of stretcher, roll the patient onto blanket. Support
> head and torso. If working alone do not twist or turn
> casualty over. Pull by shoulders if face down, ankles if
> face up, in direction in which body is lying. On rough
> ground, drag from behind, pulling by shoulders and
> resting patient's head on your forearms.

LIFTING ON YOUR OWN

Choose a method you can sustain without dropping the
casualty. Lift a light casualty by the cradle method: one
arm under thighs, the other under armpit. Alternatively,
provided the casualty's arms are not hurt, use the crutch
method: place and hold one of their arms round your
neck; put your arm round their waist, grasping their
clothing at the hip.

The fireman's lift can be used with an unconscious
or conscious casualty, but is not suitable if the victim
is heavy.

*IF CASUALTY IS UNCONSCIOUS: Place face down. Kneel at
head. Slide hands under shoulders. Lift under the armpits to a
kneeling position, then to upright. Raise their right arm with
your left hand. Continue as for conscious
casualty (overleaf).*

HEALTH

IF CASUALTY IS CONSCIOUS: Grasp victim's right wrist. Bend your head under his arm so your shoulder is level with his lower abdomen.

Bend your knees, allowing the weight to fall across your shoulders. Place your right arm between or around legs.

Transfer his right wrist to your right hand and lift, taking weight on your right shoulder.

Stand up and adjust the weight across your shoulders. The casualty is head-down — not suitable for facial or head injuries.

LIFTING WITH A SLING: The best one-man-carry method for long distances.

Make a continuous loop to act as a sling wide enough not to cut into the casualty and long enough to go over your shoulders and twice across victim's back. Place the sling beneath the victim's thighs and lower back so two loops protrude. Lie between victim's legs and put your arms through loops. Tighten the slack. Grasp victim's hand and leg on the injured side.

Turn away from injured side, rolling so that victim lies on top. Adjust the sling to make load comfortable and rise to kneeling position (if the belt is loose or the load insecure, return to the previous position and adjust). You should be able to proceed with both hands free.

HEALTH

EMERGENCY CHILDBIRTH

Labour can be precipitated by stress. Signs include low backache, regular contractions and discharge of blood-stained mucus. This stage may last several hours; the second stage begins when contractions grow stronger and more frequent. Waters may break at any time. Sterilise scissors or knife and three 20cm (8in) lengths of thread. Have plenty of hot water available. Helpers must be healthy (free of colds, infections, or sores) and should scrub hands thoroughly for 4 minutes.

In the second stage, the mother should adopt the most natural position, e.g. a supported squat, but she should not lie down. She should keep her knees drawn up, pulling them up further as she bears down during contractions. If a bowel movement occurs, wipe clean from front to back. She must stop pushing and pant when baby's head appears. Tear any membrane covering the face. If the umbilical cord is round baby's neck, ease it over the head or loop over shoulder. Support baby's head in palm of your hands; as shoulders appear support body under armpits and lift towards mother's abdomen. Be prepared for baby to be *very* slippery. Ensuring that no tension is put on the cord, place baby between or by mother's legs, head lower than body. If baby does not appear head-first and delivery is held up for more than 3 minutes after shoulders emerge, pull very gently.

Clear the baby's mouth with a clean swab. Do not smack. If it does not cry and isn't breathing, begin very gentle mouth-to-mouth resuscitation. When the baby cries, lay it by its mother's breast.

HEALTH

The third stage of labour is the delivery of the placenta (10–30 minutes after birth). When it is expelled and the cord has stopped pulsating, the blood should flow out of cord into the baby. The cord will turn from blue to white. Tie a piece of sterile thread around it 15cm (6in) from baby's navel, then another at 20cm (8in). Check first tie is secure, or baby may lose blood. Sever cord between two ties with sterile scissors. Place a sterile dressing over the cut end. Leave for 10 minutes, and check there has been no bleeding. Tie a further thread 10cm (4in) from baby. Wash the mother.

BITES

MAMMAL BITES: Danger from infection is the main risk. Anti-tetanus shots and rabies vaccine should be obtained before travelling. Rabies is untreatable without vaccine and almost always fatal. Symptoms: irritability, dislike of light, violent aversion to water and paralysis. Ensure the victim does not transmit the disease to anyone else. Cleanse all bites, washing for at least 5 minutes to remove saliva. Then deal with bleeding, dress and bandage. Even if the bite heals, report it when you are rescued. You should be examined by a doctor.

SNAKE BITES: Most species inject venom very deeply. Do not consider sucking or cutting the wound. To prevent poison spreading make the victim relax, apply pressure at the wound site and immobilise affected part. Apply a bandage – not a tourniquet – above the bite and bandage down over the bite (e.g. for an ankle bite, start bandaging at the knee). This should apply a firm pressure, but the

HEALTH

limb should not darken or swell up. A splint will prevent flexing. If bite is on torso, apply pressure with wad of fabric. Place wound in cool water, e.g. a stream or use ice to cool. Try not to move the victim. Check pulse and breathing, stand by to give artificial respiration. (See also p. 342 ff.)

SPIDER BITES: Treat as for snake bites. A cold compress helps reduce pain (ice wrapped in cloth is ideal).

STINGS: Scorpions inject a powerful venom. Bee, wasp and hornet stings may cause severe allergic reactions, especially if there are multiple stings. Bee stings should be removed from the skin as quickly as possible by stroking sting with side of a needle then extracting with tweezers. Do not squeeze the poison sac as this will release more venom. Apply a cold compress.

GENERAL POISONING

Do not induce vomiting – it can do more harm than good. It is only suitable if poisonous berries have very recently been swallowed: gently put a finger to the back of victim's throat. Never induce vomiting if corrosive substances, petrol or solvents are involved.

Try to find out what has been swallowed. Burns round mouth indicate a caustic substance is involved. You must discover in advance the properties of chemicals to which you are exposed and appropriate remedies in cases of accident. Keep airway open: place victim in recovery position. Be prepared for vomiting, fits or convulsions. If breathing stops, give artificial respiration but avoid traces of poison around mouth.

HEALTH

Mix tea and charcoal – with milk of magnesia, if available. This antidote absorbs poison in the system.

Some plants, e.g. poison ivy, poison sumac and poison oak, cause skin irritation. Skin that has been in contact with the plant should be thoroughly washed with soap and water. Remove and wash clothing. Use alcohol to neutralise oil left on the skin.

 If handling a plant produces a severe reaction, do not put your hand to your face or touch other parts of the body until it has been well washed. Rashes and swellings can interfere with breathing, vision and urination.

GENERAL DISORDERS

Small digestive upsets are relatively insignificant, but symptoms which suggest more serious conditions should not be ignored. If food is adequate the best treatment is to fast for a day and rest. Take plenty of fluids.

Treat fever with rest and aspirin, and find its causes.

Pneumonia is more serious and is indicated by inflammation of lungs with chills and fever, breathlessness, cough with green-yellow phlegm or blood, and pain in breathing. Keep the patient warm and give them frequent sips of hot water.

DISEASES

Infectious diseases are caused by bacteria (e.g. cholera, dysentery, tuberculosis), viruses (colds, 'flu, measles) and rickettsiae (e.g. typhus). Such contagious diseases are unlikely to occur unless you have brought them with you or you catch them from humans you encounter.

HEALTH

The survivor is more likely to be exposed to waterborne diseases, or those carried by insects and animals. Tropical diseases are less familiar and will therefore be dealt with here in more detail. Where drugs are not available, treatment is largely a matter of dealing with symptoms and making the patient comfortable.

Prevention is better than treatment. To avoid disease:

- Get all suitable immunisation before travelling.
- Purify drinking water.
- Clean hands when preparing or eating food.
- Wash and peel fruit.
- Sterilise eating utensils.
- Cover body to reduce risk of insect bites.
- Wash and smoke louse-ridden clothes.
- Wash body, but avoid swallowing water.
- Bury excreta.
- Protect food and drink from flies and vermin.

Isolate outbreaks of infectious diseases. Keep contact with other members of group to minimum; boil all utensils used by the patient; cover cuts and sores against exposure to infection. Wash thoroughly after treating the patient. Avoid mucus from coughs and sneezes. Take special care disposing of patient's faeces where they cannot spread infection or be disturbed.

Boil all water, even for cleaning teeth. Cover wounds and avoid standing in water in areas at risk.

HEALTH

WORLDWIDE DISEASES

LEPTOSPIROSIS: Spread by rodents and infected water. Causes serious form of jaundice. Gains entry through cuts or sores, or in contaminated drinking water.

Symptoms: Jaundiced appearance, lethargy, fever.

Treatment: Procane penicillin and Tetracycline.

INFECTIOUS HEPATITIS: Passed on through infected faeces or urine. Enters via contaminated water, and through cuts in skin.

Symptoms: Nausea, loss of appetite, abdominal pain. Skin usually turns yellowish.

Treatment: Rest and good nursing are the only treatment.

POLIOMYELITIS: Spread by contaminated drinking water.

Symptoms: Paralysis.

Treatment: Hot packs on muscles and good nursing.

BACILLARY DYSENTERY: Spread by flies, contaminated water and contact with faeces containing the bacillus.

Symptoms: Blood-streaked faeces, sudden high temperature.

Treatment: Antibiotics, rest, and plenty of fluids to counter risk of dehydration due to loss of body fluids.

ENTERIC (TYPHOID) FEVER: Caused by a salmonella bacillus.

Symptoms: Similar to dysentery, with headaches, abdominal pains, fever, loss of appetite, pains in limbs and delirium.

Treatment: Antibiotics. Inoculation will prevent it.

CHOLERA: A threat anywhere in insanitary conditions.

Symptoms: Vomiting, loss of pulse at wrist, cold clammy skin and muscle cramps.

Protection: Can be obtained by regular innoculation with cholera vaccine.

HEALTH

WARM CLIMATE DISEASES

WATERBORNE DISEASES

BILHARZIA: Disease of bowel or bladder caused by microscopic worm endemic in parts of Africa, Arabia, China, Japan and S. America. Enters body through infected drinking water or through broken skin.
Symptoms: Irritation of urinary tract.
Treatment: Niridazole in recommended doses.

HOOKWORMS: Gain entry through infected drinking water or penetrate bare skin (usually feet). Larvae may cause pneumonia. The worms live in the intestine.
Symptoms: Anaemia and general lethargy.
Treatment: Alcapar and Mintazol in recommended doses. A decoction of bracken is a powerful de-wormer.

AMOEBIC DYSENTERY: Transmitted through contaminated water and uncooked food.
Symptoms: Fatigue, listlessness. May produce a temperature. Faeces may be solid but will smell foul and carry blood and jelly-like red mucus.
Treatment: Plenty of fluids, rest and treatment with Flagyl.

INSECTBORNE DISEASES

To reduce risk keep skin covered, sleep under a mosquito net, use insect repellents, and do not camp near swamps or stagnant water. A course of tablets, begun before exposure, can protect against malaria.

MALARIA: Not restricted to the tropics. Transmitted through saliva of female anopheles mosquito. It kills over a million people a year in Africa alone.

Symptoms: Recurrent fever. Although sweating, patient feels intensely chilled and shivers violently. There are various strains with severe headaches, malaise and vomiting accompanying the fever and leaving patient weak and exhausted.

Treatment: A number of drugs are available, including Larium, Paludrine, and now Malarone which has proved to be 98 per cent effective. Ask your doctor which is most appropriate for you.

DENGUE: Spread by mosquito.
Symptoms: Headaches, pains in the joints and a rash. Full recovery may take weeks. One attack usually confers immunity.
Treatment: Rest. There is no vaccine or cure.

YELLOW FEVER: Prevalent in Africa, South America.
Symptoms: Headaches, limb pains and fever. Heart-beat may be slow. In severe cases: pain in legs, back and neck. Rapid liver damage may lead to jaundice and kidney failure.
Treatment: Rest and nursing. There is no effective drug. Obtain vaccination before travelling.

TYPHUS: Epidemic typhus is carried by body lice, while endemic typhus is transmitted by the rat flea.
Symptoms: Headache, nausea, and a rash from the armpits to the chest, abdomen and thighs. Victims may recover after about 12 days, or fall into delirium, coma, or death.
Treatment: Antibiotics. There is also a vaccine available.

> Small parasites which burrow beneath skin, e.g. larvae of warblefly, or the chigoe, should be removed before they can open up a route for further infection. Chigoes penetrate the skin of the feet or lower leg leaving red pinpricks in the skin. Remove creatures with a needle and apply antiseptic ointment to the affected area.

HEALTH

WARM CLIMATE AILMENTS

PRICKLY HEAT: Heavy sweating, coupled with rubbing by clothing, produces blockages in sweat glands.
Symptoms: Uncomfortable skin irritation.
Treatment: Remove clothing, wash body with cool water and put on dry clothes. Taking more liquid may make it worse. Antihistamine relieves discomfort.

HEAT CRAMPS: Often first warning of heat exhaustion.
Symptoms: Shallow breathing, vomiting, dizziness.
Treatment: Rest in shade. Drink water with a pinch of salt.

HEAT EXHAUSTION: Caused by exposure to heat and humidity. Can occur without direct exposure to sun.
Symptoms: Pale face, cold and clammy skin, weak pulse; with weakness, dizziness, and perhaps cramps. Delirium or unconsciousness may follow.
Treatment: As for cramps.

HEATSTROKE: The most serious result of heat exposure.
Symptoms: Hot dry skin; flushed, feverish face, but sweating stops. Temperature rises, pulse rapid and strong. Severe head-ache, often with vomiting. Unconsciousness may follow.
Treatment: Lay in shade, head and shoulders slightly raised. Remove outer clothing. Cool body by wetting underclothes with tepid (not cold) water and fanning. Do not fully immerse in water — sprinkle it over patient. Lay in well-ventilated hollow. When consciousness returns administer water to sip. When temperature returns to normal, replace clothing, keep warm.

    Immersion in cold water is very dangerous, but in extreme cases, where risk of death or brain damage outweighs shock, use after initial cooling takes effect, lowering slowly into water.

Massage extremities to increase blood flow. Remove from water as soon as temperature falls. Cover patient if it plummets. You may need to cool and cover several times before temperature stabilises.

COLD CLIMATE HAZARDS

Prolonged exposure to cold is dangerous anywhere.

HYPOTHERMIA: Loss of temperature due to exposure. Brought on by exhaustion, inadequate clothing or shelter, lack of food, lack of knowledge and preparation. Wet clothing or immersion in cold water will aggravate it, as will anxiety, stress, and injuries that immobilise.

Symptoms: Irrational behaviour: sudden bursts of energy followed by lethargy. Slowing of responses, sudden uncontrolled fits of shivering. Loss of coordination. Headaches, blurred vision and abdominal pains. Collapse or unconsciousness.

Treatment: Prevent further heat loss. Shelter from elements. Replace wet garments with dry, one item at a time. Apply warmth (other bodies, warm rocks). Place warmth in pit of stomach, small of back, armpits, back of neck, wrists, between thighs. Give warm fluids and sugary foods, but only if fully conscious. Do not administer alcohol. The patient is not cured when temperature returns to normal: recovery takes time.

> If heat is lost rapidly – rewarm rapidly.
> If heat is lost slowly – rewarm slowly.

FROSTBITE: Occurs when skin and flesh freeze. Affects all exposed parts of the body and regions furthest from heart: hands, feet, face. First sign is often a prickly feeling, then waxy patches on skin which feel numb (later turning hard, pebbly, and painful, swelling,

HEALTH

reddening and blistering before deadening and dropping off in final stage).

Prevention: *Keep a constant lookout for signs: act at first appearance of waxy skin. Grimace to exercise face, flex hands, stamp feet. Never go out without adequate clothing. Avoid getting wet. Never touch metal with bare hands. Avoid spilling petrol on bare flesh in sub-zero temperatures.*

Treatment: *Frostnip affects only the skin: warm the affected part (it will be painful when thawed). Deep frostbite should be gradually thawed with warm water at about the temperature which your elbow can comfortably bear. Do not rub with snow or expose to an open fire. Protect affected area from greater injury. Advanced frostbite may form blisters which can turn to ulcers. Do not burst blisters and never rub affected part. Use 'animal warmth' to warm gradually; severe pain indicates it has been warmed too quickly.*

SNOW BLINDNESS: Temporary blindness. Can occur even in bright overcast periods with no direct sunlight.

Symptoms: *Eyes become sensitive to glare; blinking and squinting begins. Vision takes on pink/red hue. Eyes feel gritty.*
Treatment: *Get into dark place and blindfold eyes. Apply cool damp cloth to forehead. The condition is self-correcting.*

TRENCH FOOT: Occurs when feet are immersed or are damp and cold for long periods. To prevent: keep feet dry, wear well-fitting boots, exercise feet and legs.

Symptoms: *Pins and needles, then numbness interspersed with sharp pains. Feet appear purple with swelling and blisters.*
Treatment: *Dry the feet, but do not rub or damage blisters. Elevate feet and keep warm. Do not apply artificial heat. Do not massage. Rest and warmth are the cure.*

NATURAL MEDICINE

Natural remedies can be used when medical supplies are exhausted, or to supplement your store. Urine can be used as an antiseptic to wash out wounds. Maggots will keep a wound open and clean until better treatment can be given (make sure they do not devour good tissues).

PLANT PREPARATIONS

Many modern drugs are derived from plants but the processes are complex, and attempts to use such plants in treatment could be very dangerous. What follows is a list of plants and medical uses to which they can be put in simple preparations. Identify plants carefully. As a general rule, plants are most potent when in flower. Different parts may have different uses. Larger or stronger doses may do more harm than good.

TO MAKE AN INFUSION: Cut and crush herb, pour boiling water over it, stir and leave to cool. No need to strain – herbs will sink to bottom. If you can't boil water, use half the amount of cold and stand vessel in sun. Use a scant handful of herbs to ½ litre (¾ pint) water (30g to 50cc/ 1oz to 20fl oz). If there is no sun or water, suck or chew leaves to extract the juices, then spit out the pulp.

TO MAKE A DECOCTION: Cut, scrape and mash roots. Soak in water (handful to 85cc/1½ pints) for half hour. Bring to boil, simmer until liquid reduces by one third.

TO MAKE A POULTICE: Mash up roots, leaves or entire plant and make into a flat pad. Add water if too dry. Apply to affected part (stiff joints, sprains, abscesses) and cover with large leaf. Bind in position.

HEALTH

EXPRESSED JUICE: Reduce stem and leaves to juicy mush by crushing with hands, rocks or sticks. Squeeze juice only into a wound and spread pulp around infected area. Keep in place with large leaf and bind.

REMEDIES FOR COMMON PROBLEMS

STOPPING BLEEDING:

Giant puffball: *Packed as poultice*

Plantain: *Pounded leaves as poultice*

CLEANSING RASHES / SORES / WOUNDS: Use externally to bathe 2 or 3 times a day or, if indicated, as a poultice.

Burdock: *Decoction of root; crushed raw root & salt for animal bites*

Chickweed: *Expressed juice of leaves*

Comfrey: *Decoction of root as poultice*

Dead-nettle: *Infusion of flowers and shoots*

Dock: *Crushed leaves*

Elder: *Expressed juice of leaves*

Oak: *Decoction of bark*

Scurvy grass: *Crushed leaves*

Shepherd's purse: *Infusion of whole plant, except roots, as poultice*

Silverweed: *Infusion of whole plant, except roots*

Sorrel: *Crushed leaves*

Tansy: *Crushed leaves*

Watercress: *Expressed juice*

FEVERS: These plants will induce perspiration to break a fever.

Elder: *Infusion of flowers and fruit*

Lime: *Infusion of flowers*

ACHES / PAINS / BRUISES: Use externally where indicated.

Birch: *Infusion of leaves*

Borage: *Infusion of whole plant, except roots*

Burdock: *Decoction of root*

Chickweed: *Infusion of whole plant, except roots*

HEALTH

Comfrey: *Decoction of root applied to swellings*
Cowberry: *Infusion of leaves and fruits*
Dock: *Crushed leaves (bruises)*
Poplar: *Infusion of leaf buds*
Sorrel: *Crushed leaves applied to bruises*
Tansy: *Crushed leaves applied to bruises*
Willow: *Decoction of bark (headaches)*

COLDS / SORE THROATS / RESPIRATORY COMPLAINTS:

Angelica: *Decoction of root*
Bilberry: *Infusion of leaves and fruits*
Borage: *Infusion of whole plant, except roots*
Burdock: *Decoction of root*
Comfrey: *Infusion of whole plant*
Horseradish: *Raw root*
Lime: *Infusion of flowers*
Nettle: *Infusion of leaves*
Oak: *Decoction of bark; use as gargle*
Plantain: *Infusion of leaves and stems*
Poplar: *Infusion of leaf buds*
Rose: *Decoction of hips*
Willow: *Decoction of bark*

STOMACH UPSETS:

Bilberry: *Decoction of fruit*
Bracken: *Infusion of leaves*
Bramble: *Infusion of leaves*
Dandelion: *Decoction of whole plant*
Horseradish: *Infusion of root*
Mint: *Infusion of whole plant, except root, with crushed charcoal.*

DIARRHOEA: *Take two or three times daily until symptoms subside.*

Bilberry: *Decoction of fruit*
Bistort: *Infusion of whole plant, except roots*
Bramble: *Infusion of leaves or decoction of fruit*
Cowberry: *Decoction of fruit*
Great burnet: *Infusion of leaves and shoots*

HEALTH

   Hazel: *Infusion of leaves*
   Mint: *Infusion of whole plant, except roots*
   Oak *Decoction of bark*
   Plantain: *Infusion of leaves and stems*
   Silverweed: *Infusion of whole plant, except roots*

CONSTIPATION:
   Barberry: *Expressed juice of fruit*
   Couch grass (Elymus): *Decoction of root*
   Dandelion: *Decoction of whole plant*
   Elder: *Expressed juice of fruit*
   Rowan: *Expressed juice of fruit*
   Rose: *Decoction of hips*
   Walnut: *Decoction of bark*

HAEMORRHOIDS: *Apply externally, 2 or 3 times a day.*
   Bilberry: *Expressed juice of fruit*
   Oak: *Decoction of bark*
   Plantain: *Expressed juice*
   Poplar: *Decoction of leaf buds*
   Silverweed: *Infusion of whole plant, except roots*

EXPELLING WORMS:
   Bracken: *Infusion of roots*
   Tansy: *Infusion of leaves and flowers, use sparingly in small amounts*

SOME USEFUL HERBAL PREPARATIONS

• Headaches: Willow leaves and bark make a
decoction containing salicin, a constituent of aspirin.

• Healing: Expressed juice of comfrey leaves aids
tissue regrowth.

• Strawberry roots contain a descaler to clean teeth.

• Delphinium seeds can be crushed to treat head lice.

• Birch bark can be distilled to produce a tar oil which
soothes skin complaints.

TROPICAL MEDICINAL PLANTS

The following are a few of the many plants which may be of use, but lacking accurate data on medicinal plants you will do better to take medicines with you. Never experiment with plants you cannot positively identify.

Key
● Habitat ◆ Leaves ▲ Height ❖ Flowers

Copperleaf ● India, SE Asia ▲ 2–3m (6–10ft). ◆ heart-shaped, often variegated: red, pink and green. A decoction of roots and leaves of this shrub is laxative and restorative.

Alstonia ● India, Philippines, Indonesia, Australia. Boil bark in water for tonic to reduce fever, relieve diabetes and kill internal parasitic worms.

China Bark (Red Bark) ● tropics. Large trees, red-brown trunk. Decoction of quinine-containing bark for malaria.

Horseradish Tree ● tropics. Use expressed juice of roots and leaves to treat skin eruptions and inflammations.

Kibatalia arborea ● Asia. Tree. Bark, when cut, yields a latex-like sap. Use this sap, in small amounts, to treat worms.

Sida cordifolia ● India to Taiwan. An erect, downy annual. ▲ to 1m (3ft) tall, ◆ oblong toothed. ❖ yellowish. Use an infusion of leaves for coughs/fevers. Seeds are mildly laxative.

Pergularia extensa ● tropical Africa. Stems with stiff spreading hairs. ◆ broadly oval, up to 15cm (6in) long. ❖ small, greenish-white. Use tender leaves and shoots as a potherb or in a strong infusion to treat tapeworm and diarrhoea. Use a poultice of leaves on boils, abscesses and wounds.

Baobab (see p. 112) Use leaves to promote sweating to relieve colds, fevers and asthma and a decoction of the bark to suppress malaria.

Acacia (see p. 112) Scrape gum off the bark. Use to treat worms and diarrhoea.

Medicinal plants

These medicinal plants are found in temperate climates. Many are common and all are quite safe. They have been grouped under their most common applications.

General and antiseptics

1 **Eyebright** ● grassy places, mountains in Eurasia. ▲ to 30cm (12in) ◆ oval, often downy. ❖ white, tinged violet or purple veined with yellow spot. *Strained infusion of whole plant for eye infections. Also eases hay fever, catarrh and nasal congestion.*

2 **Garlic** ● temperate and tropical parts. ◆ long, strap-like. ❖ small, pink or white, on top of tall stem. The smell will lead you to them. *Bulb is antiseptic, use externally as expressed juice diluted with water for wounds and swellings. Eat garlic to treat and prevent colds.*

3 **Wild Thyme** ● dry, grassy places, western Eurasia. Mat-forming. ◆ oval, small. ❖ red-purple. *Use as infusion for coughs and colds, or as potherb.*

4 **Figwort** ● woods, clearings, scrub in Eurasia. ▲ to 90cm (36in). ◆ pointed oval. ❖ red-brown. Square stems. *Apply as decoction to reduce swellings, sprains, boils, to dissipate blood clots and to treat haemorrhoids.*

HEALTH

Bleeding

1 **Self-heal** ● dry, grassy waste places in Eurasia. Downy creeping plant. ◆ pointed oval. ❖ violet. *Use expressed juice to staunch bleeding or by infusion for internal haemorrhage.*

2 **Dove's foot Crane's bill** ● dry grassy wasteland. ◆ deeply lobed. Hairy stem. ❖ small, pink 5-petalled. *Use expressed juice to staunch bleeding or as decoction for internal haemorrhage.*

3 **Marsh woundwort** ● damp places, woods and shady wasteland. ▲ to 90cm (36in). Strong-smelling, hairy. ◆ toothed, heart-shape. ❖ White-blotched, dark pink to purple spikes. Similar species occur by woodland edges and shady waste places. *Use expressed juice to staunch bleeding, or infusion to bathe aches, sprains and wounds.*

4 **Sanicle** ● woodland in Eurasia. ▲ to 50cm (20in) ◆ hand-shaped, deeply lobed. ❖ tiny, white or pink. *Use expressed juice to staunch bleeding or by infusion for internal haemorrhage.*

5 **Greater periwinkle** ● woods, scrubland and rocky areas in Eurasia. ▲ to 50cm (20in) ◆ broad, spear-shaped. ❖ large, blue-violet. *Use expressed juice externally to staunch bleeding.*

HEALTH

Intestinal problems

1 **Mountain avens** ● mountainous rocky and northern Arctic areas. Resembles a creeping wild strawberry
◆ well-lobed, paler below.
❖ large white, yellow-stamened. *Use an infusion of stems, leaves and flowers for diarrhoea or as gargle.*

2 **Balm** ● grassy areas in warmer parts of Eurasia. ▲ to 60cm (24in).
● toothed, oval, green-yellow.
❖ small, white, occurring at leaf bases. *Use infusion of whole plant for fever and nausea. Can also be used to ease painful menstruation.*

3 **Water mint** ● near fresh water. ▲ to 80cm (32in).
◆ Aromatic, hairy, toothed, pointed oval. ❖ clusters, pink. *Use infusion of leaves for diarrhoea, and heated to induce perspiration in fevers. If too strong, infusion becomes emetic. Similar mints are also effective.*

4 **Elm** Tall trees ◆ large, oval, toothed. Green, disc-shape fruit. Often suckers at base of the trunk. *Use decoction of bark for diarrhoea and skin eruptions.*

HEALTH

5 **Cleavers** or **Goosegrass**
● Widespread on moist, woody and waste land. Straggling with long, prickly stems. ◆ narrow, prickly. ❖ small, white. *Use an infusion to ease constipation. Give frequent doses, mixed with marsh mallow for cystitis.*

6 **Agrimony** ● Dry, grassy places. ▲ to 90cm (36in). Downy stem. ◆ toothed, spear-shaped leaflets. ❖ yellow, on tall spike. *Use infusion of whole plant for constipation and acid stomach. Frequent small doses for cystitis.*

7 **Lesser celandine**
● wet woodland, damp areas. ▲ to 20cm (8in). ◆ shiny, dark green, heart-shaped. ❖ yellow. *Apply expressed juice externally for haemorrhoids; do not confuse with poisonous relative, the buttercup.*

8 **Solomon's seal** ● wood or scrubland. Small, patch-forming, with arching stems. ❖ tube-shaped, green-white. *Use decoction of root externally for haemorrhoids and bruises. Infusion for nausea. When boiled, root sets hard as makeshift splinting agent. An infusion or poultice of powdered root eases bruising. Berries are poisonous.*

HEALTH

Fevers, coughs and colds

1 **Camomile** ● grassy places in Eurasia. Aromatic, creeping. ◆ finely dissected ❖ daisy-like. *Use infusion of whole plant for fevers, headaches, migraines and colds, or expressed juice of flowers for aches and strains. Calming influence.*

2 **Colt's foot** ● bare or waste ground from late winter. ❖ large, yellow, dandelion-like. Asparagus-like stems. *Use infusion of leaves for colds and coughs.*

3 **Lungwort** ● mixed woods and scrub in Eurasia. ▲ to 30cm (12in). ◆ downy, pale-spotted spear-shaped. ❖ bell-shaped pink or purplish-blue. *An infusion of the whole plant for chest complaints and diarrhoea. For coughs use with equal parts of colt's-foot.*

4 **Horehound** ● dry scrubland in Eurasia. Thyme-scented, downy; squarish stems. ▲ to 50cm (20in) ◆ roundish, crinkly, greenish-white. ❖ white, in whorls. *Use infusion of whole plant for chills and respiratory disorders; oil expressed from leaves soothes earache. Good cough remedy for infants. In large doses it is a laxative.*

5 **Yarrow** ● grassy places. Downy, aromatic. ▲ to 60cm (24in) ◆ dissected, feathery, dark green. ❖ white or pink, tiny. *Use infusion of whole plant, but not roots, for colds and fevers. Hastens clotting of blood in an injury and reduces blood pressure and bleeding in haemorrhoids.*

HEALTH

6 **Musk mallow** ● grassy, scrubby places. ▲ Hairy stem to 60cm (24in) ◆ deeply divided. ❖ large, pink, five-petalled. Widespread, many varieties. *Use as marsh mallow (below).*

7 **Tree mallow** ● rocky coastal areas Europe to Asia Minor. ▲ to 3m (10ft). Hairy stem, woody at base. ◆ ivy-shaped. ❖ pink-purple, streaked darker purple. *Use as marsh mallow (below).*

8 **Marsh mallow** ▲ to 90cm (36in). Downy grey. ◆ large lobed. ❖ pale pink. Root edible cooked. *Use infusion of whole plant for chest complaints or one of root to relieve giddiness from loss of blood and to clean wounds. Rub insect bites with bruised leaves; boil leaves as poultice for skin eruptions.*

9 **Great mullein** ● dry, warm grassy places. ▲ to 2m (6.5ft) Covered in pale woolly down. ◆ large spear-shaped. ❖ yellow, 5-petalled, in a dense spike. *Use infusion of flowers and leaves for coughs and chest complaints, or decoction of root as gargle. Powder flowers for pain-relieving tea.*

10 **St John's wort** ● open woods, grassland. ▲ to 60cm (24in). ◆ small, oblong, translucently spotted. ❖ golden-yellow flower which exudes a red juice when crushed. *Use infusion of whole plant for colds and chest complaints.*

HEALTH

BITES AND STINGS

These creatures are not a major problem but should be treated with respect.

1 **Scorpion** ● tropical/sub-tropical regions, lives under tree bark, rocks, etc. Colour varies from yellow to brown or black. Most are nocturnal. Cornered or crushed scorpions may sting repeatedly. *Venom is neuro-toxic, causing respiratory or cardiac problems. Seldom fatal in adults.*

2 **Recluse Fiddleback spider** ● Asia, US, S. America, Europe. Brown with 'violin' mark on centre of mid-section. *Bite causes burning sensation at first, then pain increases, wound turns red and blisters. May be fatal if kidneys are affected. Can lead to amputation if untreated.*

3 **Black Widow Hourglass spider** ● warm areas, worldwide. Small, dark, recognisable by red, yellow or white hourglass-shaped markings on abdomen. *Bites cause dull pain in limbs, chest and abdomen. Nausea, cramps, vomiting follow. Fatal in children.*

4 **Funnelweb** ● Australia. Small, black spider. Spins funnel-shaped web. *Fangs can penetrate clothing. A bite can kill an adult in 90 minutes.*

5 **Tarantula** ● Large hairy spider. Despite menacing appearance, the poison is mild and causes skin irritation.

1 ☠

2 ☠

3 ☠

4 ☠

5 ☠

6 **Centipede** ● worldwide under stones, in piles of wood and damp places. Most are small and harmless, but some tropical and desert kinds may reach 25cm (10in). Their feet have sharp claws which can puncture skin and cause infections. Some species' bites cause swellings and infections. *Do not swat with bare hands. Brush off in the direction they are moving.*

7 **Hornet** Swarms guard nests ferociously. Very aggressive, the killing of a single worker can disturb the whole colony. They will chase over some distance, inflicting numerous stings. Avoid. *Painful sting – several at once could be fatal.*

8 **Tick** ● common in tropics; flat-bodied and round. *Do not pull off: head will remain and cause infection. Use heat, petrol, alcohol or hot water to make it drop off.*

9 **Leech** ● jungles and moist areas. Blood-sucking worm-like creature. Waits, thread-like, on vegetation before attaching itself to a victim. *Do not pull off: remove with fire or a pinch of salt. Leeches often carry infections.*

10 **Vampire bat** ● Central and South America. Small, nocturnal, sucks blood of sleeping victims. *Bites may carry rabies. Keep covered at night in these areas.*

HEALTH

POISONOUS SNAKES: SAFETY RULES

• Do not approach, provoke or handle snakes – even if they seem to be dead. Some only move to strike when prey is close – and they can strike faster than you can!

• Watch where you step: after eating, and when shedding skin, snakes are sluggish, and a well-camouflaged one is easily trodden on.

• Look closely before parting bushes or picking fruit. Some snakes are arboreal.

• Stay calm: do not move suddenly or corner a snake.

• Back off slowly. Most snakes will be eager to escape

• Do not put hands or feet in places you can't see. Use tools or sticks, not hands, to turn over logs and rocks.

• Wear stout boots.

• Check bedding, clothes, and packs before putting them on – snakes may use them as shelter.

• If you have to kill a snake, use a long stick to make a single, chopping blow to the back of the head. Make it effective first time – a wounded snake is highly dangerous.

• Not every snake is poisonous, nor do poisonous species always inject venom when they bite. Effects of bites vary depending on age, health and fitness of victim. Most bites are on arms or on unprotected legs.

• Spitting snakes: a few cobras spit poison as well as bite. This is not dangerous unless the poison reaches an open cut or the eyes. If this happens, wash out immediately with water or, in an emergency, with urine.

• What to do if bitten by a snake: see pp. 319–20.

POISONOUS SNAKES

North and South America

1 **Rattlesnake** Chunky body, wide head. Rattle at end of tail usually but not always sounded as warning. Widespread in USA and Mexico. The largest are the various diamondbacks, with distinctive blotches. 45cm–2.1m (18in–7ft). *Very dangerous.*

2 **Copperhead** Stout body, buff or orange-brown with rich-brown bands and copper-red head. Mainly in eastern USA. 60–90cm (24–36in) long. Fairly timid, it vibrates its tail if angry. *Bites rarely fatal.*

3 **Cottonmouth (Water moccasin)** Thick brown or brown-olive body, yellowish belly, sometimes blotched. Inside of mouth is white. 60–130cm (24–51in). Aquatic, found in or by freshwater in the southern USA. *Belligerent – do not annoy! Victims may suffer tissue damage necessitating amputation.*

4 **Cascabel (Tropical rattlesnake)** Diamond-shaped marks, two dark stripes on neck and rattle on tail. 1.5–2m (5–6ft). Nocturnal. Dry areas; South and Central America. *Aggressive, one of the world's most dangerous snakes.*

HEALTH

5 **Fer de Lance** Brown with paler
geometric markings. 1.3–2m (4–6ft).
Various related species in South and
Central America. Some are
arboreal. *The cause of many deaths.*
Tend to loop body before striking.

5 ☠

6 **Bushmaster** Large-headed,
pink-brown with dark brown
triangles. 2–2.6m (6–8ft).
Nocturnal. Lowland forests in Central
and S.America. Often in burrows.
Vicious when cornered, one of the
most feared of all New World snakes.

6 ☠

7 **Coral snake** Slender, strikingly
coloured with bands of black and red,
yellow and white. Southern USA
to South America. Similar species
in south-east Asia. 45–90cm
(18–36in). *Small-mouthed, reluctant*
to bite, but deadly.

7 ☠

Europe

1 **Adder** Only poisonous snake of
N. Europe. Found on heaths, moors
and in open areas. Olive-grey to red-
brown with zigzag pattern. 30–75cm
(12–30in). *Timid, but strikes quickly and*
repeatedly if alarmed. Bite rarely fatal.

1 ☠

HEALTH

Africa and Asia

1 **Puff adder** Thick-bodied, large-headed, short-tailed. 90–130cm (36–51in). Straw-brown with darker markings. Found in savannah and semi-arid areas, often near water, Africa and Arabian peninsula. *Very poisonous – bite causes extensive internal bleeding.*

2 **Saw-scaled viper** Rough-scaled, pale reddish to sandy-brown with darker markings and light blotches. 40–55cm (16–22in); in arid areas from North Africa to India. *Vicious; causes many fatalities.*

3 **Russell's viper** Brownish, with three rows of spots formed of white-bordered black rings with a reddish-brown centre. 102–127cm (40–50in). Found in most areas of Asia from Pakistan east to Taiwan. *Responsible for the majority of viper bites in the area. Highly venomous.*

4 **Malay pit viper** Fawn, reddish or grey marked with geometric patterns, the belly yellowish or spotted greenish-brown. 60–80cm (24–32in). South-east Asia and Indonesia. *Bites are common. This snake has many relatives in area, so avoid any that resemble it.*

HEALTH

5 Cobra When alarmed, recognisable by raised head and spreading hood. Common, especially in rocky and semi-arid areas of Asia, Middle East to Far East. 1.5–2m (5–6ft). *Highly toxic venom.*

6 Mamba Small-headed, very slender, usually with large green or greyish scales. 1.5–2.1m (5–7ft); in Africa south of the Sahara, usually in trees. The large Black Mamba is mostly terrestrial. *Often quick to strike, Black Mambas deliver large doses of venom which affect the brain and heart. Bites fatal in almost all untreated cases.*

7 Boomslang Very slender, varying from green to brown or black. 1.3–1.5m (4–5ft). Hard to spot, lives in trees in savannah parts of Africa south of the Sahara. *Highly venomous; it inflates its throat when alarmed.*

8 Krait Small-headed, some have black and white or black and yellow bands. 90–150cm (36–60in). In open and forest areas, India to Indonesia. Nocturnal. *Slow to strike, but its venom is especially powerful. Bite is almost painless. Symptoms may take several hours to develop, by which time it may be too late. Can be fatal.* Its ocean-dwelling relative, the banded sea krait, is found in the Bay of Bengal, off Japan and around the coasts of Australia and New Zealand. Venom is twice as toxic as that of cobra.

HEALTH

Australasia

Of the 23 most poisonous snakes in the world, 20 are Australian, including all the top ten.

1 **Death adder** Thick-bodied, brownish, reddish or grey with darker banding. 45–60cm (18–24in). In sandy areas of much of Australia, Papua New Guinea and some nearby islands. Well camouflaged. *Highly venomous.*

2 **Australian black snake** Slender, blue-black with bright red belly. 1.5–2m (5–6ft). In or near freshwater. *Rarely fatal. Flattens neck when aroused.*

3 **Eastern brown snake** Slender, yellowish-grey to brown with a pale belly. 1.5–2m (5–6ft). Found in dry areas of eastern Australia. *Easily roused and when antagonised, strikes repeatedly. The world's second most poisonous snake.*

4 **Tiger snake** Thick-bodied, large-headed, tawny-ochre bands with greenish-yellow, grey or orange-brown. 1.3–1.6m (4–5.5ft). Found in semi-arid areas from Southern Queensland down to New South Wales (where it's black rather than brown). Nocturnal on warm summer nights. *Aggressive, the world's fourth most poisonous snake.*

HEALTH

5 **Taipan** Uniformly light to dark brown with yellowish-brown on sides and belly. Found from Kimberleys through Arubauland to Queensland. Up to 3.5m (11ft). *Ferocious when provoked.World's third most poisonous snake.* Its relative the western taipan or small-scaled snake is considered to be the most lethal land snake in the world.

6 **Yellow-bellied sea snake** One of most widely distributed of all sea snakes, it averages 72–88cm (28–35in). Like most other sea snakes, it occurs in the Indian and Pacific Oceans. Some sea snakes are partly terrestrial, living in estuaries and coastal swamps. *The highly toxic venom of the yellow-bellied sea snake causes respiratory paralysis. Can be fatal.*

LIZARDS

1 **Gila monster** Large rounded head, thick chunky body, short stumpy tail and brightly patterned in yellow. Found in deserts of Arizona, Mexico and nearby areas. 37–45cm (15–18in). *The bite is poisonous but likely only when handled.*

2 **Beaded lizard** resembles the gila monster but is darker and larger, with a slenderer tail, and spots rather than a mottling of colour; in a few arid parts of Mexico and Central America. *Docile, but the bite is poisonous. Do not handle.*

HEALTH

CROCODILES AND ALLIGATORS

• Crocodiles and alligators are amphibious, living on the banks of lakes, streams and swamps. Not all species are considered dangerous, but do not take chances.

• Most float almost submerged with only eyes and nostrils breaking the surface of the water. They are lazy creatures, but will attack large mammals including man, pulling their prey beneath the surface to drown. On land, despite their short legs, they are capable of a considerable show of speed over short distances. They hunt mainly at night, sunning themselves during the day.

• Do not swim, especially at night, in crocodile or alligator areas, and never during the rainy season (when most documented attacks have occurred).

• When in croc country, stick to 'safe' areas. Do not allow children to go near the water or roam unsupervised, do not clean fish near the water, and do not go near nests or groups of baby crocodiles – the mother may not be far away.

American alligator Southeastern USA (Florida and Louisiana). Average length: 4m (13ft).

African crocodile Throughout tropical Africa (including offshore islands) in salt and freshwater. 5m (16ft).

Saltwater crocodile India, Malay archipelago, Australia, in coastal rivers and swamps as well as saltwater. Grows to 7m (23ft). An infamous man-eater.

Mugger (Marsh crocodile) Still common in parts of India (and considered sacred). Up to 3m (10ft) in length.

Black caiman Amazon and Orinoco basins. Largest of the caimans, it is big enough to pose a threat to man.

HEALTH

DANGEROUS WATER CREATURES

RIVERS

1 **Electric eel** Native to Orinoco and Amazon river systems of S. America. 2m (7ft) long and 20cm (8in) thick. Rounded body, olive to black, pale belly. Often prefer shallow water. *The shock from a large one can be 500 volts, enough to knock a man off his feet and to pose a threat to swimmers.*

2 **Piranha** Orinoco, Amazon and Paraguay river systems of South America. Vary in size, up to 50cm (20in) long. All are deep-bodied and thickset, having large jaws with razor-sharp interlocking teeth. *Can be very dangerous, particularly in the dry season when the water levels are low.*

SEAS AND RIVERS

3 **Stingray** A danger in shallow waters worldwide. Very variable, but all have distinctive ray shape. *Venomous spines in the tail can inflict severe injury. Amputation or death may result.*

SALTWATER

4 **Rabbitfish** or **Spinefoot** Occur mainly on reefs in Indian and Pacific Oceans. 25–30cm (10–12in). Edible but with sharp spines in most fins. *Venomous. Handle with care.*

1 ☠

2 ☠

3 ☠

4 ☠

HEALTH

TROPICAL WATERS

1 **Tang** or **Surgeonfish** Found in all tropical waters, where they often form large schools. 20–25cm (8–10in). Deep-bodied, small-mouthed, colourful. *Small venom glands in dorsal spines, but danger comes from razor-sharp tail, which in some species opens like a flick knife.*

2 **Toadfish** Occur in tropical, sub-tropical and temperate waters. 3–4cm (7–10in). Dull-coloured and large-mouthed. Lie buried in sand. *Sharp, very poisonous spines on side of head.*

3 **Scorpionfish** or **Zebrafish** On reefs in the tropical Indian and Pacific Oceans. 10–20cm (4–8in). Very variable, but usually reddish with long, wavy fin rays and spines. *A sting is intensively painful. Heart failure may result.*

4 **Stonefish** Occur in tropical Indo-Pacific waters. 40cm (16in). Their drab colours and lumpy shape make them difficult to see. *When trodden on, dorsal spines inject venom that is agonisingly painful, causing convulsions and paralysis. Recovery may take months, and stings are sometimes fatal.*

HEALTH

The sharks shown here have been known to attack man (see pp. 268–69).

1 **Great White Shark** or **White Pointer** Off Southern Africa, N. America, southern Australia and NZ. Up to 6m (18ft). Grey above, white below, thick-bodied; black eyes, with a stubby conical snout.

2 **Mako** or **Blue Pointer** or **Mackerel Shark** Warm temperate waters of Australia, NZ, South Africa. Averages 2–3m (6–10ft); sturdy body; ultramarine blue above, creamy-white below. *A fast swimmer, capable of leaping 6m (18ft) out of the water.*

3 **Tiger Shark** Tropical to subtropical waters, often close inshore. 3–3.5m (10–11ft); heavy bodied, wide head, abrupt snout, long tail; barred or botched above when young, evenly greyish when mature, white below. *Powerful and aggressive.*

HEALTH

4 **Barracuda** Tropical waters. Not a shark but a thin, torpedo-like fish, growing up to 2m (6ft). Bluish-barred above, brilliant silver below; with protruding mouth and sharp teeth. *Very fast, often in shoals, usually dangerous only when there is blood in the water.*

5 **Hammerhead Shark** Tropical and subtropical waters. Up to 6m (18ft); hammer-shaped head.

6 **Bull Shark** Tropical west Atlantic. Up to 4m (13ft); stout, grey above and white below. *Aggressive, dangerous in its liking for shallow water.*

7 **Nurse** Eastern Australian waters. Over 4m (13ft). Heavily built, large-finned, grey above, white below.

PROTECTION AGAINST SHARKS: Follow product instructions for shark repellent. May not be fully effective. Use only when situation is dire. Dissipates in water and becomes ineffective. Choose moment well. Can only be used once.

HEALTH

OTHER SEA CREATURES

1 **Portuguese Man-of-War** Mainly sub-tropical, it is common in Gulf Stream. Especially common in waters of high salinity, e.g. those around Australia and Florida. Floating bladder may be only 15cm (6in) long, but tentacles with their stinging cells can stream out for 12m (40 ft). *Stings are very painful and may cause breathing and swimming difficulties. Even dead ones can sting.*

2 **Blue-ringed octopus** Small, sometimes only fist-sized, found in shallow waters and pools off Australia. Venom causes swelling, dizziness and respiratory paralysis. *Apply artificial respiration. Treat all tropical reef octopuses with caution.*

3 **Cone shell** Sub-tropical and tropical gastropod with venomous harpoon-like barb which pokes through the narrow end of the shell. Varying shell patterns. *Do not touch. Can cause temporary paralysis and breathing difficulties leading to death within six hours.*

4 **Auger** or **Terebra** Found in temperate and tropical seas, it has a stinging barb, much thinner and longer than that of the cone shell. *Sting is not as serious as the cone's, but do not eat.*

5 **Weeverfish** Tapering, dull-coloured, 30cm (12in) long. Lie buried in shallow sandy bays along the coasts of Europe south to West Africa and the Mediterranean. *Venomous spines on back and gills cause disabling pain. Soothe it by applying very hot water. Risk of secondary infections and gangrene. Can be fatal.*

Poisonous to eat

1 **Porcupine fish** Occurs in all shallow tropical waters. 50–60cm (20–24in). Varieties differ somewhat in appearance, but when alarmed all inflate into a spiny ball. *The flesh is poisonous.*

2 **Puffer fish** Occurs in tropical and warmer temperate waters, a few kinds in rivers in south-east Asia and tropical Africa. Stout-bodied, rounded, 15–75cm (6–30in) long, most kinds with spines; when alarmed they puff into a ball. *Their blood, liver and gonads are poisonous; even a tiny quantity of the poison can kill.*

3 **Triggerfish** Occurs in huge variety, mostly in shallow tropical seas. Deep-bodied, compressed, usually under 60cm (24in), with very large, stout dorsal spines. *Many kinds are poisonous to eat. Avoid them all.*

HEALTH

SOME OTHER DANGEROUS SEA CREATURES

• Sea wasp (box jellyfish): a cube-shaped jellyfish 25cm (10in) across, clusters of tentacles at the corners up to 9m (30ft) long. Venom can be fatal. Avoid all jellyfish streamers, even when washed up on the beach.

• Many fish with dangerously sharp spines are hard to detect, except at close quarters. The spines usually occur on the back but may also be on fins on the side of the fish. Even a small spine can inflict a bad prick with consequent risk of infection. Large spines – and some spiny catfish grow as large as a man – are as effective as stiletto knives. Wade/step with caution.

• Sea urchins can also inflict painful injuries and sea anemones can sting.

• Toadfish, stonefish and scorpionfish (see p. 351) are edible. If you land one, strike it on the head and handle only when dead, and then with great care.

POISONOUS TO EAT

• Many inshore fish, living in reefs and lagoons, are poisonous to eat. Most of these are confined to the tropics, but wherever you are, be wary of eating any fish that you cannot positively identify.

• Some fish that are otherwise good to eat are inedible when taken from reefs and lagoons, where they will have absorbed poisonous substances.

• The most poisonous kinds, such as puffer fish, usually have rounded bodies with hard, shell-like skins covered in bony plates and spines. They also commonly have parrot-like mouths, small gill openings and either lack pelvic fins or have only a small one.

DISASTER STRATEGIES

Accidents and isolation are not the only causes of a survival situation. Many natural and man-made forces can produce disasters in which your survival skills and strategies will come into play.

PREDICTING DISASTER

Meteorological stations around the world study weather conditions 24 hours a day and play a major role in warning of disasters. Monitor weather broadcasts for advance warning of severe weather conditions and disasters such as flooding, hurricanes, volcanic eruptions and earthquakes.

DROUGHT

In temperate regions, if rainfall drops far below the normal, periodic drought may be produced. The resulting death of vegetation causes deprivation right through the food chains that are based upon it. If the drought becomes severe, dead and dying animals may pollute what water supplies still remain.

Fire risk

Corpses of dead animals should be buried in deep graves. Dry ground can be very hard, but burying is the best way to remove these possible sources of infection. The bodies could be burned, but since drought leaves everything tinder dry, a fire could easily get out of hand and, without water to check the flames, fire spreads rapidly. If you must have a fire, dig down to bare earth and keep the fire small and attended at all times.

DISASTER STRATEGIES

Hygiene

Lack of water for washing and sanitation poses a health risk. Sweating will help to keep pores open and free of dirt, but, even when you need all available water for drinking, try to clean your hands after defecation and before preparing food. Make a latrine near the camp (see pp. 195–96).

Store and conserve water

If a monsoon does not come, or a hot dry summer causes a parching of the earth, take precautions by storing as much water as possible and using it wisely. Keep it covered and shaded to avoid evaporation.

Dig a pit for a storage cistern in a shady spot, avoiding tree roots. Line it with a polythene sheet or with cement if available (but don't fill it up until the cement has had a chance to dry thoroughly). If there is clay in the area, dig a pit and line it with clay. If the clay or concrete is built into a partial dome, it will help to keep the contents cool and leave a smaller opening to keep covered.

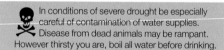

In conditions of severe drought be especially careful of contamination of water supplies. Disease from dead animals may be rampant. However thirsty you are, boil all water before drinking.

Never waste water. Water used for cooking can later be used for washing.

Boil all drinking water. If a well runs dry you may gain more water by digging deeper, but the further you dig, the more you deplete the water stored in the earth.

Try to eat foods with a high moisture content (such as fruit) and which require little preparation or clearing up afterwards.

Flies may be a serious problem – ensure that all foodstuffs are covered. Protect your supplies from dust, which may become a hazard as top soil is blown away.

 When nature is disturbed by a severe drought, animals are known to act abnormally. Crazed by thirst, normally docile creatures may attack you.

FIRE

The best protection from fire is prevention. Many fires are caused by carelessness with lighted cigarettes and burning matches. The sun shining through a piece of glass can start a blaze in a dry season.

FOREST FIRES

If you are present where a fire starts (or where a camp fire accidentally spreads) in woodland, or on heath or grassland, your first action should be to smother it.

The first sign of an approaching forest fire will be the smell of smoke. Then you will probably hear the fire before you see flames. You may notice unusual animal behaviour before you realise the cause.

Escape route

If caught in an area where fire is raging, and when it is far too late to put it out yourself, do not immediately flee – unless the fire is so close that there is no choice.

DISASTER STRATEGIES

Even though you may feel that clothing hampers your movement, do not discard it, for it will shield you from the full force of radiated heat.

Smoke will indicate the direction of the wind – the fire will be travelling fastest in that direction. If the wind is blowing away from you, towards the fire, move into the wind. Head for any natural fire break – such as a swathe through the trees, where the flames should be stopped. A river is the best break – even if the flames can leap it you will be reasonably safe in the water. In forestry plantations look for the firebreaks.

> Do not run wildly. Stop and think. Choose your escape route. Check the surrounding terrain and the wind direction to assess the possible spread of fire.

If the wind is blowing towards you the fire is likely to travel more quickly – and the flames can leap across a larger gap. Fire travels faster uphill so do not make for high ground. Try to go around the fire if you can, but some forest fires burn on a front several kilometres wide, making it impossible. If you can neither skirt nor outdistance the blaze take refuge in a large clearing, deep ravine, watercourse or gully.

Going to earth

If you can semi-immerse yourself in a creek, so much the better. However, if there is no natural break or gully in which to shelter and the fire is too deep to think of running through, you may have to seek the protection of the earth itself.

People have survived fires by digging themselves in and covering themselves with earth, allowing the fire to burn over the top of them. The risk is great, not just from heat but from suffocation: fire burns up oxygen.

Scrape as much of a hollow as you can, clearing away grass and foliage, and throwing the earth on to a coat or cloth if you have one. Lie face down and pull the cloth over you with its earth covering. Cup your hands over your mouth and nose and breathe through them. This won't increase the amount of oxygen, but it will cool down and filter the very hot air and sparks, which can damage the respiratory system. Try to hold your breath as the fire passes over.

STAY IN A VEHICLE

Don't try to drive through thick smoke. If caught in a fire in a vehicle, park in a clear area. Pull off the road, but don't risk getting bogged down. Turn on the headlights and stay inside the car. Wind windows tightly shut. Turn off the ventilation system and seal the air vents. The car will give you some protection from radiant heat. It is possible to survive by staying in a vehicle until the glass begins to melt, by which time the fire will have moved beyond you. There is a danger of a petrol tank exploding but, if the fire is intense, your chances are much better inside the vehicle than outside.

Fighting a forest fire

In forestry plantations you should see racks of fire-beating equipment at intervals along the main routes. This consists of bundles of twigs, tied in a broom, and spade-shaped beaters with rubber blades. They can be effective in putting out the beginnings of a blaze.

DISASTER STRATEGIES

Despite the name, do not beat rapidly with fire-beating equipment. Instead, smother the fire by bringing the beater down over the flames to extinguish them.

If no equipment is available use a coat or blanket to smother the fire, or use a leafy branch to beat it out.

Fight fire with fire

Provided it is still some distance away, it may be possible to use fire to create protection when there is no way of getting out of the path of a forest fire or going through it.

The technique is to burn a patch of ground before the main fire reaches it. With nothing left to ignite, the flames cannot advance, giving you a place of refuge. The main fire must be sufficiently far away for your fire to burn a space it cannot jump before it arrives.

Light your own fire along as wide a line as possible, at least 10m (33ft) wide, but 100m (330ft) would be better. It will burn in the same direction as the main fire, creating a break which you can move into. Make sure you determine the wind direction correctly.

BEWARE

Winds may be swirling and fires create their own draughts, so you may still have to make a dash through your own flames. The main fire must be far enough away for your own fire to burn and pass. Do not underestimate the speed at which flames travel – they may be approaching faster than you can run. Do not light another fire unless you are desperate and fairly certain of the outcome.

DISASTER STRATEGIES

Escaping through fire

Sometimes the best escape route may be to run through the flames. This is impossible if they are very intense and the area covered by the fire is great. In a large clearing or on heath land, however, it may be possible to run through less dense fire to refuge on the already burned-out land.

Thick vegetation burns fiercely – so choose the spot for your breakthrough with care. Make your mind up, then do not delay. Dampen a piece of cloth to cover your nose and mouth. Cover as much exposed skin as you can (including your head) with a blanket, curtain or overcoat. If you have water available, tip some over you to damp down clothing, hair and any flesh you have not been able to cover. Take a deep breath. Cover your nose and mouth to keep out smoke and run.

If your clothes catch alight do not stay on your feet when out of the fire. Flames and smoke will travel up your body, over your face and into your lungs.

Do not run if your clothes are ablaze – this will only fan the flames. Roll on the ground and try to wrap yourself in something that will smother the flames – a mat, blanket or overcoat.

If someone else comes running out of a fire with their clothes alight, push them to the ground and use the same methods of denying the flames oxygen. Do not hug them to you, or your clothes may catch fire.

DISASTER STRATEGIES

FIRES IN BUILDINGS

Block gaps round doors and windows. Close all blinds and curtains. Stay away from outside walls and don't be panicked into running out of the house when the fire reaches it.

Once the fire has passed, avoid excessive smoke inhalation, but go outside and put out any small fires.

VEHICLE FIRES

The greatest danger with cars is the risk of the fuel tank being ignited. The aim is to control the fire before it can reach the tank. Everything has a flash point and a fuel tank is more at risk than most things. Usually a fuel line (if not armoured) will catch fire first, acting as a fuse which eventually ignites the tank.

If a car catches fire in a confined space, smoke and toxic fumes will soon build up. Try to put the fire out first – but if that is not practicable remove the car from the building before it further endangers life and property. Do not get into the car. You can do everything from outside, including steering. If possible, push or pull the car out. If your car has a starter button, select a low gear or reverse and use the starter to bounce the car out. With conventional ignition, turn the key in short bursts. Be prepared for the car to jerk forward violently.

In a crashed car, doors may jam. If it catches fire get through any window or kick the windscreen out. If the fire is inside the car use the extinguisher or smother it with a rug or coat. Synthetic materials used in upholstery in many cars burn rapidly and give off thick smoke and toxic gases. These will persist even when the flames are extinguished, so get out into the air as soon as possible.

> **KEEP YOUR FIRE EXTINGUISHER HANDY!**
> There's no point having your fire extinguisher in the boot or trunk – keep it within immediate reach. Impact could distort the boot lid and prevent your opening it.

FIRES IN THE AIR

Aeroplanes are equipped with automatic extinguishers for engine fires and hand-held extinguishers in the cabin. Action should be taken immediately. On civil airlines summon a flight attendant immediately you suspect fire – the staff know where equipment is and how to use it. Avoid creating panic among other passengers. If you see smouldering or flames, smother with an airline blanket or clothing.

The main fire dangers are before take-off when there is volatile fuel and vapour around the plane, and especially when landing under difficult circumstances when fuel tanks could be ruptured and electrical or friction sparks ignite aviation spirit. Every safety precaution is taken to ensure that fire is not a hazard. You can help.

FLOOD

Flooding can occur for many reasons. It may be caused by the overflowing of rivers, lakes and reservoirs caused by heavy rains (not necessarily rainfall at the place where the flood occurs); by the build-up of sea or lake water due to

DISASTER STRATEGIES

the effects of submarine earthquake, hurricanes and freak high-tides and winds; or by the collapse or dams or dykes.

Heavy rain can rapidly produce torrents where there was a dry riverbed, or a build-up in a narrow channel or behind a barrier which then gives way to a rushing wall of water that envelops everything in its path.

Persistent rainfall over a long period after a dry spell and heavy storms should alert you to keep clear of water channels and low-lying ground, but a flood can affect much wider areas. It is always safer to camp on a spur. If the water is rising, move to higher ground. In hilly areas, keep out of valley bottoms which are particularly prone to flash floods.

Food is not likely to be a problem, at least at first, for animals will also head for high ground. Both predators and prey are likely to concentrate on getting to safety – but beware of injury from panic-stricken animals in the water.

Drinking water may be difficult to obtain, for the water swirling around you may be contaminated. Collect rainwater to drink, and boil any other water before you use it.

Flooded buildings

If you are in a building when the water begins to rise, stay where you are. You will be less at risk than if you are trying to evacuate on foot. Turn off gas and electricity and prepare emergency food supplies, warm clothing, and drinking water in well-sealed containers. Collect a torch, whistle, mirror and brightly coloured cloths for signalling, and add them to your gear with a camp stove, candles, and matches.

Move to an upper floor, or on to the roof in a single-storey building. If you are forced to occupy the roof, erect a shelter. If it is a sloping roof, tie everyone to a chimney-stack or other solid structure. If the water continues to rise, prepare some kind of raft. If you have no ropes, use bed sheets. Unless the water rises so high you are forced to evacuate, stay until it stops rising.

Evacuation

Seek shelter on higher ground. You don't have to be at the bottom of a hill to be on low ground!

When walking or driving to a safer location remember that a small drop in the level of the roadway down a hill can make a difference to the water depth.

If your car stalls, abandon it. You and your vehicle could be swept away.

Do not attempt to cross a pool or a stream unless you are certain that the water will not be higher than the centre of the car's wheels or your knees. If you must cross, use the river-crossing techniques explained on pp. 252–56. If crossing bridges which are underwater take especial care if flood has already swept part of the bridge away.

Flash floods

In a sudden heavy rainfall keep out of valley bottoms and stream beds both during and after rainfall. You don't have to be at the bottom of a hill to be caught by water rushing down it carrying mud and debris.

Coastal flooding

This is usually a combination of high tides and winds which make them even higher. Flood warnings will usually be given and evacuation is the best action.

Flood aftermath

Do not go outside until you know it's safe. More storms could be on the way.

As flood waters recede they leave a scene of devastation littered with debris and the bodies of flood victims. With decay and the pollution of the water comes the risk of disease. Take extra precautions: burn all animal corpses – do not risk eating them – and thoroughly boil all water before using. Some crops may still be available after the flood waters recede and birds that have escaped the flood will be safe and good to eat.

TSUNAMI

A tsunami, or tidal wave, is linked with an earthquake beneath the ocean, creating a series of waves which can reach more than 30m (98ft) high and travel vast distances causing damage along coasts. Not all earthquakes cause a tsunami, but any earthquake could.

Keep away from shores and take to higher ground when there are tremors. Do not go to look for a tsunami – if you are close enough to see one, you are too close to escape it, unless high above its level. There is no defence against a moving wall of water. Evacuate.

A tsunami is not one wave but a series. Do not return to the danger area after the first wave as you may be killed by the onslaught of a second or third.

AVALANCHE

There are several types of avalanche.

SOFT-SLAB AVALANCHE

Snow falling on lee slopes, often below a cornice, fails to settle and compact like the snow below. A gap forms behind. It may feel hard and safe but any disturbance or loud noise can set the whole slab in motion.

AIRBORNE AVALANCHE

Frequently the result of new snow falling on an already hard crust or in cold dry conditions. This may begin as a slab avalanche, but gathers momentum and more powdered snow to reach very high speeds. Cover nose and mouth to stand a chance of survival – death is caused by drowning from inhaling snow.

WET-SNOW AVALANCHE

More common in times of thaw, often following a rapid temperature rise after snowfall. It moves more slowly than an airborne avalanche, picking up trees and rocks in its path. When it stops it freezes solid almost instantly, making rescue very difficult.

Lay flat and use crawl stroke to keep on top of slide (the debris can form a very deep layer). Get rid of your pack and other burdens. Cover nose and mouth to avoid swallowing snow. When you come to rest, make as big a cavity around you as you can before the snow freezes, and try to reach the surface. Slip off any kit you have not been able to discard – it will hamper your extraction. Save your energy to shout when you hear people.

DISASTER STRATEGIES

HURRICANE

A hurricane is a wind of high speed – above force 12 on the Beaufort Scale – which brings torrential rain and can destroy any flimsy structures. It is a tropical form of cyclone, which in more temperate latitudes would be prevented from developing in the upper levels of the air by the prevailing westerly winds.

Hurricanes are known by various names around the world:
Hurricane: Caribbean and North Atlantic, eastern North Pacific, western South Pacific.
Cyclone: Arabian Sea, Bay of Bengal, southern Indian Ocean.
Typhoon: China Sea, western North Pacific.
Willy-willy: Northwest Australia.

Hurricanes develop over the ocean when sea temperatures are at their highest, especially in late summer. Warm air creates a low pressure core around which winds may rotate at speeds up to 300kph (186mph) or more, circling anticlockwise in the northern hemisphere, clockwise in the southern. The strongest winds are usually 16–19km (10–12 miles) from the centre of the hurricane but the centre, or eye, brings temporary calm. The eye may be up to 500km (300 miles) in diameter. Hurricanes can occur at any time of year: in the northern hemisphere, the main season is June to November, and in the southern, November to April (especially January and February). Hurricanes are not a feature of the South Atlantic.

Pattern of the hurricane

Out at sea hurricanes will build up force and begin to veer towards the Pole, the wind speed usually being greatest on the poleward side of the eye.

Hurricane warnings

Satellite surveillance enables meteorologists to track hurricanes and to warn of their approach. Some move very erratically, so monitor forecasts in hurricane areas.

Without radio to alert you, the growth of swell can indicate a hurricane, especially when coupled with other conditions such as highly coloured sunsets or sunrises; dense banners of cirrus cloud converging towards the vortex of the approaching storm; and abnormal rises in barometric pressure followed by an equally rapid drop.

DISASTER STRATEGIES

HURRICANE PRECAUTIONS

- Get out of the hurricane's path if you can. Hurricane warnings are usually issued when one is expected within 24 hours and will give you plenty of time to evacuate its path, if you are prepared.
- Keep away from the coast and from river banks.
- Board up windows and secure any objects outdoors that might be blown away.
- At sea take down canvas, batten down hatches and stow all gear.

If you are in a solid building and on high ground stay where you are – travel in a hurricane is extremely dangerous. The safest place is usually in a cellar or under the stairs. Do not shelter near an internal chimney breast – the chimney may collapse.

DISASTER STRATEGIES

Store drinking water — water and power supplies may be cut off by the storm — and have a battery-operated radio to listen for any instructions.

If you are not in a sturdy structure, evacuate to a hurricane shelter. Shut off power supplies before you leave.

> Do not drive in a hurricane. Cars offer no protection from high winds and flying debris.

Seeking shelter

Outdoors, a cave will offer the best protection. A ditch will be next best. If unable to escape, lie flat on the ground where you will be less of a target for flying debris. Crawl to the lee side of any really solid shelter such as a stable rocky outcrop or a wide belt of large trees. Beware of small trees and fences which could be uprooted.

> Stay where you are when the hurricane appears to have passed – there will usually be less than an hour of calm as the eye passes and then the winds will resume in the opposite direction. If sheltering outdoors move to the other side of your windbreak in preparation or move to better shelter if close by.

TORNADO

Tornadoes are the most violent of atmospheric phenomena and the most destructive over a small area. Wind speeds have been estimated at 620kph (385mph).

The diameter of the twister at ground level is usually only 25–50m (80–160ft) but, within it, the destruction is enormous. Everything in its path except the most solid structures is sucked up into the air. The difference in pressure outside and inside a building is often the cause of collapse. Tornadoes can sound like a spinning top or engine and have been heard up to 40km (25 miles) away. They travel at 50–65kph (30–40mph).

TORNADO PRECAUTIONS

• Take shelter in the most solid structure available – ideally in a storm cellar or cave. In a cellar stay close to an outside wall, or in a specially reinforced section. If there is no basement, go to the centre of the lowest floor, into a small room or shelter under sturdy furniture – but not where there is heavy furniture on the floor above. Keep well away from windows.

• Close all doors and windows on the side facing the oncoming whirlwind and open those on the opposite side. This will prevent the wind getting in and lifting the roof as it approaches, and equalise the pressure to prevent the house 'exploding'.

• Do not stay in a caravan or car, it could be drawn up in the storm. Outdoors you are vulnerable to flying debris and to being lifted up.

• You can see and hear a tornado coming. Get out of the way. Move at right angles to its apparent path. Take shelter in a ditch or depression, lie flat and cover your head with your arms.

LIGHTNING

Lightning can be especially dangerous on high ground or when you are the tallest object. In a lightning storm keep away from hill brows, from tall trees and lone boulders. Make for low, level ground and lie flat.

DISASTER STRATEGIES

Insulation

If you cannot get away from tall objects, sit on dry material which will provide insulation. A dry coil of climbing rope makes good insulation. Do not sit on anything wet. Bend your head down and hug your knees to your chest, lifting your feet off the ground and drawing in all your extremities. Do not reach down to the ground with your hands, that could give a contact to conduct the lightning. If you have nothing which will insulate you from the ground lie as flat as you can.

Stay low

You can sometimes sense that a lightning strike is imminent by a tingling in the skin and the sensation of the hair standing up on end. If you are standing up, you should drop to the ground at once, going first to the knees with the hands touching the ground. If you should be stuck, the charge may take the easiest route to the earth through your arms – missing the torso and possibly saving you from heart failure or asphyxiation. *Quickly lie flat.*

Do not hold metal objects when there is lightning about and keep away from metal structures and fences. However, do not jettison equipment if you will lose it altogether (when climbing, for instance). A dry axe with a wooden handle may spark at the tip, but is well insulated.

Proximity to large metal objects can be dangerous, even without contact, for the shockwave caused by the heated air – as the lightning passes – can cause damage to the lungs.

Shelter

One of the best places to shelter in a lightning storm is at least 1m (3ft) inside a deep cave with a minimum of 1m (3ft) space on either side of you.

Do not shelter in a cave mouth or under an overhang of rock in mountainous country. Lightning can spark across the gap. Small openings in the rock are frequently the ends of fissures which are also drainage routes and automatic lightning channels.

EARTHQUAKE

Earthquakes come suddenly, with little warning. Minor earth tremors can happen anywhere, but major quakes are confined to known earthquake belts.

With monitoring by seismologists, earthquakes can be predicted and evacuation may be possible. Animals become very alert, tense and ready to run.

A succession of preliminary tremors, known as foreshocks, often followed by a seismically quiet period, usually precede a major quake, which they can actually trigger. These initial tremors may not be noticeable.

DISASTER STRATEGIES

EARTHQUAKE PRECAUTIONS

• Stay tuned to a local radio station for up-to-date reports and advice if you have warning of a possible earthquake.

• Turn off gas, electricity and water if advised to do so.

• Remove large and heavy objects from high shelves.

• Have ready in case needed: freshwater and emergency food, a torch, first aid materials and a fire extinguisher.

EARTHQUAKE PRECAUTIONS

In a building

Stay indoors. Douse fires. Stay away from glass, including mirrors, and especially from large windows. An inside corner of the house, or a well-supported interior doorway, are good places to shelter. A lower floor or a cellar gives the best chance of survival. Make sure there are plenty of exits. Get under a table or large piece of furniture which will give both protection and an air space. In a shop keep away from large displays of goods. In high-rise offices never go into a lift. Staircases may attract panicking people. Get under a desk.

In a car

Stop as quickly as you can, but stay in the car – it will offer some protection from falling objects. Crouch down below seat level and you will be further protected if anything falls on the car. When the tremors cease, keep a watch for any obstructions and hazards such as broken cables and undermined roadways or bridges which could give way.

Outdoors

Lie flat on the ground. Do not try to run. You will be thrown about and could be swallowed in a fissure. Keep away from tall buildings and trees. Do not deliberately go underground or into a tunnel where you could be trapped by collapse. If you have managed to get to an open space do not move back into buildings for, if minor tremors follow, they could collapse any structure left unstable by the first quake.

On a hillside it is safer to get to the top. Slopes are liable to landslide and there would be little chance of survival. People have been known to survive by rolling into a tight ball on the ground.

Beaches – provided they are not below cliffs – are initially fairly safe but, since tidal waves often follow a quake, you should move off the beach to high open ground as soon as the tremor has finished. Further tremors are unlikely to be as dangerous as a tsunami.

Be calm and think fast: speed is essential if an earthquake strikes. There is little time to organise others. Use force if necessary to get them to safety or pull them to the ground.

AFTER THE EARTHQUAKE

Check yourself and others for injuries. Apply first aid if necessary.

Rupture of sewage systems, contamination of water and the hazards of the bodies trapped in the wreckage can all make the risk of disease as deadly as the earthquake itself. Bury all corpses, animal and human. Take special precautions over sanitation and personal hygiene. Filter and boil all water. Check that sewage services are intact before using lavatories.

Do not shelter in damaged buildings or ruins. Build a shelter from debris. Be prepared for after-shocks. Open cupboards carefully – objects may tumble out. Clean up spilled household chemicals and potentially harmful substances. Do not strike matches or lighters, or use electrical appliances, if there is any chance of a gas leak. Sparks ignite gas.

DISASTER STRATEGIES

VOLCANO

Active volcanoes are found in the areas of the world which are also most prone to earthquakes.

ERUPTION HAZARDS

Although it is possible to outrun most basalt lava flows they continue relentlessly until they reach a valley bottom or eventually cool off. They crush and bury anything in their path. Lava flows are probably the least hazard to life, for the able-bodied can escape them. Other hazards are more dangerous.

Missiles

Volcanic missiles, ranging from pebble-sized fragments to lumps of rock and hot lava, can be scattered over vast distances. Volcanic ash can cover an even greater area.

If evacuating from close to the volcano, hard helmets offer some protection. Over a wider area, evacuation may not be necessary, but protection should be worn against the ash and any accompanying rain.

Ash

Volcanic ash is pulverised rock forced out in a cloud of steam and gases. Abrasive, irritant and heavy, its weight can cause roofs to collapse. It smothers crops, blocks transport routes and watercourses and, combined with toxic gases, can cause lung damage to the very young, the old and those with respiratory problems. Only very close to an eruption are gases concentrated enough to poison healthy people. However, when ash is combined with rain, sulphuric acid (and other acids) are produced in concentrations which can burn skin, eyes and mucous membranes. Wear goggles which seal the area around the eyes (rather than sunglasses, which will offer no protection). Use a damp cloth over the mouth and nose, or, better still, industrial dust masks. On reaching shelter remove clothing, thoroughly wash exposed skin and flush eyes with clean water.

Gas balls

A ball of red-hot gas and dust may roll down the side of a volcano at speeds of more than 160kph (100mph). Unless there is an underground shelter nearby, the only chance of survival is to submerge yourself under water and hold your breath for the half-minute or so it will take to pass.

Mud flows

The volcano may melt ice and snow and cause a glacial flood or – combined with earth – create a mud flow, known as a lahar. This can move at up to 100kph (60mph), with devastating effect. In a narrow valley a lahar can be as much as 30m (98ft) high. They are a danger long after the major eruption is over and are a risk even when the volcano is dormant if it generates enough heat to produce meltwater retained by ice barriers. Heavy rains may cause it to breach the ice.

Volcanoes usually show increased activity before a major eruption. Sulphurous smells from rivers, stinging acidic rain, loud rumblings or plumes of steam from the volcano are all warning signs.

DISASTER STRATEGIES

> Remember that if evacuating by car: ash may make roads slippery, even if it does not block them. Avoid valley routes which could become the path of the lahar.

VEHICLES

Transport has an important role to play in disaster strategy. Make sure you know how to get the best use out of your vehicle in any situation.

BEFORE SETTING OFF

For desert travel, fit long-range fuel tanks and make provision for storing drinking water. Carry further supplies of both in jerry cans. A jack is no use in soft sand and an air bag should be carried which is inflated by the exhaust. Extra filters will be needed in the fuel line and air intake. Sand tyres must be fitted and sand channels carried to get you moving again when bogged down in loose sands.

For high altitudes adjust the carburettor. In scrub country, thorn gaiters will reduce puncture risks. Antifreeze and suitable wheels and chains are needed for snow and ice. The engine will need special tuning to match climatic conditions and its own spares. Carry a spare wheel and a good tool kit.

IN HOT CLIMATES

Overheating: Stop and allow the engine to cool. If you are driving on a particularly tricky stretch and stopping is out of the question, switch on the heater. This will give greater volume to the cooling water and, although the inside of the car will get even hotter, the engine will cool.

When convenient stop and open up the bonnet. Do not undo the radiator cap until the temperature drops. Check the radiator and all hoses for leaks. If the radiator is leaking, adding the white of an egg will seal small holes. If there is a large hole, squeeze the section of the copper piping flat to seal it off. It will reduce the size of the cooling area but, if you drive very steadily, you will be able to keep going.

METAL GETS HOT: Be careful! All metal parts of a car can become hot enough to cause blisters.

 Never leave an injured person or an animal in a closed car in a hot climate – or even on a sunny day in temperate regions. Always keep windows open to ensure ventilation. Heat exhaustion kills even in the shade, as the sun will move.

CARE IN SANDY CONDITIONS: When adding fuel, sand and dust can get into the tank. Rig a filter over or just inside the inlet to the tank.

IN COLD CLIMATES

If you are trapped in a blizzard, stay in the car. If you are on a regular traffic route you will probably soon be rescued. Going for help could be too risky.

Run the engine for heat if you have fuel. Cover the engine so that as little heat as possible is lost, but make sure the exhaust is clear. Do not risk exhaust fumes coming into the car. If you feel drowsy stop the engine and open a window. Do not go to sleep with the engine running. Switch off the heater as soon as you have taken the chill off, starting it again when the temperature drops. If there is no fuel, wrap up in any spare clothing, rugs, etc. and keep moving inside the car.

If you have to leave the car to go a short distance, e.g. if you know help is very close, rig up a signpost — a bright scarf on a stick will help you find the car again.

When the blizzard stops, and provided it is daylight (otherwise wait until morning), it is worth walking out if there is a clear guide to the route (such as telegraph poles).

If you are miles from anywhere and the snow is building up to bury the car, get out and build yourself a snow cave. When the blizzard stops scrape large signs in the snow and use other signals to attract attention.

STARTING: Try to park on a gradient so you can use a bump start to back up the starter. Once you get the engine going keep it running, but check the handbrake is firmly on and never leave children or animals in an unattended vehicle with the engine running.

DEMISTING: Don't try to drive looking through a small clear patch on a misty screen. Rub onion or raw potato on the inside of the screen to stop it misting up.

Cover the outside of the windscreen and windows with newspaper to prevent frost building up on them. If damp, however, paper will stick.

COVER THE ENGINE: Wrap a blanket round the engine to help prevent it from freezing up, but remember to remove it before you start the engine. Cover the lower part of the radiator with cardboard or wood so that it does not freeze as you go along. If very cold, leave covered. Otherwise, remove to prevent overheating.

COVER METAL: Don't touch any metal with bare hands. Your fingers could freeze to it and the skin could be torn off. Where handling metal components with gloves is awkward, wrap fingers with adhesive tape. Treat radiator cap and dip stick in this way to ease your daily checks.

DIESEL ENGINES: Diesel contains water and freezes solid at low temperatures. Always cover front of engine, but check for overheating. Wrap engine at night or when left standing. Some drivers light small fires under frozen tanks. Only you can judge if the risk is worth taking.

GENERAL

CLUTCH SLIP: Often caused by oil or grease getting on the clutch plates. To degrease, use the fire extinguisher. Squirt it through inspection plate opening.

BROKEN FAN BELT: Improvise with tights, a tie or string.

HIGH-TENSION LEADS: If a high-tension lead breaks, you may be able to replace it with a willow twig. Any plant stem with water content will carry current from the coil to distributor. Spit on ends and insert them into push-fit contacts. When you switch on, there is a deadly current of about 1300 volts: do not touch. Replace the twig frequently, as it dries out.

DEAD BATTERY: Set the vehicle moving by a tow, a push or by letting it run downhill. Select second gear and release the clutch to bump start.

DISASTER STRATEGIES

CREDITS

CREDITS

This book was edited and designed by
Anne O'Brien and Stephen Kirk

All colour illustrations by Norman Arlott
Other illustrations were drawn by
Steve Cross, Chris Lyon,
Andrew Mawson, Tony Spalding

The editors would also like to thank
the following for their assistance:
Belinda Bouchard, Ronald Clark, Mark Crean,
Johnny Pinfold, William Spalding

Department of Community Affairs,
State of Florida, USA

Department of Emergency Management,
State of Washington, USA

Federal Emergency Management Agency,
Washington, DC, USA

Greater London Council Fire Brigade Department, UK

Health and Safety Commission, UK

Office of Emergency Services,
State of California, USA